Enlightenment and Conservatism in the Dutch Republic

SPECULUM HISTORIALE

STUDIËN OP GESCHIEDTHEORETISCH, GESCHIEDFILOSOFISCH
EN IDEEËNHISTORISCH GEBIED

Enlightenment and Conservatism in the Dutch Republic

The Political Thought of Elie Luzac (1721-1796)

Wyger R.E. Velema

1993

Van Gorcum, Assen/Maastricht, The Netherlands

Publication of this book was made possible by grants from the Netherlands Organization for the Advancement of Research (N.W.O) and the Dr Hendrik Muller's Vaderlandsch Fonds.

CIP-DATA KONINKLIJKE BIBLIOTHEEK, DEN HAAG

Velema, Wyger R.E.

Enlightenment and Conservatism in the Dutch Republic: The Political Thought of Elie Luzac (1721-1796) / Wyger R.E. Velema. – Assen [etc.] : Van Gorcum. – Portr. – (Speculum historiale, ISSN 0169-8931; 13)
With bibliogr.
NUGI 641/654
Subject headings: Dutch Republic; Enlightenment; History of Political Thought; Luzac, Elie.

ISBN 90-232-2743-3

Printed by Van Gorcum, Assen, The Netherlands.

"It is not what happens to people that is significant,
but what they think happens to them"

A. Powell, *Books do Furnish a Room*

Parentibus

CONTENTS

ACKNOWLEDGMENTS

In researching and writing this book over a period of many years in two different countries I have accumulated more debts than it is possible fully to acknowledge here. It was H.M. Beliën who, at the University of Amsterdam, first introduced me to the charms of eighteenth-century intellectual history. My interests became more clearly focused during a subsequent period of study at the University of Groningen, where I greatly profited from the inspired and inspiring scholarship of E.H. Kossmann. After I left Groningen, he continued to encourage my research in many ways. My greatest thanks, however, go to J.G.A. Pocock, who supervised the dissertation on which this book is based with great kindness and infinite patience and whose approach to the past has been a constant source of inspiration to me. During my years at the Johns Hopkins University I have also had many helpful conversations with M. Walker, O. Ranum, and J.B. Schneewind. Back in the Netherlands, the sometimes lonely task of research and writing was eased by the interest and encouragement of E.O.G. Haitsma Mulier.

The initial stages of my research were made possible by a Fulbright grant and by various fellowships from the Johns Hopkins University, an institution I shall always remember for its stimulating and scholarly atmosphere. My research in the Netherlands was funded over a twenty-eight month period by the Netherlands Organization for Scientific Research. That same Organization and the *Stichting Dr. Hendrik Muller's Vaderlandsch Fonds* made the publication of this book possible.

Although I have in places drawn on previously published articles (as listed in the bibliography), it is only a substantial part of Chapter V that has appeared before in more or less similar form: Wyger R.E. Velema, "Elie Luzac and Two Dutch Revolutions: The Evolution of Orangist Political Thought" in: M.C. Jacob and W.W. Mijnhardt, ed. *The Dutch Republic in the Eighteenth Century. Decline, Enlightenment, and Revolution.* Copyright © 1992 by Cornell University. I thank the publisher, Cornell University Press, for permission to use this material. The jacket illustration, an anonymous portrait of Elie Luzac (ca. 1770), is reproduced by courtesy of *Stedelijk Museum "de Lakenhal"*, Leiden.

In the final stages of the production of this book, G.T. Moran has expertly assisted me with my English. Willem Melching, who knows all there is to know about computers, has with great patience and friendship helped me with the technical side of things. My oldest debt, intellectual and otherwise, is to my parents. It is to them that I dedicate this book. It could, finally, never have been written without the unfailing support of my wife Pauline.

A NOTE ON THE TEXT

The fact that this book is written in English whereas the sources on which it is based are largely in French and in Dutch poses a problem of presentation. In Anglophone scholarship this problem is usually solved by translating all citations and by giving a reference to the original in a footnote. In Dutch monographs, on the other hand, it is a widely accepted practice to incorporate citations in a wide variety of languages into the main body of the text. I have opted for a compromise between these two approaches. To increase the readability of the text, I have translated all citations into modern English. In the interest of historical scholarship, I have put the originals on which my translations are based into the footnotes, maintaining their original and often idiosyncratic spelling and punctuation. I have only done so, however, in the case of authors (mainly Luzac himself) whose work is not easily accessible, not in the case of well-known authors such as Montesquieu, Wolff, or Rousseau, whose work is readily available in modern editions or reprints. The reader who wishes to follow the main line of my argument may simply ignore the citations in the footnotes; they are there for those who wish to savor the eighteenth-century originals for themselves. I realize that my decision has resulted in some pages cluttered with footnotes and therefore less than elegant in their typography, but I am convinced that the scholarly advantages of this mode of presentation far outweigh the aesthetic disadvantages.

All translations in the text, unless otherwise indicated, are my own. I have left the French titles appearing in the text (e.g. Rousseau's *Contrat social*) untranslated. Where I deemed it to be virtually untranslatable, I have incorporated an occasional French term in the main body of the text (e.g. Montesquieu's *moeurs*). The full titles of the works referred to in the footnotes may be found in the bibliography at the end of the book.

ix

INTRODUCTION

There was a time in the historiography of eighteenth-century Europe when Enlightenment and conservatism were considered to be direct opposites. The title of the present study would, in those days, have seemed a contradiction in terms. The Enlightenment was seen as a unitary and cosmopolitan movement of an anti-religious nature. Its liberal and reasonable politics necessarily brought it into conflict with the authoritarian, irrational, and antiquated political structures of the *ancien régime*. The Enlightenment, in this view, was at the basis of the late eighteenth-century democratic revolutions.[1] Conservatism was interpreted as a reaction against the onslaught of the combined perils of Enlightenment and revolution, or - which amounted to the same thing - against the birth of the modern world. Conservatism was traditionalism made conscious, a transformation brought about by the massive challenge to the *status quo* that the late eighteenth century witnessed.[2]

In recent years, however, historians have largely abandoned this interpretation of eighteenth-century intellectual history. It has, to start with, become highly problematical to write about *the* Enlightenment. Recent scholarship has emphasized that the intellectual developments the term was used to cover were in fact highly diverse. M.C. Jacob has made it clear that there was a Radical as well as a Newtonian Enlightenment. The Enlightenment in Protestant cultures was greatly different from that in Catholic cultures. Within the Protestant world, Enlightenment was by no means the same as *Aufklärung* or *Verlichting*. H.F. May, to give a final example, has deemed it helpful to distinguish no less than four varieties of Enlightenment within one single eighteenth-century culture.[3] One of the consequences of this proliferation of Enlightenments has been that it is no longer possible to take the link between Enlightenment and late eighteenth-century revolutions for granted. That link has also been rendered problematical by another historiographical development. Increasingly, the purely modern and enlightened nature of the late eighteenth-century challenge to the *ancien régime* has come to be doubted. A clear connection between late eighteenth-century radicalism and older varieties of republican thought has been established. Not only, apparently, were there enlightened conservatives, there were also unenlightened

---

1. The last great representative of this interpretation was Gay, *Enlightenment*.

2. The *locus classicus* is Mannheim, "Conservative Thought".

3. Jacob, *Radical Enlightenment*; Porter and Teich, ed. *Enlightenment in National Context*; May, *Enlightenment in America*.

revolutionaries.[4] Taken together, these two historiographical revisions force us to rethink the whole development of late eighteenth-century political thought. Whereas in the old interpretation modern and enlightened revolutionaries valiantly struggled against narrow-minded conservatives, in the new historiography it is not uncommon to find enlightened conservatives defending an established order defined as modern against what are perceived to be regressive and primitivist revolutionary attacks.

Unfortunately, the themes touched upon here seem to have had very little impact on the study of Dutch eighteenth-century intellectual history. Scholarship on the Dutch Enlightenment, it is true, has undergone a remarkable transformation in recent years. Until the 1970s, it was generally held that the Dutch Republic had not known an Enlightenment worth the name.[5] This conviction resulted from the mistaken identification of Enlightenment with certain forms of philosophical and political radicalism to be found in eighteenth-century France. Once this preoccupation with the French example was abandoned, it became possible to discover a Dutch Enlightenment. A new historiographical consensus rapidly emerged. The Dutch Enlightenment, it is now generally accepted, was a Protestant Enlightenment.[6] With some exaggeration it may be said that, in the course of two decades, Dutch historiography has moved from the bizarre conclusion that nobody was enlightened to the equally startling one that almost everybody was.

The general characterization of the Dutch Enlightenment as predominantly Protestant is not, to be sure, unfounded. The problem is that it obscures many of the most important issues. The term is, for one thing, used to cover such a wide range of phenomena - from Leiden Newtonianism to Wolffian natural law and from physico-theology to spectatorial literature - that it tends to draw a veil over significant intellectual divisions. It is, in other words, necessary to go beyond this new consensus and to study the many varieties of Enlightenment to be found in the Dutch Republic in detail.[7] Such studies, moreover, would do well to pay attention to the hitherto neglected political dimensions of Dutch enlightened thought. Indeed, the current emphasis on the Protestant and

---

4. Pocock, *Machiavellian Moment* and *Virtue, Commerce, and History*.

5. E.g. Zwager, *Nederland en de Verlichting*.

6. E.g. Buijnsters, "Lumières hollandaises"; Bots and De Vet, "Les Provinces-Unies et les Lumières".

7. A most valuable recent socio-cultural study attempting to present a more diversified image of the Dutch Enlightenment is Mijnhardt, *Tot Heil van 't Menschdom*.

unitary nature of the Dutch Enlightenment makes it altogether impossible to understand how the Patriot era could witness the emergence of radically opposed political groups, both claiming to represent true Enlightenment.[8]

The present study is intended as a contribution to the international and national historiographical debates just outlined. On the most general level, it seeks to demonstrate the existence of a certain international variety of rational, tolerant, and liberal Protestant Enlightenment. It follows this Moderate Enlightenment in its conflicts first with the sensationalism and radicalism of the French High Enlightenment and later with the revolutionary political thought of the late eighteenth century. In the more limited context of Dutch history, this study is intended to deepen our understanding of the Dutch Enlightenment by studying one of its varieties in detail. More specifically, it aims to bring out the political dimensions and implications of a certain mode of Dutch enlightened thought and the fundamental nature of its conflict with the radicalism of the Dutch Patriot movement that emerged in the final decades of the late eighteenth century. It is, in other words, a study in Enlightenment and conservatism.

To address these topics in the Dutch Republic, there is no more logical choice than to study the work of Elie Luzac (1721-1796). Not only is he widely regarded as one of the most remarkable representatives of Dutch enlightened thought, he is also generally considered to be among the most talented late eighteenth-century Dutch conservatives. Yet despite these estimates, very few aspects of his thought have ever been studied in any depth. This is perhaps not as surprising as it might at first seem to be. Born in Noordwijk as the son of a second generation Huguenot *émigré* who ran a successful boarding school, Elie Luzac developed an astonishing range of activities from an early age on.[9] Not only did he acquire an international reputation as a printer, publisher, and bookseller, he also became a distinguished lawyer. First and foremost, however, he was an enormously prolific author who left posterity, to quote E.H. Kossmann, "an oeuvre of perplexing proportions and an equally per-

---

8. A somewhat similar plea for a new approach to the study of the Dutch Enlightenment may be found in Hanou, *Sluiers van Isis*, vol.1, 52-64 and, by the same author, "Kanttekeningen bij de studie van de Verlichting".

9. Although not entirely dependable, the most important source for Luzac's biography remains Cras, "Beredeneerd verslag". For general overviews see the various articles by J. Marx cited in the bibliography.

plexing shapelessness".[10] In his long career as a writer between 1747 and 1796 Luzac addressed almost every conceivable eighteenth-century topic in well over twenty thousand printed pages, enough to scare away many later potential students of his work. Indeed, anyone wishing to study the life and work of this exceptional man is forced to make a number of choices.

The present study, it should be emphasized, is neither a biography of Elie Luzac, nor even a full intellectual biography. Primarily based on Luzac's printed work, it is an analysis of a certain variety of enlightened and conservative political thought in the second half of the eighteenth century. Its methodology was inspired by what is known as the Cambridge school or the "new history of political thought". The practitioners of the new history of political thought - J. Dunn, J.G.A. Pocock, Q. Skinner, and by now a host of others in the Anglo-American world - claim to be writing "a history of political theory with a genuinely historical character".[11] Their enterprise is best understood by contrasting it with two older approaches to the subject: on the one hand the ahistorical philosophical commentary on a series of highly abstract, chronologically arranged canonical texts; on the other hand, the study of political thought as epiphenomenal to social, economic, and political "reality", in other words reductionism. To avoid the drawbacks of both these approaches the Cambridge school proposes to make language the central concern of the historian of political thought or - more accurately - political discourse. It is argued that the meaning of a text cannot be known unless its character as a language performance carried out by its author within durable language structures is reconstructed. In order to do this successfully, the historian has to familiarize himself thoroughly with the political languages or rhetorics available at a given time and place. The specific texts or series of utterances to be studied may then be located in the context of these "paradigms" and may be seen to adopt, adapt, combine, ignore, or reject the latter. This rigorously historical approach allows the historian to understand the meaning of texts in their own, that is primarily linguistic, contexts and thus to understand past political discourse as it bore meaning

---

10. E.H. Kossmann, "Comment on Pocock" in: Pocock, "Problem of political thought", 32. Kossmann is the only author to have attempted a general interpretation of Luzac's political thought. See his 1966 inaugural lecture *Verlicht Conservatisme: over Elie Luzac*.

11. Skinner, *Foundations*, vol.1, xi.

in the minds of contemporaries.[12]

The first two chapters are strictly chronological. Chapter one deals with Luzac's formative years. It discusses his early thought against the background of the contemporary learned world and demonstrates that he shared the rational, tolerant, and liberal Protestant values of an international community of enlightened Huguenots, best described as representing a Moderate Enlightenment. Chapter two addresses the way in which this Moderate Enlightenment was driven into a defensive position by the philosophical and later the political radicalism of leading representatives of the French High Enlightenment. More specifically, it analyzes Luzac's response to the writings of Montesquieu, d'Alembert, and Rousseau. Chapter three abandons strict chronology to discuss Luzac's mature views on the science of morals or modern natural law, views heavily influenced by the work of Christian Wolff. It reconstructs his account of the history of the *science des moeurs*, analyzes his substantive contributions to natural law, and discusses his position in the contemporary Dutch debate about the relative merits of Roman and natural law. Chapters four and five are devoted to Luzac's approach to Dutch politics and society. Chapter four seeks to establish that Luzac regarded commerce and the Stadholderate as the central themes to be addressed in writing about the Dutch Republic. It is against the background of both his general intellectual outlook and his more specific opinions about the nature of the Dutch Republic that Luzac's total rejection of the late eighteenth-century Patriot movement may be understood. His anti-Patriot political conservatism is the subject of the fifth and final chapter.

---

12. There is a sizable and rapidly expanding literature on this methodology, but see especially Tully, ed. *Meaning and Context;* Hampsher-Monk, "Review Article: Political Languages in Time"; Tuck, "History of Political Thought".

CHAPTER I

A RATIONAL AND MODERATE ENLIGHTENMENT

Luzac's response to the intellectual and political upheavals of the second half of the eighteenth century was to a large extent determined by the outlook he developed as a young man. The purpose of this first chapter is to reconstruct his early thought and to place it in a contemporary context. It will be shown how Luzac's first experiences in publishing led him to adopt very decided opinions on the freedom of intellectual exchange. This will lead on to a second section which attempts to analyze Luzac's position in the contemporary learned world. Against that background it will then be possible to understand the main themes in his early writings.

1. Enlightenment and the Liberty of the Press

In the final months of 1747 one of the most notorious eighteenth-century materialist tracts was published in Leiden: Julien Offray de la Mettrie's *l'Homme machine*. The publication of this small but explosive volume not only gave rise to lengthy polemics against materialism, but it also sig- nalled the arrival on the public scene of Elie Luzac, until then a relatively unknown publisher and student at Leiden University. Luzac, who per- sonally knew La Mettrie and had probably met him during the French- man's second stay in Leiden in 1747, took a considerable risk in putting his publisher's name on the title page of *l'Homme machine*. But even though he certainly was aware of the hazards involved in publishing material of this nature, the uproar and scandal caused by *l'Homme machine* shocked him deeply. It forced him to develop both practical and argumentative strategies to deal with the consequences of his action. It taught him some enduring lessons about the perils of religious, and especially clerical intolerance. The episode, in fact, was of supreme importance in the maturing of Luzac's views and therefore deserves our close attention.

To be on the safe side, Luzac took several precautions before he published *l'Homme machine*. First of all, he appended a brief preface to the book, in which he explained his reasons for undertaking its publica- tion. True religion, Luzac there remarked, was immune to attempts to undermine it by argument. This proposition was even more powerful in reverse form: any attempt to suppress anti-religious arguments would in fact strengthen the position of unbelief. People would come to feel that what was being withheld from them might be interesting, or at least had to be taken seriously, and they would therefore begin to doubt the truths of religion. A completely open and rational debate, on the other hand, would inevitably and invariably result in the total defeat of the atheists. "I compare atheists to those giants who desired to climb the heavens: their fate will always be the same". The readers moreover should bear in mind the fact that the whole content of the treatise was based on no more than a highly uncertain hypothesis. Finally, there was also the practical consideration that had Luzac himself not consented to publish the book, somebody else would gladly have done it.[1] Apparently unconvinced that these remarks would pacify future opponents of the book, Luzac took great care to hide the identity of its author, who had already been forced to leave France for Holland after the publication of his *Politique du médecin de Machiavel* in 1746.[2] In his preface Luzac, who was in close touch with La Mettrie, claimed not to know the author and to have received the manuscript from an anonymous writer in Berlin. To limit the financial risks for the publisher, La Mettrie's book was published at his own cost, although Luzac advanced most of the money.[3]

None of these precautions turned out to offer Luzac, or for that matter La Mettrie, sufficient protection. No sooner had circulation of *l'Homme machine* started then its publisher was called before the Walloon Consistory of Leiden. On December 18, 1747, the Consistory declared *l'Homme machine* to be a book "filled with the most appalling atheism and libertinism". In order to put an immediate stop to the circulation of the book and to prevent such things from happening again in the future the Consistory ordered Luzac "1. to hand over all copies of the said book still in his possession and all those he could retrieve, so that they can be burned. 2. to disclose the name of the author of the book. 3. to apologize for contributing to the circulation of this wicked book by printing it and solemnly to promise never again to print or sell any book attacking Divinity, religion, or good manners". Luzac promptly gave in to the first demand. He promised to hand over all his copies of the book to the Consistory for destruction by fire. In the other two matters he asked for a two-day reprieve before answering, which was granted. On December 20, Luzac was back before the Consistory. He repeated his solemn promise to hand over all the copies of *l'Homme machine* at his disposal and indeed he subsequently delivered a large number of them. In the matter of the

1. *Homme machine*, "Avertissement de l'Imprimeur" ("Je compare les Athées à ces Géans qui voulurent escalader les Cieux: ils auront toujours le même sort.").

2. Vartanian, *La Mettrie*, 6.

3. *Corr. Rey*, Luzac to Rey, Leiden, April 1, 1748.

revelation of the identity of the book's author, however, he declared "that he was incapable of doing so". But he was more than willing to state that he was deeply sorry to have printed such a scandalous book. He would also gladly refrain from doing such a thing ever again. The Consistory, so the text proceeds, was satisfied with this declaration.[4]

Luzac was, of course, completely insincere. On that very same day he wrote to his Amsterdam colleague Marc-Michel Rey, later to become one of the most prominent publishers of the European Enlightenment, that the Consistory was planning to burn *l'Homme machine*, but that this would not prevent him from putting further copies into circulation at some future point in time.[5] He indeed proceeded to do so, for in March and April 1748 we find him sending numerous copies of the book to Rey.[6] But even his apparently trustworthy partner in clandestinity Rey turned out to be less than entirely discreet. During his struggles with the Walloon Consistory Luzac came to realize that his persecutors strongly suspected La Mettrie of the authorship of *l'Homme machine*. Their information, he gathered, came from a letter written to them by the Amsterdam Walloon pastor and publicist David Renaud Boullier. And Boullier, so Luzac thought, could only have come by this information through Rey. Fortunately La Mettrie had, before his authorship became more widely known, left the Dutch Republic for Prussia, where he settled as a guest of King Frederick.[7] Still, Luzac severely reprimanded Rey: "Allow me to tell you that you have acted wrongly in supplying this theologian with information against Mr. de la Mettrie, who is now invulnerable in his position at the Prussian court, but who would have run a great risk without my firmness and prudence".[8]

---

4. Archives de l'Eglise Wallonne de Leyde, nr. 46, 1740-1765, 89-91 ("...rempli de l'Athéisme et du Libertinage le plus affreux..."; "1. de lui remettre tous les Exemplaires du susdit Livre, qu'il a chez lui, et tous ceux, qu'il pourra recouvrer, afin qu'ils soient brulez. 2. de lui nommer l'Autheur de ce livre. 3. de lui temoigner le regret, qu'il a d'avoir favorisé le debit de ce mechant Livre en l'imprimant, et de lui promettre solennellement de ne plus jamais rien imprimer et debiter aucun Livre, qui attaque en quelque manière que ce soit la Divinité, ou la Religion, ou les bonnes Moeurs."; "...qu'il étoit hors d'état de le faire..."). See also Valkhoff, "Luzac", 13-14.

5. *Corr. Rey*, Luzac to Rey, Leiden, December 20, 1747. On Rey see Fajn, "Marc-Michel Rey" and Vercruysse, "Marc-Michel Rey imprimeur philosophe ou philosophique".

6. *Corr. Rey*, Luzac to Formey, Leiden, March 30 and April 1, 1748.

7. Vartanian, *La Mettrie*, 7-8.

8. *Corr. Rey*, Luzac to Rey, Leiden, February 25, 1748 ("Vous avez mal fait, permettez moi de Vous le dire, d'avoir donné à ce Théologien des informations contre Monsr. de la Mettrie, qui présentement Medecin ordinaire de la Maj. Prussienne, s'en moque, mais qui

La Mettrie's sudden departure from Holland did not mean the complete end of his relationship with Luzac. During the next few years Luzac continued to show great interest in his various publications.[9] In the fall of 1750 we even find him visiting La Mettrie in Potsdam.[10] But his growing irritation with the philosopher's refusal to pay his financial debt finally caused Luzac to bring their relation to an end. In May 1751 Luzac engages the services of a German lawyer to recover his debt.[11] Shortly thereafter he even contemplates going directly to Frederick the Great to make the ungrateful author pay up. "Without me", he bitterly remarks, "he would have gone to the scaffold like a miserable bandit".[12] But when the frivolous and unreliable materialist died after overindulging in *pâté de faisan aux truffes* on November 11, 1751, Luzac still had not received his payment.[13]

This, however, was the least of Luzac's problems. He had reconciled himself at an early point to a financial loss, cheerfully writing to Rey that "fortunately only my income has suffered from the animosity of the theologians".[14] He had learned some valuable practical lessons. He had come to realize, even more than before the publication of *l'Homme machine*, that absolute discretion was required to maintain the anonymous status of a controversial author. It had also become abundantly clear to him that putting the true publisher's name on the title page of a book was not always a smart idea, even in a country internationally renowned for its freedom of the press and its lack of rigid censorship. He would never forget these lessons in his future career as a publisher and as a publicist. The task still remaining and to his own mind extremely important, however, was the elaboration of an intellectual defense of his actions with

auroit couru grand risque sans ma fermeté et sans ma prudence.").

9. E.g. *Corr. Formey*, Luzac to Formey, Leiden, March 3, 1750.

10. Provinciale Bibliotheek Leeuwarden, Hs 1152, s.n., Luzac to Herman Cannegieter, [undated, but probably 1750].

11. *Corr. Formey*, Luzac to Formey, Leiden, May 4, 1751.

12. *Ibidem*, [undated, but probably June 1751] ("Sans moi il eut monté sur l'Echafaut comme un miserable bandit.").

13. On the circumstances of La Mettrie's death see Vartanian, *La Mettrie*, 12.

14. *Corr. Rey*, Luzac to Rey, Leiden, March 4, 1748 ("...par bonheur l'animosité des Théologiens n'a fait du tort qu'à ma bourse."). The circulation of *l'Homme machine* would continue to be interrupted by clerical and governmental intervention. In 1750, for instance, the Consistory of the Reformed Church in The Hague protested against the appearance of a copy of the book at a public auction. It was thereupon seized and destroyed by the States. See A.H. Huussen jr., "Freedom of the press and censorship in the Netherlands 1780-1810" in: Duke and Tamse, ed. *Too Mighty to be Free*, 112-113.

more substance than the short preface to *l'Homme machine*. Despite its brevity, the preface itself had caused a scandal, especially in that segment of the Republic of Letters to which Luzac himself belonged: the liberal Protestant wing of the descendants of the Huguenot refuge.[15] Pierre Roques, pastor of the French church in Basel, was so shocked by its content that he published a lengthy refutation in the *Nouvelle Bibliothèque Germanique*.[16] In this "Examen de l'avertissement de l'imprimeur qui a publié le livre intitulé, l'Homme machine", Roques took great care, both in his argumentation and in his choice of authorities to be cited, to emphasize his enlightened position. Freedom of the press, he argued, was a great good. It was absurd, as all too often happened, to forbid all works not completely conforming to "the religion of the country and of the dominant sect".[17] Yet, the liberal pastor continued, this freedom also had its clear limits. No books against religion in general, no books against the incontestable rules of morality, and no books inciting to rebellion should be allowed to be published. It was against this rule that Luzac had sinned. "If Mister Elie Luzac...had thought about these limits set by reason, religion, and sound politics, he would never have printed in this scandalous way what is perhaps the most impious brochure ever to have appeared".[18] *L'Homme machine* was a most dangerous tract, filled with atheism of a Spinozist variety and inciting to a "libertinage des moeurs".[19] And atheism was much more than a monstrous error: it was a grave crime against both God and human society. It had always been forbidden and justly so, Roques emphasized, adducing the authority not of theologians, but of "the greatest jurisconsults" - Grotius, Pufendorf and Barbeyrac.[20] The dogmatic atheist was mankind's most cruel enemy.

Why then had Luzac soiled his printing presses with this publication? Roques judged the arguments put forward in Luzac's preface to be totally unconvincing. That religion was immune to this kind of attack might be

---

15. The helpful term liberal Protestantism has been coined by S.S.B. Taylor in his article "The Enlightenment in Switzerland" in: Porter and Teich, ed. *Enlightenment in National Context*, 72-89.

16. *Nouvelle Bibliothèque Germanique*, vol. 5, second part, 1748-1749, 328-357. The piece is signed April 3, 1748.

17. *Ibidem*, 329 ("...la Religion du Païs, et de la Secte dominante.").

18. *Ibidem*, 330-331 ("Si le Sieur Elie Luzac...avoit réfléchi sur ces bornes que la Raison, la Religion, et la saine Politique prescrivent, il n'auroit point mis scandaleusement sous sa presse...la Brochure la plus impie qui ait peut-être jamais paru...").

19. *Ibidem*, 331-340. The quotation is on 336.

20. *Ibidem*, 340-344 ("Les plus grands Jurisconsultes...").

true at the highest level, he conceded, but weak and unenlightened minds might very well be damaged. Attacks of this kind would moreover furnish new weapons to those already inclined to libertinage. And even if no harm was done in any direct way, there was still no reason whatsoever to allow God to be publicly insulted in print.[21] It was also wrongheaded to think that people's faith would be weakened if they were prevented from reading "the impieties of the libertines".[22] As to the merits of open debate, there had already been more than enough of that. If even the excellent works of Nieuwentijt, Derham, and Ray did not suffice to silence the atheists, nothing would.[23] Their pernicious writings simply had to be banned. Roques contemptuously dismissed Luzac's final argument, the fact that somebody else would certainly have printed *l'Homme machine* had he not done it himself. First of all, Luzac could not possibly know this for certain. But more importantly, it did not absolve him from moral responsibility.[24] Luzac had in short, Roques concluded, been guilty of "inexcusable conduct".[25]

But condemnation did not stop in Basel. In Berlin Luzac's correspondent and business partner Jean Henri Samuel Formey, with whom he shared so many convictions, also raised his voice. Formey strongly condemned Luzac's decision to publish *l'Homme machine* and loudly protested against the content of the preface. He accused Luzac of "a false moral heroism which is entirely chimerical if separated from religion". In his reply Luzac vehemently denied separating morality from religion, although he found it necessary to specify exactly what was to be understood by religion in this context: "the cult of a first cause to which we owe our being and the duration of our existence, and all that goes with it".[26] To this he added that Roques's attack on his preface was so weak as to be almost ridiculous. He would send Formey, who had taken over the editorship of the *Nouvelle Bibliothèque Germanique* in the meantime,

21. *Ibidem*, 346-347.

22. *Ibidem*, 349 ("...les impiétés des Libertins.").

23. *Ibidem*, 349-351. Bernard Nieuwentijt, William Derham, and John Ray were all prominent early eighteenth-century practitioners of the then highly fashionable mode of apologetics known as physico-theology. On this extremely important intellectual current see Bots, *Tussen Descartes en Darwin*.

24. *Nouvelle Bibliothèque Germanique*, as in note 16, 347-348.

25. *Ibidem*, 357 ("...une conduite insoutenable...").

26. *Corr. Formey*, Luzac to Formey, Leiden, April 11, 1750 ("...un faux heroisme de morale qui n'est qu'un phantome si on le separe de la Religion..."; "...le culte d'une cause première à qui nous devons l'Etre, et la durée de notre existence, avec tout ce qui l'accompagne.").

a reply with which he could do as he pleased. Luzac's reply, "Response de l'imprimeur à Mr... sur son examen de l'avertissement qui se trouve à la tête du livre intitulé, l'Homme machine", appeared in the spring issue of 1750.[27] It was accompanied by some remarks by Formey in which the latter made it very clear that he disagreed with its content and that in his own view nothing, including the publication of dangerous books, should ever be done to undermine religion and morality, the two main pillars of society.[28]

In his answer to Roques Luzac refused simply to reiterate the arguments he had used in his preface to *l'Homme machine*. The whole point of the controversy, he now stated, came down to this: it had to be demonstrated that publishing *l'Homme machine* was a morally reprehensible action and that the publisher could and should have known this.[29] And that, he submitted, was impossible to do. He would first briefly indicate the weakness of Roques's position and then proceed to defend his own. As to Roques's position, he had completely failed to make it clear which books ought to be banned and which books ought to be permitted. His general religious, moral, and political criteria were so vague as to be utterly useless. Where, given the unspecific nature of these criteria, would the prohibition of books stop? Cleverly drawing into the debate the name of a philosopher highly respected in liberal Protestant circles, Luzac at this point remarked that he had often heard Leibniz accused of Spinozism. Did Roques wish to prohibit further publication of works by this author? More generally, how many people actually agreed as to what constituted good morals?[30]

Much more important, however, was Luzac's defense of his own moral position. From Roques's essay and learned quotations, Luzac remarked with heavy irony, it was clear that the pastor was intimately familiar with the thought of Grotius's, Pufendorf, and Barbeyrac. Roques would therefore certainly agree with him that according to these great men an action was morally wrong only if by its very nature it caused a bad effect. The publication of *l'Homme machine* could therefore only be

27. *Nouvelle Bibliothèque Germanique*, vol. 6, second part, 1750, 431-441. The piece is signed Et. Luzac, which led Vartanian (*La Mettrie*, 98) to suppose that it was written by Etienne Luzac on behalf of Elie. But the Et. was a printing error and Elie did write the article himself. The matter is cleared up in *Corr. Formey*, Jean Luzac to Formey, Leiden, August 28, 1750.

28. *Nouvelle Bibliothèque Germanique*, as in note 27, 429-431.

29. *Ibidem*, 433.

30. *Ibidem*, 433-435.

called morally wrong if the nature of that book in itself and necessarily caused a bad effect. But that was patently untrue. Had Roques himself, who no doubt had perused the controversial publication several times, been corrupted by his readings? Obviously not. It was therefore as absurd to call the publication of the tract morally wrong as it was nonsensical to doubt the moral integrity of a wine merchant on the ground that some of his clients later abused their purchases to drink themselves into a stupor.[31] Or, as Luzac wrote to Formey in this same matter, "there must be a necessary link between effect and cause and that connection is absent between the production of a book and the uses a capricious public chooses to make of it".[32]

Having thus made his main point, Luzac still needed to deal with Roques's contention that the practical argument for deciding to publish *l'Homme machine* was worthless. How did Luzac know, Roques had asked, that somebody else would gladly have published the book? Just look at the number of pirate editions circulating, Luzac could now simply answer. But that was not the most important thing. The fundamental fact was that as soon as a publisher could reasonably expect that a manuscript would be published somewhere else, probably even in a different country, he made himself guilty of harming his country if he turned it down. Publishing, Luzac stressed, was an extremely important part of Dutch commerce. It generated jobs and brought money into the country and thus contributed greatly to national prosperity. Why give up these advantages with no moral gain in return? What good would a ban on the publication of, for instance, Pierre Bayle's famous *Dictionnaire historique et critique* have done? "None. On the contrary, it would have robbed several families of their work, the country of valuable production, while the profits would have gone elsewhere".[33] The curt dismissal of practical arguments for publishing was therefore completely unjustified.

Pierre Roques had died before Luzac's reply was published. The polemic therefore ended with Luzac's contribution, although his disagreement with Formey lasted somewhat longer. Luzac kept blaming Formey for the fact that he had prefaced his refutation of Roques with a clear

---

31. *Ibidem*, 436-438.

32. *Corr. Formey*, Luzac to Formey, [undated, but probably 1749] ("...il faut une liaison nécessaire de l'effet à sa cause, et l'on ne peut dire qu'il y a cette liaison entre la production d'un livre et l'usage que le public en fait, car cet usage depend de ses caprices.").

33. *Nouvelle Bibliothèque Germanique*, as in note 27, 438-440. The quotation is on 440 ("Aucun: au-contraire on auroit privé plusieurs familles de cette partie de leurs travaux, le Païs des fonds qu'il a produit dans son sein, pendant qu'on auroit fait passer chez l'Etranger toute la valeur des Exemplaires qui y seroient entrés.").

endorsement of the very principles that Luzac was about to reject. This, clearly, had unnecessarily prejudiced the readers against Luzac's arguments. In the end, however, Luzac forgave Formey, who must have done it, so he thought, to do the friends of the deceased pastor a favor.[34] To Luzac, however, these brief polemics had been no more than preliminary exercises. In order to bring the whole matter of the publication of *l'Homme machine* to an intellectually satisfactory ending something more substantial was needed. First of all, he wanted to make it absolutely clear that publishing *l'Homme machine* did not mean agreeing with its content.[35] As early as the final months of 1747 therefore we find him engaged in printing a refutation of La Mettrie's materialism.[36] It appeared anonymously early in 1748 under the title *l'Homme plus que machine*. Having learned his lessons, Luzac put "à Londres" on the title page and had Rey handle the original distribution of the book. It was a resounding success. So much so, that in April 1748 he had to encourage Rey to speed up the Dutch distribution. "In Leiden and elsewhere there is a great demand for *Hommes plus que machines*. Please, Sir, be sure to send this brochure into the country before the interest slackens".[37] In August of that same year, the first printing had almost sold out and Luzac was producing new copies.[38] The book was translated into English and appeared in London in 1752 as *Man more than a machine*.[39] A second edition of the original French version was published by Luzac in 1755.[40] The book was also reprinted several times in editions of La Mettrie's *Oeuvres philosophiques*.[41] In modern scholarship there has long been a controversy about the true authorship of this treatise, but there can be no

34. *Corr. Formey*, Luzac to Formey, Leiden, July 19 and August 9, 1750. On the exchange between Roques and Luzac see also Vartanian, *La Mettrie*, 98-99 and Marx, "Elie Luzac", 76-80.

35. Cf. Luzac's remark (*l'Homme plus que machine*, ed. 1755, 120) that he would never have written his refutation of La Mettrie "si l'on n'avoit jugé à propos de m'attribuer des sentimens, tout à fait contraires aux miens...".

36. *Corr. Rey*, Luzac to Rey, Leiden, December 23, 1747.

37. *Ibidem*, Arnhem, April 6, 1748 ("On demande à Leiden et partout des Hommes plus que Machines. Faites moi le plaisir, Monsieur, de ne pas attendre que le feu soit rallenti pour envoier cette brochure dans nos Provinces.").

38. *Ibidem*, Leiden, August 14, 1748.

39. *Man more than a machine...In answer to an wicked and atheistical treatise, written by M. de La Mettrie, and entitled Man a machine*. London, printed for W. Owen, 1752.

40. *l'Homme plus que machine: Ouvrage, qui sert à refuter les principaux argumens, sur lesquels on fonde le materialisme*. Seconde édition. Gottingue, chez l'auteur, 1755.

41. Vartanian, *La Mettrie*, 105.

doubt that it was Luzac himself who wrote it.[42] Not only did the 1755 edition, published at a safe distance from Leiden in Luzac's new Göttingen printshop, appear with his own name on the title page, he also explicitly claimed the authorship on two occasions.[43] But more important for our present purposes is the second substantial work Luzac wrote as a consequence of the La Mettrie affair.

It was an elaborate, principled and by mid-eighteenth-century standards extremely radical defense of the freedom of expression, including the freedom of the press, entitled *Essai sur la liberté de produire ses sentimens*.[44] Given the explosive nature of its content, Luzac carefully kept his identity a secret, although he admitted his authorship to the trusted Formey.[45] The title page bore a programmatic imprint ("In free country. For the public good. 1749. With privilege from all true philosophers") and a motto from Jean Barbeyrac's introduction to Pufendorf's *Droit de la nature et des gens* condemning "the illusions of the heart and the tyranny established in the world in the realm of opinions" as the great barriers to our knowledge of human morals and duties. Luzac dedicated the essay to the English nation as the only nation known to him to enjoy a complete and unfettered freedom of expression. Small wonder, he added, that England had produced such a brilliant succession of prominent scholars. "You do not know that rage to force convictions: you do not proscribe a Descartes or leave a Bayle to his fate. Happy people! That you may be admired and imitated!"[46] Although a regrettable number of attempts had been made to do so, Luzac remarked in his preface, it was in the end impossible to repress the freedom of thought successfully. It

---

42. Hastings, "Did La Mettrie"; Vartanian, "Elie Luzac's refutation"; Falvey, "La Mettrie, l'Homme plus que machine".

43. *Corr. Formey*, Luzac to Formey, Leiden, June 29, 1756. Luzac provided the information for Formey's dictionary of Francophone authors. It appeared in 1757 as *La France littéraire* and listed Luzac as the author of *l'Homme plus que machine*. The second occasion was a letter by Luzac to "Messieurs les directeurs des Nouvelles Litteraires de Göttingue", Bremen, June 12, 1748. Gemeentearchief Leiden, Familiearchief Van Heukelom, Portefeuille T.

44. The Dutch eighteenth-century debate on the liberty of the press has never been adequately or exhaustively analyzed. For a recent contribution see Huussen, "Freedom of the Press" in: Duke and Tamse, ed. *Too Mighty to be Free*, 107-126.

45. *Corr. Formey*, Luzac to Formey, Leiden, February 11, 1749.

46. *Essai*, "Dédicace" ("Au pays libre. Pour le bien public. 1749. Avec privilège de tous les véritables philosophes"; "...les illusions du Coeur, et la tyrannie établie dans le monde au Sujet des Sentimens..."; "On ne connoit pas chez vous un rage de forcer la persuasion: on n'y voit pas un Des Cartes proscrit et un Bayle sans appui. Peuple heureux! Qu'on vous admire: qu'on se contente de Vous imiter!").

was the actual expression of the products of this thought that was much more vulnerable to the omnipresent *esprit de domination*. In this essay he would therefore solely try to answer the question "whether the freedom of expression can by right be limited or even be altogether denied to man".[47]

In the first chapter Luzac addressed the issue whether or not any person had a natural right to limit the freedom of expression of another person, "abstracting from every state of empire".[48] The basis of his argument, he stated, was the existence of a Supreme Being and the principles resulting from that existence. Both by his own nature and by the divine will man was obliged to contribute to the general good and, within the limits set by that first duty, to strive for his own happiness. It was therefore clear that man was not allowed to express opinions harmful to society. But who was to be the judge of this? It was individual man himself, who for that very reason had been endowed with intelligence by God. In his search for what was beneficial or harmful to society man absolutely needed to know the opinions of others on this subject. The duty to contribute to the general good therefore clearly resulted in the right to enounce and absorb opinions.[49] Moreover, had not Barbeyrac convincingly demonstrated that according to the principles of good morals a man must follow his own sincerely held opinions, even if they were misguided? Everybody therefore had a right to express his opinions as long as he thought them to be beneficial, or at least unharmful, to society. The only conceivable reason to forbid the expression of such opinions would be the knowledge that the person uttering them was doing so against his own conviction or conscience. But such knowledge was obviously impossible to obtain. Nobody therefore had a natural right to limit another man's freedom of expression.[50] The same matter could also be looked at from a slightly different angle. Since the general good requires the discovery of the truth, everybody is obliged to seek after it. But the truth cannot be found without an examination of all possible points of view. It is therefore evident that nothing should be done to limit the expression of opinions.[51] All of this, Luzac now provocatively stated,

47. *Ibidem*, 8 ("...si la liberté de produire ses Sentimens peut être limitée de droit, ou être ôtée tout-à-fait à l'homme.").

48. *Ibidem*, 10 ("...abstraction faite de tout état d'empire...").

49. *Ibidem*, 9-13.

50. *Ibidem*, 13-15. The Barbeyrac passage Luzac is referring to can be found in Pufendorf, *Devoirs de l'homme*, vol.1, ch.1, §5, note 1.

51. *Essai*, 17-18.

was equally true with regard to atheists.[52] By what right should they be denied the expression of opinions they themselves believed to be useful to society? What was even more, who was to say that they were wrong in their convictions? After all, eminent and respected philosophers had been heard to admit that the existence of a Supreme Being was no more than highly probable. The fact that most people firmly believed in the existence of such a Being did not make that proposition true to all others and it certainly did not entitle the majority to force it upon the minority. Moreover, Luzac added repeating a by now familiar argument, we can never be certain of the truth of our convictions unless we listen to all counter-arguments.[53]

The next question to be asked and answered was whether or not the freedom of expression could be harmful to society. At this point Luzac gave the argument we previously encountered in his polemic with Roques an extended treatment. The expression of an opinion, he maintained at length and with a wealth of sometimes extreme examples, could in itself never be harmful to society. It was only the bad use to which an opinion was put by its recipients that could cause such societal harm. But there was no reason to suppose that such a bad use would regularly occur and certainly not in the case of potentially very harmful opinions. Take for instance the opinion that the virtues are no more than a chimera. Clearly its widespread practical application would wreak havoc on society and for that reason some people would no doubt want to forbid its expression. Not so Luzac. Because of the very fact that this opinion was so evidently wrongheaded, he maintained, people would find it quite easy to dismiss it on the basis of a reasoned judgment. A prohibition therefore was both superfluous and unjustified.[54] After this he repeated his conviction, already expressed in the essay's first chapter, about the existence of a close relationship between the general good, the freedom of expression, and the search for truth.[55] Finally, he briefly pointed to the dangers to society resulting from a limitation of the freedom of expression. Not only

---

52. Luzac explicitly continued to conduct his argument from the position of a believer, but he pointed out that, from a totally different perspective, atheists would have to arrive at the same conclusion. Since they did not recognize the existence of a Supreme Being, they recognized no duties. Recognizing no duties in turn implied that they would never have a valid reason to limit the freedom of others, including the freedom of expression of believers. *Ibidem*, 19-20.

53. *Ibidem*, 18-28.

54. *Ibidem*, 29-44 and 79-83.

55. *Ibidem*, 44-53.

would it cause the greatest minds to keep their thoughts to themselves, it would also undermine the faith of lesser minds in evident truths.[56] But despite all these arguments and despite the enlightened nature of the present century, Luzac observed at the end of the second chapter, many a sovereign still lends a willing ear to those in favor of bridling the freedom of expression.[57]

This observation directly led him to his next chapter, treating the question of whether or not sovereigns had the right to limit the freedom of expression of their subjects. Luzac announced that he would only discuss this matter in the context of unlimited sovereignty. The conclusions to be drawn for other forms would, so he trusted, be obvious.[58] From the existence of a Supreme Being it can be deduced, thus ran his argument, that sovereigns, just like their subjects, are obliged to seek the general good and that of their own state in particular. They have a right to direct the will of their subjects towards that goal. The subjects, in their turn, have to obey. Strictly speaking this could be taken to mean that sovereigns have the right to limit their subjects' freedom of expression, should they judge it to be harmful to the good of society.[59] And in some cases, Luzac could not resist adding, this would indeed be a great blessing. It would, for instance, benefit every European nation if sovereigns outlawed those abominable catechisms in which people were taught nothing but superstition and inhumanity and which helped to make the misguided dogma of corrupt human nature into a self-fulfilling prophecy. It would also be a huge advance if sovereigns decided to silence the clergy, quite often consisting of "turbulent and factious people, without education or honor", who constantly disturbed the public peace with their meddlesomeness and who should be taught, if necessary the hard way, to limit themselves to what they were paid for: "to teach the religion of the country".[60] But although he clearly saw the advantages of such limits to the freedom of expression, Luzac at this point broke off his praise of anti-clerical governmental action. Instead, he went on to point out that although the sovereign might have an undoubted right to guide his subjects towards the general good, it was also true, as he had just demonstrated, that the expression of opinions could never be harmful to that general

56. *Ibidem*, 53-58.

57. *Ibidem*, 60.

58. *Ibidem*, 65.

59. *Ibidem*, 65-69.

60. *Ibidem*, 69-72 ("...gens turbulens, factieux, sans éducation, et sans honneur..."; "...enseigner la Religion du Pays...").

good. Indeed, the very opposite was true. It was easy to draw the conclusion.[61]

Having shown that it was both unjust and useless to limit the freedom of expression, Luzac observed that nonetheless governments frequently resorted to prohibitions. He therefore devoted a final chapter to a brief investigation of the causes of this regrettable phenomenon. It was of course possible, he remarked, to attribute the widespread suppression of the freedom of expression to ignorance. One could then simply suppose that most sovereigns did not realize or understand that a complete freedom in this area could never be harmful to their societies.[62] But such an explanation, he immediately added, put far too favorable an interpretation on the behavior of the average repressive sovereign. The root cause of the suppression of the freedom of expression was a much darker one. It was bad government by the sovereign and his dependents, the fear that this would be publicly exposed, and the related apprehension that this exposure would result in a curtailment of power.[63] Good governments, Luzac stressed, had no reason whatsoever to fear openness and would always gladly be obeyed by their subjects. In this context he repeatedly adduced the example of Prussia's Frederick the Great, a sovereign whose early enlightened policies he greatly admired.[64] The more a government was based on might instead of right, Luzac ended his chapter with a general maxim, the more it would feel the need to limit the freedom of expression.[65] The overall conclusion of the essay left nothing to be desired in clarity: "It is therefore no more than a bad principle which brings people to curtail the freedom of expression. The good of society does not demand it. It is not done by right and it is useless. That, I believe, is sufficient to prove that everybody should be left entirely free to express their opinions".[66]

Luzac's essay is eloquent testimony to the fact that the idea of an

---

61. *Ibidem*, 72-74.

62. *Ibidem*, 98-99.

63. *Ibidem*, 99-110.

64. *Ibidem*, 109-111. For recent discussions of the nature of Frederick's regime see Schieder, *Friedrich der Grosse* and T.C.W. Blanning, "Frederick the Great and Enlightened Absolutism" in: Scott, ed. *Enlightened Absolutism*, 265-288.

65. *Essai*, 115.

66. *Ibidem*, 124 ("Ce n'est donc qu'un mauvais principe, qui engage les hommes, à porter atteinte à la liberté de produire ses Sentimens. Le bien de la Société ne le demande pas. On n'y a point de droit, et on le fait sans fruit. Voilà, je crois, tout ce qu'il faut pour prouver, qu'on doit laisser jouïr un chacun de la liberté de produire ses Sentimens.").

expansion and intensification of the process of communication was, as Hans Erich Bödeker has recently suggested, absolutely crucial to Enlightenment culture's self-understanding.[67] It is hard to find, anywhere in mid-eighteenth-century Europe, a more principled and determined plea for the search for truth by means of an entirely open process of intellectual exchange, free from both internal hierarchy and external repression. Yet despite this very real radicalism of Luzac's essay, it should be realized that its whole argument depended on certain implicit assumptions and that it functioned within a specific historical context. In order fully to understand Luzac's intentions it is important to bring this out. The subject matter of the essay was the freedom of rational intellectual communication at a high level of abstraction. In the very opening sentences of the first chapter Luzac made it clear that he would not be dealing with "novels, defamatory pamphlets, and other productions of that nature" and in the course of his argument he repeatedly stressed that everything he wrote only applied to publications "where one is content with reasoning naturally about matters", not to publications filled with "indecent expressions".[68] He was, in other words, writing about the exchange of opinions within a limited and highly educated elite. To be even more precise, he was writing about the collective search for truth within an idealized Republic of Letters.[69]

The limits to the essay's objectives are also clear from what might be called its apolitical nature. As we have seen, Luzac believed that unlimited freedom of expression would lead to the discovery of the truth and to general enlightenment. Obviously, any sensible sovereign should refrain from interfering with this process and could, in fact, greatly profit by it, for the free process of communication could potentially contribute to the formulation of enlightened policies or could at least help to prevent dreadful errors. But the thought that unlimited freedom of expression should lead to the formation of a unified public opinion which in turn should directly determine governmental policy was far beyond Luzac's intellectual horizon in 1749.[70] That the essay's main aim was no more

---

67. Bödeker, "Aufklärung als Kommunikationsprozeß".

68. *Essai*, 9, 86, 119 ("Des Romans, des Libelles, et autres productions de cette nature..."; "...où on se contente de raisonner naturellement des choses."; "...expressions indécentes...").

69. An informative discussion of some important aspects of the eighteenth-century Republic of Letters can be found in Gay, *Enlightenment*, vol.2, 57-84.

70. On the development of eighteenth-century conceptions of public opinion see J.W.A. Gunn, "Public Opinion" in: Ball, et al. *Political Innovation*, 247-265; Gunn, *Beyond Liberty and Property*, 260-315; Baker, *Inventing the French Revolution*, 167-199.

than the creation of a free area of rational intellectual exchange, preferably protected by the power of the state, was also evident from its
preoccupation with the perils of clerical power. Having recently experienced the clergy's intolerant fanaticism at first hand, Luzac left no
rhetorical device unused to make it clear that the clergy, with the important exception of the "veritable theologians", was the main threat to the
enlightened search for truth. No group, he pointed out, was more willing
to limit the freedom of expression than "the administrators of
churches".[71] It was only the state that potentially could curb the power
of these zealous theologians, with their extremely dangerous and influential private empire "with its own laws, proclaimed by certain men of
inspired wisdom, against whom the sovereigns may not act, and to whom
the people owe a blind and total obedience".[72] Pierre Bayle had, indeed,
been absolutely correct in pointing out that in all likelihood superstition
was more dangerous to a state than atheism.[73]

The essay's presuppositions and preoccupations are perfectly understandable from the historical context in which it was written. Luzac
himself at the time moved primarily in an enlightened and liberal Protestant Republic of Letters. In view of the personal attacks he had sustained
during the La Mettrie affair, it is not surprising that he identified the
clergy as one of the main enemies of the freedom of expression. But it is
even more important to stress the fact that his essay was written some
twenty-five years before the nature of public debate in the Dutch Republic was transformed by the emergence of political newspapers, the birth of
a certain vicious brand of political journalism, and the participation of
half educated segments of the population in politics.[74] The essay had
certainly not been intended to support such phenomena. It was therefore
highly ironic that it was actually translated and used by Luzac's political

---

71. *Essai*, 116-117 ("...véritables Théologiens..."; "...les Administrateurs des Eglises...").

72. *Ibidem*, 75-76 ("...qui a ses Loix en propre, émanées de la part de certains hommes,
doués d'une sagesse inspirée, contre lesquels les Souverains ne doivent rien ordonner, et
auxquels le peuple doit l'obéissance la plus aveugle, préférablement à tout autre...").

73. *Ibidem*, 76.

74. N.C.F. van Sas, "Opiniepers en politieke cultuur" in: Grijzenhout, et al, ed. *Voor
Vaderland en Vrijheid*, 97-130 and by the same author "Drukpers, politisering en open-
baarheid van bestuur in de patriottentijd. Enkele kanttekeningen" in: Van der Zee, et al., ed.
1787, 174-184. On the development of the English debate about the freedom of the press
under the impact of similar circumstances see most recently E. Hellmuth, "'The palladium of
all other English liberties': Reflections on the Liberty of the Press in England during the
1760s and 1770s" in: Hellmuth, ed. *Transformation of Political Culture*, 467-501.

opponents in 1782.[75] And it is highly understandable that early in the nineteenth century H. Collot d'Escury, author of one of the first histories of Dutch culture, while praising Luzac as one of the most important Dutch eighteenth-century writers, at the same time with hindsight reprimanded him for an altogether excessive liking for the freedom of expression. But then, the Baron added on second thought, Luzac had written his essay before the rise of that fateful journalism which had caused so many political disasters in Europe.[76]

2. *Luzac's Republic of Letters*

Any attempt to place Luzac in an intellectual milieu should probably start with the following simple facts. In December 1735 the young Luzac arrived in Leiden as an apprentice in the business of his uncle Jean Luzac (1702-1783), bookseller and, from 1738 on, printer of the *Gazette de Leyde*, a publication later to become famous as one of Europe's most important late-eighteenth-century newspapers. With this apprenticeship as a useful basis Elie started out on his own in the publishing business as early as 1742.[77] In the meantime he had, on October 15, 1739, been enrolled as a *Litterarum Studiosus* at Leiden University, where he would continue his studies for most of the 1740s.[78] Luzac's training at Leiden University provided him with a first introduction to the contemporary world of learning and brought him valuable contacts with several prominent Dutch scholars. His activities as a publisher, and from 1748 on as a publicist, made him a participant in a European-wide Republic of Letters. These things combined gave him, at a relatively early age, a central position in a dense web of intellectual exchange. They helped to make him, in the words of J. Marx, into "one of the greatest figures of eighteenth-century European cosmopolitanism".[79]

Although Leiden University may have been past its international prime by the mid-eighteenth century, it was still one of the important European centers of learning.[80] In Dutch intellectual life it continued to play a

75. *Onderzoek over de vryheid, van zyne gevoelens mede te deelen.* Amsterdam, 1782.

76. Collot d'Escury, *Holland's Roem*, vol.5, 359-365.

77. Versprille, "Remarks", 1-2. On Jean Luzac see Popkin, *News and Politics*, 12-13.

78. *Album Studiosorum Academiae Lugduno Batavae*, 975.

79. Marx, "Imprimeur", 779.

80. Two valuable eyewitness accounts of Leiden University in respectively 1725-1727 and 1759 can be found in Lindeboom, ed. *Haller in Holland*, *passim* and Kernkamp, ed. "Bengt Ferrner's dagboek", 462-486.

significant role throughout the century.[81] When in 1749 Luzac dedicated a book to his Leiden preceptors, he listed the following names: J. Alberti, J.C. Rücker, A. Weiss, H.D. Gaubius, P. van Musschenbroek, and J. Lulofs.[82] Not all of these men, however, had been of equal importance to his intellectual formation. For, as H.C. Cras wrote in his manuscript account of Luzac's writings, his favored fields were at first mathematics and physics and later philosophy and natural law.[83] And in 1749 Luzac described himself as primarily a "student of philosophy".[84] It is therefore of particular importance to devote some attention to Van Musschenbroek and Lulofs.

Petrus van Musschenbroek (1692-1761) was the last of a triumvirate of brilliant Leiden practitioners and popularizers of Newtonian science.[85] Together with his predecessors Herman Boerhaave (1668-1738) and Willem Jacob 's-Gravesande (1688-1742), Van Musschenbroek gave Leiden its great international reputation as the foremost continental center of Newtonian "experimental philosophy" in the first half of the eighteenth century. It attracted such famous visitors as Haller, La Mettrie, and Voltaire and hundreds of lesser known foreign students.[86] 's Gravesande and Van Musschenbroek passionately advocated a strict adherence to the Newtonian *regulae philosophandi*: observation and experiment as the basis of all science, the ordering of the data thus obtained by the strictest rules of mathematics and logic, and the avoidance of *a priori* hypotheses.[87] But their insistence on these rules, it should be emphasized, did not mean that they entirely discarded theology and metaphysics. Indeed,

81. On the role of universities in the Dutch Republic in general see Frijhoff, *Société Néerlandaise*.

82. *Disquisitio politico-moralis*, dedication. For information on the public lectures of these professors see the *series lectionum* in Molhuysen, ed. *Bronnen Leidsche Universiteit*, vol.5, Appendix, 77 ff.

83. Cras, "Beredeneerd verslag", 3.

84. *Corr. Formey*, Luzac to Formey, Leiden, August 22, 1749 ("...étudiant en Philosophie...").

85. See on this Leiden brand of Newtonianism in general: Cassirer, *Philosophy of the Enlightenment*, 60-64; Sassen, *Geschiedenis van de Wijsbegeerte*, 223-231; Gay, *Enlightenment*, vol.2, 135-136; Van Berkel, *Voetspoor van Stevin*, 70-77.

86. For brief accounts of the life and work of these three Leiden Newtonians see Kox, ed. *Van Stevin tot Lorentz*, 71-105. For more detailed discussions: Lindeboom, *Herman Boerhaave*; De Pater, ed. *Willem Jacob 's-Gravesande*, 13-58; De Pater, *Petrus van Musschenbroek*.

87. De Pater, ed. *Willem Jacob 's-Gravesande*, 17-18; Kox, ed. *Van Stevin tot Lorentz*, 86-87.

these representatives of the Newtonian Enlightenment were convinced that their research would contribute to the greater glory of the Christian God.[88] In this respect, their work showed a great similarity to that of the physico-theologians, who enjoyed immense popularity in the eighteenth-century Dutch Republic and whose most eminent representative was Bernard Nieuwentijt (1654-1718).[89] But apart from this link between experimental philosophy and natural theology, both 's-Gravesande and Van Musschenbroek also remained interested in metaphysics. 's-Gravesande even wrote a highly successful *Introductio ad philosophiam, metaphysicam et logicam continens*, a book also used by Musschenbroek in his teaching.[90]

Luzac fully absorbed the Newtonian science as taught in Leiden. He would always remain an admirer of Newton and he was intimately familiar with the written work of both 's-Gravesande and Van Musschenbroek. But his real guiding star at Leiden University was Professor Johan Lulofs (1711-1768), who, as 's-Gravesande's successor, taught mathematics and astronomy, and from 1744 on also metaphysics and ethics. According to the *series lectionum*, Lulofs started lecturing on the nature of the celestial bodies in 1742, then switched to the history of philosophy in 1745. In 1747 he was proving the existence and perfection of God from the works of creation.[91] In his private lectures he discussed Pufendorf's *De officio hominis et civis*.[92] Luzac developed a close personal relationship with Lulofs. Lulofs critically read the manuscript of *l'Homme plus que machine* and Luzac, in turn, dedicated the book to him as the person who had introduced him to the study of philosophy.[93] In later

---

88. On the broader religious implications of the Newtonian Enlightenment see Jacob, *Radical Enlightenment*, 87-108 and, by the same author "Christianity and the Newtonian Worldview".

89. Bots, *Tussen Descartes en Darwin, passim*; Van Berkel, *Voetspoor van Stevin*, 77-80; Vermij, ed. *Bernard Nieuwentijt*, 13-39; Vermij, *Secularisering en Natuurwetenschap, passim*.

90. De Pater, ed. *Willem Jacob 's-Gravesande*, 29-30 and 152-153; Wielema, "'s-Gravesande en de metafysica".

91. Molhuysen, ed. *Bronnen Leidsche Universiteit*, vol.5, Appendix, 143, 159, 161: "Johannes Lulofs de natura corporum coelestium aget" (Sept. 1742); "Johannes Lulofs diebus lunae et veneris historiam philosophiae enarrabit" (Sept. 1745); "Johannes Lulofs diebus lunae et veneris existentiam et perfectiones dei ex operibus creationis demonstrabit" (Feb. 1747).

92. Sassen, *Lulofs*, 92.

93. Gemeentearchief Leiden, Luzac to "Messieurs les directeurs des Nouvelles Litteraires de Göttingen", Bremen, June 12, 1748; *l'Homme plus que machine*, ed. 1755, Dedication.

years, Luzac would publish work by Lulofs and would always praise him, both in private correspondence and in publications, as one of the most important Dutch scholars.[94] Lulofs's work had a number of characteristics that appealed to Luzac. First of all, Lulofs strongly emphasized the use of mathematics in all fields of human knowledge, as evidenced by his 1744 inaugural lecture *On the most useful, but hitherto rare marriage of mathematics and metaphysics.*[95] Secondly, he actually applied this mathematical method in the development of a natural theology, in which reason and revelation, although certainly not considered as mutually incompatible, were strictly separated.[96] But perhaps most important was Lulofs's general optimism and his great confidence in the growth of human happiness. Inspired by among others the German philosopher Christian Wolff (1679-1754), who was also to be of crucial importance to Luzac's work, Lulofs foresaw that the application of this new method of systematic reasoning would bring about a golden age in all branches of human knowledge.[97]

In a formal sense, Luzac's relationship with Leiden University was somewhat strained. From 1750 on the regulation that people engaging in a trade or commerce were not allowed to remain *membra universitatis* was enforced with greater strictness than before.[98] Despite his protests, Luzac's name was therefore struck from the *album studiosorum* in that year.[99] In the end, however, the Senate allowed him to enroll briefly as a *iuris studiosum honoris ergo inscripta* in 1759 in order to defend his dissertation and to earn a doctorate in law.[100] Informally, Luzac's ties with the Leiden academic community would always remain strong. At the very end of the century he was still publishing the works of such Leiden professors as Friedrich Wilhelm Pestel and Adriaan Kluit. Leiden University, however, was only one of many possible points of entry into the contemporary learned world. As we have seen from the La Mettrie affair, a much wider field was opened to Luzac by his activities as a publisher

---

94. E.g. *Corr. Formey*, Luzac to Formey, Hamburg, October 27, 1750; *Nederlandsche Letter-Courant*, vol.4 (1760), 110.

95. *De utilissimo sed hactenus raro matheseos ac metaphysices connubio*; Sassen, *Lulofs*, 18-21.

96. Sassen, *Lulofs*, 22-41; Bots, *Tussen Descartes en Darwin*, 51-53.

97. Sassen, *Lulofs*, 19-20.

98. Molhuysen, "Voorrechten", 24-26.

99. Molhuysen, ed. *Bronnen Leidsche Universiteit*, vol.5, 320 and Appendix, 168-169.

100. *Album Studiosorum Academiae Lugduno Batavae*, 1064 and Molhuysen, ed. *Bronnen Leidsche Universiteit*, vol.5, Appendix, 298.

and as a publicist. Each publication brought him new contacts and sometimes even briefly put him in the very center of European intellectual controversy. Thus, to give but one more brief example, he was actively involved in the famous quarrel between Maupertuis and Koenig on the principle of the least action. Not only did he publish Maupertuis's *Essai de cosmologie*, but also the most scandalous pamphlet related to this whole episode, Voltaire's *Diatribe du Docteur Akakia.*[101] For Luzac, the whole affair resulted in a close friendship with the celebrated Swiss Wolffian philosopher Samuel Koenig, who spent the last part of his life in the Dutch Republic.[102] In October 1750, Luzac described Koenig to Formey as "one of the most important philosophers". Shortly thereafter, we find the two men contemplating a French translation of Christian Wolff's *Institutiones iuris naturae et gentium*. Although they did not complete that project, the collaboration between them lasted until Koenig's death in 1757.[103]

In 1753, meanwhile, Luzac had expanded his publishing activities into the Holy Roman Empire by opening a printshop in Göttingen, having previously refused a request by Frederick the Great to do the same thing in Berlin.[104] The business in Göttingen involved him in an interminable legal controversy with the Hannover government.[105] It finally had to be closed down in 1760, but it had greatly helped to expand his international contacts, already substantial before 1753 because of his vast correspondence and frequent travels to Germany, where he not only visited bookfairs, but also set up meetings with scholars.[106] But at least as important to Luzac's place in the Republic of Letters was his active involvement in the publication of two mid-century learned journals. Between 1750 and 1758 he closely collaborated with Formey in the publication of the

101. On the Maupertuis-Koenig affair and Voltaire see Harnack, *Geschichte der Preussischen Akademie*, vol.1, 331-344 and Calinger, "Newtonian-Wolffian controversy", 324-328. On Luzac's role see Marx, "Elie Luzac", 86-89.

102. On Koenig see Galama, *Wijsgerig Onderwijs*, 159-160 and Sassen, *Geschiedenis van de Wijsbegeerte*, 236-237.

103. *Corr. Formey*, Luzac to Formey, Leiden, October 1, 1750 ("...un des premiers Philosophes..."); Hamburg, November 7, 1750; Leiden, January 24, 1758.

104. Provinciale Bibliotheek Leeuwarden, Luzac to Herman Cannegieter, [undated, but probably 1750].

105. Luzac's troubles in Göttingen can be followed in detail in the *Corr. Formey* between May 7, 1753 and September 8, 1760. The papers relating to the legal controversy have been preserved in the Universitätsarchiv Göttingen, Archiv Luzac.

106. E.g. Provinciale Bibliotheek Leeuwarden, Luzac to Herman Cannegieter, [undated, but probably 1750].

Bibliothèque Impartiale.[107] From 1759 to 1763 he published, and largely wrote, his own journal with news from the world of learning, the *Nederlandsche Letter-Courant.*[108] These two ventures necessitated the critical digestion of a constant stream of intellectual information from all over Europe for over a decade. They help us understand how Luzac came to belong to that highly select group of eighteenth-century Dutchmen who rapidly acquainted themselves with important intellectual developments outside their own country. Thus, to give but two examples, he quickly reacted to the programmatic statements underlying the French *Encyclopédie* and he was the only Dutch author to write an early and substantial response to the work of Rousseau.[109] Finally, to round off this brief account of the various forms Luzac's literary sociability took, it should be pointed out that he was an eager participant in the essay competitions held by learned societies. This led him to write on such fashionable topics as the nature of moral duties for the Berlin Academy of Sciences and on the contribution of revelation to human ethics for the Leiden *Legatum Stolpianum.*

From the above it should be clear that by his tireless energy and great intellectual curiosity Luzac quickly succeeded in establishing himself in an important position in the world of learning. Answering an enquiry by Formey, he confidently remarked as early as 1750 that "there are hardly any learned people in our country...whom I do not know".[110] Yet the varied nature of his activities and the wide range of his contacts in the mid-century Republic of Letters should not obscure the fact that Luzac had a very specific intellectual orientation and belonged to a clearly recognizable sub-group in the international world of learning. The Luzac family had moved to the Dutch Republic in the late seventeenth century, driven out of southern France by Louis XIV's revocation of the Edict of Nantes. The Republic was not the only place where substantial numbers of Huguenots settled. They also flocked to London, Geneva, and especially Berlin, where they were welcomed with special privileges. These *émigrés*, surrounding their old country in a huge semi-circle, formed an international network of communication. Primarily by means of their dominance in the market of learned journals, they came to play the role

---

107. On this periodical see Marx, "Une revue oubliée" and Marx, "Bibliothèque Impartiale".

108. See on this journal Stouten, "On tolerance" and Van Manen, "Nederlandsche Letter-Courant".

109. Luzac's response to the French Enlightenment will be discussed in Chapter II.

110. *Corr. Formey*, Luzac to Formey, Leiden, March 3, 1750 ("...il n'y a presque point de Personnes lettrées dans notre pays...que je ne connoisse...").

of cultural intermediaries in early eighteenth-century Europe.[111] The story of the earliest phases of their exile has been told numerous times and its intellectual aspects have been exhaustively explored by Erich Haase.[112] It is less frequently recognized that, although the exiles show-ed remarkable skill in adapting to the national cultures of their various new countries, the consciousness and reality of a Huguenot Republic of Letters extended far into the eighteenth century. This phenomenon is of crucial importance for a proper understanding of many of Luzac's early writings, for they directly belong to the liberal Protestant wing of the mid-century international Huguenot community, a group that could also be described as representing a Moderate or Conservative Enlight-enment.[113]

The thought of this community, in which Jean Henri Samuel Formey (1711-1797), the Perpetual Secretary of the Berlin Academy of Sciences, was the central figure, was characterized by a number of salient fea-tures.[114] While these enlightened Huguenots emphatically remained Protestant, they were vehemently opposed to all forms of religious enthusiasm and fanaticism. This antipathy sometimes, as in the case of Luzac himself, resulted in a marked anti-clerical strain. It certainly led to decided rejection of governmental religious persecution. Although they were strongly interested in and highly receptive to the new natural science, these liberal Protestants never came to adopt the extreme anti-rationalism that would come to dominate the French Enlightenment in its later stages. Instead, they favored the *connubium rationis et experientiae* as taught by Christian Wolff.[115] But above all, they were interested in developing and propagating the *science des moeurs* or modern natural

111. De Beer, "Huguenots and the Enlightenment"; Richter, "Aufklärung und die Berliner Hugenotten"; Gibbs, "Role of the Dutch Republic".

112. Von Thadden and Magdelaine, ed. *Die Hugenotten*; Bots, et al., ed. *Vlucht naar de Vrijheid*; Haase, *Einführung in die Literatur des Refuge*.

113. The term Moderate Enlightenment has been used, in a somewhat different context, by May, *Enlightenment in America*, 3-101; see also Sher, *Church and University*. For the term Conservative Enlightenment, covering similar phenomena, see below, note 116.

114. On Formey see Voisine, "J. Formey"; Marcu, "Formey and the Enlightenment"; Marcu, "Encyclopédiste oubliée"; Roth, "Encyclopédie réduite"; Krauss, "Correspondance de Formey"; Krauss, "Akademiesekretär"; Marx, "Liaison dangereuse"; Schwarzbach, "Voltaire et les Huguenots de Berlin". A comprehensive study of the work and correspondence of Formey would be highly desirable. For his enormous bibliography see Cioranescu, *Biblio-graphie*, vol.2, 811-814.

115. H.W. Arndt, "Rationalismus und Empirismus in der Erkenntnislehre Christian Wolffs" in: Schneiders, ed. *Christian Wolff*, 31-47.

law. Their Protestant faith, although still very real, had far distanced itself from the original emphasis on man's sinful nature. It had, to a large extent, come to consist of optimistic prescriptions for good morals and virtuous living and it was firmly oriented towards this world, not towards the afterlife. Religious fanaticism on the one hand, total scepticism or moral Pyrrhonism on the other hand, were perceived as the greatest threats to this mode of thought.[116] This preference for and systematic study of the *science des moeurs* in the mid-eighteenth century enlightened Huguenot community had been pioneered early in the eighteenth century by Jean Barbeyrac (1674-1744), who produced lavishly annotated Francophone editions of Grotius's *De iure belli ac pacis* and Pufendorf's *De iure naturae et gentium* and *De officio hominis et civis*.[117] By the mid-eighteenth century the attention had shifted from Grotius and Pufendorf to Christian Wolff, the philosopher regarded as having brought the systematic and scientific study of morals to previously unknown heights. Formey was a convinced Wolffian who achieved great fame with his popular rendering of the master's philosophical doctrines in the form of a novel, *La belle Wolffienne*.[118] His French translation and abridgement of Wolff's natural law was published in Amsterdam in 1758: *Principes du droit de la nature et des gens, abrégé du grand ouvrage Latin de Ch. Wolff*.[119] His circle included Jean Des Champs (1709-1767), who wrote a *Cours abrégé de philosophie Wolffienne, en forme de lettres*.[120] To this same group also belonged the Swiss Wolffian Emer de Vattel (1714-1767), whose 1758 *Le droit des gens ou des principes de la loi naturelle* would go through more than fifty subsequent editions.[121]

What these men finally also had in common was a strong interest in

---

116. On the origins of certain forms of Enlightenment in the abhorrence of fanaticism and enthusiasm see Pocock, "Clergy and Commerce" and Pocock, "Conservative Enlightenment". On the importance of scepticism in the genesis of modern natural law see R. Tuck, "The 'modern' theory of natural law" in: Pagden, ed. *Languages of Political Theory*, 99-119 and Tuck, "Moral Science".

117. On Barbeyrac see Meylan, *Barbeyrac*, and Othmer, *Berlin und die Verbreitung des Naturrechts*.

118. 6 vols. The Hague, 1741-1753. Reprinted Hildesheim, etc., 1983. See Thomann, "Influence du Ius Naturae", xliii.

119. Thomann, "Influence du Ius Naturae", xlii.

120. 3 vols. Amsterdam and Leipzig, 1743-1747. On Des Champs see Janssens-Knorsch, *Jean Des Champs*.

121. On Vattel see Thomann, "Influence du Ius Naturae", xxxvi-xxxvii; A. Dufour, "Die école romande du droit naturel. Ihre deutsche Wurzeln" in: Thieme, ed. *Humanismus und Naturrecht*, 133-143; Whelan, "Vattel's Doctrine of the State".

all things French. Even the third generation descendants of the original Huguenot *émigrés* remained highly conscious of the tragic expulsion of their forbears from France. The fact that it was the learned *lingua franca* for most of the eighteenth century moreover made it easy and convenient for them to retain French as their first language. But more generally it might be said that developments in France remained their most important point of reference. The main tenets of their liberal Protestantism had been formulated in the first half of the eighteenth century, with Catholic and absolutist France as the prime example of what was to be avoided. But in the course of the century this Moderate Enlightenment was being over-taken, primarily from within France, by a sensationalist, anti-Christian, and ultimately politically revolutionary brand of Enlightenment. The intel-lectual universe of these enlightened Huguenots therefore to a large extent took shape in a constant dialogue with various extreme views emanating from their old country. The mid-century was the crucial turning point. The *science des moeurs*, having originated in an anti-absolutist setting, was now confronted by radical *philosophes*. Liberal Protestantism, having been inspired by the Catholic intolerance of Louis XIV's France, now came under attack from anti-Christian French sensationalists and mate-rialists. The result was great confusion. The Moderate Enlightenment suddenly found itself on the defense against a previously unknown enemy and threatened to disintegrate.

During the 1750s and 1760s Luzac was very much a part of the world just described. Through his journals, he had close contacts with such London-based representatives of the Huguenot Republic of Letters as Matthieu Maty and Jean Des Champs.[122] When in 1763 Maria Massuet became his second wife he actually married into this intellectual com-munity.[123] She was the daughter of Pierre Massuet, one of the authors of the *Bibliothèque Raisonnée*, whom Luzac described to Formey as "a doctor of medicine in Amsterdam and well-known in the Republic of Letters".[124] Luzac also published several works by the noted Swiss liberal Protestant scholar Charles Bonnet and seriously considered pub-

---

122. On Maty see Janssens-Knorsch, *Matthieu Maty*.

123. Luzac's first wife, Ernestine Auguste Treu, had died in 1751. His marriage to Maria Massuet would also be short-lived, for she died in 1766. Versprille, "Remarks", 2. Luzac reported Maria Massuet's death in a letter to Formey: "Cette mort m'afflige; il n'y a qu'une resignation aux decrets de la providence, qui puisse nous donner les moyens de consolation dans ces cas accablans pour des coeurs sensibles". *Corr. Formey*, Luzac to Formey, Leiden, November 29, 1766.

124. *Corr. Formey*, Luzac to Formey, Leiden, July 22, 1763 ("...Docteur en Medecine à Amsterdam, connu dans la Republique des Lettres.").

lishing work by Vattel.[125] But his most important contact in this circle was Samuel Formey. As we saw, the two men collaborated closely in the publication of the *Bibliothèque Impartiale* during the years 1750 to 1758. But there was far more to their relationship. In hundreds of letters, mainly written during the 1750s, they exchanged news from the world of learning and, as in the La Mettrie case, personal opinions. Formey kept Luzac informed about developments in the Berlin Academy of Sciences. Luzac, in turn, provided Formey with news about the latest Dutch publications, repeatedly emphasizing that these received far too little attention in the existing Francophone journals.[126] Luzac also served as the publisher of a considerable number of Formey's writings, among them the *Philosophe chrétien*, the *Mélanges philosophiques*, the *Pensées raisonnables*, the *Philosophe payen*, and the *Principes de morale*.[127] During the 1750s Formey's works seem to have enjoyed great popularity, so much so that Luzac had to fight over the legal publishing privilege and was repeatedly deprived of legitimate income by the appearance of pirate editions.[128] He constantly, but not always successfully, tried to bring the prolific Formey to let him publish even more than he already did. Thus, for instance, he could not persuade Formey to give him the abridged edition of Mosheim's enormous church history. Despite repeated requests by Luzac, it went to the Amsterdam publisher J.H. Schneider.[129]

Luzac greatly admired Formey's capacity to present his arguments in a way that was easily comprehensible yet systematic and thorough. He warmly praised his incessant efforts to propagate the "moral and religious

---

125. On Bonnet see Marx, "Charles Bonnet" and Taylor, "Enlightenment in Switzerland" in: Porter and Teich, ed. *Enlightenment in National Context*, 85-86. On the possible publication of work by Vattel see *Corr. Formey*, Luzac to Formey, Leiden, May 17 and June 29, 1756. Luzac later critically reviewed Vattel's *Questions du droit naturel* in the *Nederlandsche Letter-Courant*, vol.9 (1763), 12-14.

126. E.g. *Corr. Formey*, Luzac to Formey, Hamburg, October 27, 1750.

127. *Le philosophe chrétien, ou discours moraux*. 4 vols. Vols. 1 and 2 Leide, 1750-1752, vols. 3 and 4 Göttingue and Leyde, 1755-1757; *Mélanges philosophiques*. 2 vols. Leide, 1754; *Pensées raisonnables. Avec un essai de critique sur le livre intitulé Les Moeurs et la Lettre de Gervaise Holmes à l'auteur de celle sur les aveugles*. Göttingue and Leyde, 1758; *Le philosophe payen, ou pensées de Pline, avec un commentaire littéraire et moral*. Leide, 1759; *Principes de morale déduits de l'usage des facultés de l'entendement humain*. 2 vols. Leide, 1762.

128. On privileges see *Corr. Formey*, Luzac to Formey, Leiden, April 8, 1760 and Van Eeghen, *Amsterdamse boekhandel*, vol.5, 127; on pirate editions see *Corr. Formey*, Luzac to Formey, Leipzig, October 12, 1754 and Leiden, September 12, 1756.

129. *Abrégé de l'histoire ecclésiastique par Mr. Formey*. 2 vols. Amsterdam, 1763; *Corr. Formey*, Luzac to Formey, Leiden, [undated], April 18 and September 7, 1761.

virtues".[130] But he had to admit that some of Formey's writings were somewhat superficial and that many of them were long winded, written too much in the "Style de Prédicateur".[131] For reasons both of content and of commerce, he kept urging the Berlin minister to lessen the religious emphasis in his texts in favor of a moral one. Thus, while he was still publishing volumes of Formey's *Philosophe chrétien*, Luzac encouraged its author to start on a *Philosophe moral*, remarking about the study of morality that "I take a very strong interest in the progress of that part of our knowledge which I consider to be both the most necessary to man and the least known".[132] Not only would such a book be of great interest and utility, Luzac added, it would also sell well, for "the public of the present time is more interested in morals than in revealed theology".[133] The two men kept discussing the project until a work of this nature finally appeared in 1762: Formey's *Principes de morale déduits de l'usage des facultés de l'entendement humain*. Although he had some points of criticism, Luzac praised the two volumes as among the best available on their subject in the French language.[134]

Luzac and Formey not only cooperated in many publishing ventures, they also engaged in highly similar forms of writing. As great admirers of Christian Wolff's philosophy, they produced the only two eighteenth-century Francophone editions of Wolff's system of natural law. As we have seen, Formey's abridged translation appeared in 1758. Luzac, of course, applauded the fact that this work was now available in French. But having read the manuscript he concluded, together with Koenig, that the translation was too arid and boring and that it would therefore scare away potential readers.[135] His own richly annotated edition of Wolff's natural law, the *Institutions du droit de la nature et des gens*, would appear in 1772. Side by side, the two men opposed the French *philosophes*. Where Formey tried to refute Diderot's *Pensées philosophiques* with his *Pensées raisonnables*, Luzac sharply attacked d'Alembert in his

130. *Nederlandsche Letter-Courant*, vol.2 (1759), 149 ("...zedelyke en godvruchtige deugden...").

131. *Ibidem*, 10 and *Corr. Formey*, Luzac to Formey, Leipzig, October 12, 1754.

132. *Corr. Formey*, Luzac to Formey, Leiden, December 16, 1755 ("...tout mon coeur est porté aux progrès de cette partie de nos connoissances que je regarde comme la plus nécessaire à l'homme, et la moins connue.").

133. *Ibidem*, August 13, 1754 ("Le Public du tems present donne plus dans la morale que dans la Théologie revelée...").

134. *Nederlandsche Letter-Courant*, vol.7 (1762), 187-190 and 197-200.

135. *Corr. Formey*, Luzac to Formey, Leiden, January 15, 1751.

Nederlandsche Letter-Courant.[136] They were also united in their fascination with and negative response to the work of Rousseau, although Luzac perceived the Genevan's writings as a much greater threat and consequently reacted more strongly than Formey.[137] But despite their intellectual affinity, their mutual interests and their practical cooperation, contacts between Luzac and Formey waned as the century progressed. The rapidly decreasing sales of Formey's works clearly showed that their brand of Enlightenment had lost its popularity. The public's taste, so Luzac observed, was moving away from the enlightened and systematic study of morality to more frivolous things.[138] In his final letter to Formey, dated July 3, 1770, Luzac expressed deep regret about the turn things were taking. "Had the taste of our century responded better to ours or had ours been more in tune with the dominant trend in the Francophone Republic of Letters, perhaps our correspondence would not have petered out".[139]

By the time Luzac wrote these last words he had already given a great deal of thought to developments in the Republic of Letters. In his very first writings, particularly in the 1749 *Essai sur la liberté de produire ses sentimens*, he had, as we have seen, given powerful expression to the ideal of an open and rational process of intellectual communication among an international elite of cultivated men. The years to follow had done much to show him that theory and practice were separated by a deep divide. From within the Republic of Letters he had been confronted with vicious quarrels, such as the one between Maupertuis, Koenig, and Voltaire, and with the stubbornness and egocentricity of the authors whose works he published. In one of his more pessimistic moments this led him to remark that, on the whole, he much preferred merchants to scholars. "When I make a general comparison between scholars and merchants, it seems to me that the former are quite wrong in despising the latter, who in many respects are more humane and sociable".[140]

---

136. On Formey and Diderot see Marcu, "Formey and the Enlightenment", 57-88.

137. Among the writings Formey devoted to Rousseau were the *Anti-Emile* (1763), *L'esprit de Julie, ou extrait de la nouvelle Héloïse* (1763), and the *Emile chrétien* (1764). See Voisine, "J. Formey" and Marcu, "Formey and the Enlightenment", 89-110.

138. *Corr. Formey*, Luzac to Formey, Leiden, August 20, 1765.

139. *Ibidem*, July 3, 1770 ("Si le gout de notre Siècle eut plus repondu au notre ou si le notre eut été plus conforme au ton regnant dans la Republique des Lettres françoises, notre correspondance n'auroit peut-être pas tarie.").

140. *Ibidem*, December 30, 1751 ("Quand je fais une comparaison générale des Savans aux Negotiants je trouve que les premiers ont bien tort de mépriser les seconds, qui me paroissent à bien des egards plus humains et plus sociables.").

Such practical difficulties, however, were not insurmountable. A much more serious problem was posed by the fact that the Republic of Letters frequently turned out to be more susceptible to the dictates of fashion than to rational argument. "The learned world", so Luzac observed, "is often very similar to the normal world; it follows fashion".[141] The French in particular, going through one literary vogue after another, seemed to have become hopeless slaves of fashion.[142] These short-lived crazes, Luzac thought, were indicative of a deeper shift of mood within the Republic of Letters. Systematic reasoning was increasingly being replaced by elegant and vapid bantering. Or, to capture the difference between the worlds of the Moderate and the French Enlightenment in the titles of two books, the *Pensées raisonnables* were being pushed aside by the *Pensées philosophiques*. A change in the climate of opinion was rapidly transforming the Republic of Letters that Luzac had so lovingly described in 1749 beyond recognition.

At the same time, another process was causing a partial disintegration of the Republic of Letters as Luzac had first come to know it. Broadly speaking, during the first half of the eighteenth century intellectual debate had primarily taken place within an international and cosmopolitan cultural elite, with Latin and increasingly French as the dominant languages. For a variety of reasons, among them the growth of the reading public, the second half of the century witnessed an increased role for the various national cultures.[143] This inward turn can be observed in a number of countries, but it was particularly pronounced in the Dutch Republic, where it coincided with a relatively sudden decline in international status.[144] Luzac's development reflected this broader trend in a remarkable way. Starting from an almost exclusive focus on the international world of learning in his initial years as a publicist, as the century progressed he became increasingly interested in participating in Dutch debates. The founding of the *Nederlandsche Letter-Courant* is of great interest in this context. Not only was it among the first learned journals in the Dutch language, but Luzac also expressly started writing and pub-

---

141. *Nederlandsche Letter-Courant*, vol.3 (1760), 396 ("Dikwyls gaat het in de geleerde wereld even als in de gemeene; men volgt 'er de mode.").

142. *Ibidem*, 397.

143. On changes in the reading public see Brouwer, "Rondom het boek".

144. This point has recently been emphasized by W.W. Mijnhardt. See *Tot Heil van 't Menschdom*, 83-88; "De Nederlandsche Verlichting" in: Grijzenhout, et al., *Voor Vaderland en Vrijheid*, 53-79; "The Dutch Enlightenment: Humanism, Nationalism, and Decline" in: Jacob and Mijnhardt, ed. *The Dutch Republic in the Eighteenth Century*, 197-223.

lishing it to call attention to the products of Dutch culture. It might be added here that Luzac's liberal Protestantism, while coming under attack elsewhere, was increasingly in tune with the mainstream of Dutch enlightened opinion in the 1760s and 1770s, in which radicalism of all sorts was eschewed.[145] Yet despite his practical disappointments, his sombre evaluation of the changing mood in the international scholarly community, and his growing interest in Dutch culture, Luzac would always keep at least one eye on the international scene. Optimist to the end, he kept hoping that the "sound philosophy" which he propagated would once again come to dominate the Republic of Letters or what was left of it.[146]

3. *God, Reason, and Happiness: Early Writings*

It is against the background of his close association with the international liberal Protestant community that the content of most of Luzac's writings from the late 1740s to the early 1760s should be understood. As indicated above, the thought in this milieu, strongly influenced by the teachings of Christian Wolff, was characterized by a rejection of the extremes of fanaticism and scepticism, by a refusal to rely completely on the senses and the consequent retention of a strong element of rationalism, by a clear separation of reason and revelation, and by an overwhelming interest in the development of natural law or the science of morality. It is the purpose of this section to demonstrate that all of these themes were prominently present in Luzac's early writings. Once that has been established, it will be easier to understand how and why he came to oppose more radical forms of Enlightenment.

In his 1748 *l'Homme plus que machine* Luzac made it clear that he rejected materialism and that he disapproved of La Mettrie's limited empirical orientation, a deviation, so he observed, not unusual in medical circles.[147] His purpose was not to write a step by step refutation of *l'Homme machine*. Instead, he wished to discuss materialist thought and some of the broader conclusions derived from it in general. The fundamental difference between materialists and immaterialists, he first of all explained, was that the former were convinced that man consisted of one

---

145. Buijnsters, "Lumières hollandaises"; Van den Berg, "Orthodoxy"; Bots and De Vet, "Les Provinces-Unies et les Lumières"; S. Schama, "The Enlightenment in the Netherlands" in: Porter and Teich, ed. *Enlightenment in National Context*, 54-71.

146. *Droit naturel, Programme*, 24-25 ("...saine philosophie...").

147. *l'Homme plus que machine*, 11-12. All references are to the 1755 edition.

single material substance, whereas the latter held that this single material substance was insufficient to explain the presence of the faculty of thought, or the soul.[148] He brushed aside the claim that this problem should be solved on the sole basis of "physical experiments" as an unacceptable *petitio principii*, for it presumed from the start that the soul was in fact material. "We shall therefore have to listen to *metaphysicians* as well as to *physicians* concerning this problem".[149] This opened the way for Luzac's first main argument. In a Cartesian vein he tried to establish that the properties of thought were incompatible with those of matter.[150] Whereas thought was active, self-transforming, and capable of a multiplicity of simultaneous actions, matter had none of these characteristics. Thought therefore had to be immaterial.[151] This conclusion was reinforced, so Luzac continued, by a second argument. The physical experiments collected and performed by doctors such as La Mettrie were incapable of proving more than the existence of a reciprocal relationship between body and soul. To take these experiments as proof that the soul was a mere mechanical function of the body was as absurd as the contention that "a musician is no more than the mechanism of his instrument, because he cannot play well when something is wrong with his instrument".[152] Luzac also deemed the analogy between men and animals, much favored by La Mettrie, to be completely irrelevant to the solution of the mind-body problem, for the causes of certain observable external behavioral similarities between man and beast remained in the dark.[153] The attributes of thought, to sum up, were completely different from those of matter. Neither medical observations nor the flawed analogy between men and animals could prove the contrary. It was therefore evident that human thought or the soul was immaterial. The exact nature of the relationship between mind and body, Luzac modestly added, remained beyond present understanding. "A wise man is not ashamed not to be able to know everything and even less ashamed to admit this. It is sufficient for him that what he espouses is proven, whereas its opposite is

---

148. *Ibidem*, 15-16.

149. *Ibidem*, 18 ("...les expériences physiques..."; "Ce seront donc les *Metaphysiciens*, aussi bien que les *Physiciens*, qu'il faudra écouter ici.").

150. For Descartes's manner of arguing in these matters see Sorrell, *Descartes*, 81-92.

151. *l'Homme plus que machine*, 20-32.

152. *Ibidem*, 33-47. The quotation is on 47 ("...un Musicien n'est que le mecanisme de son instrument, parce qu'il ne peut pas bien jouër lorsque son instrument n'est pas en ordre.").

153. *Ibidem*, 76-113.

not. That argument should make every reasonable being an im-
materialist".[154]

Having thus argued that the soul or human thought was immaterial,
Luzac went on to consider the broader implications of materialism. From
their reflections on man's constitution, he observed, the materialists
concluded that the universe too was a simple machine. They emphatically
denied the need to look for external causes to explain its existence.
Consequently, they also failed to acknowledge the existence of a Supreme
Being. Even if some of them did not positively deny the possibility of the
existence of such a Being, they still claimed that man could know nothing
about it and was under no obligation to worship it. The possible existence
of a Supreme Being was therefore a matter of very limited interest to
man.[155] Luzac first of all rejected the materialist analogy between man
and the universe. Even if man were a machine, he argued, it would not
follow that the universe had the same constitution. "That assertion
presupposes a perfect knowledge of everything that exists and is therefore
absolutely invalid".[156] Luzac dealt with the contention that the universe
could be the cause of its own existence by following the natural theology
of his teacher Lulofs, whose demonstration of the existence of God had
heavily relied on the Leibnizian principle of sufficient reason.[157] The
materialist position, Luzac claimed, would only be credible if the essence
and nature of the universe could be shown necessarily to cause its existence in a definite and unchanging form. Given the constant observable
changes in the universe, this was obviously not the case. Consequently,
the reason for its existence had to be looked for elsewhere. It had to be
sought in an unchanging, eternal first cause; in "an intelligent and perfect
being, existing by virtue of its own nature".[158] But what did all this
mean for man? Deducing a whole string of attributes from the necessary
existence of a Supreme Being, Luzac remarked that in creating man God
had clearly intended him to strive for his own happiness and that of

154. *Ibidem*, 117-118 ("Un sage ne rougit pas de ne pouvoir tout connoître, et encore moins
de l'avouër. Il lui suffit que ce qu'il embrasse soit prouvé, pendant que son opposé ne l'est
pas, et cette raison doit porter tout Etre raisonnable à avouër l'Immatérialisme.").

155. *Ibidem*, 118-120.

156. *Ibidem*, 122 ("Cette assertion suppose une parfaite connoissance de tout ce qui existe;
et n'est par consequent d'aucune valeur.").

157. Sassen, *Lulofs*, 27-28. Lulofs's *Primae liniae theologiae naturalis* was not published
until 1756, but it was an outgrowth of his lectures on the existence and perfection of God
that had started in 1747. See note 91.

158. *l'Homme plus que machine*, 122-138. The quotation is on 136 ("...un Etre intelligent,
parfait, et qui existe en vertu de sa propre nature.").

mankind in general. For man, the most pressing reason to behave in this fashion was the conviction that he had an obligation to regulate his behavior in accordance with the divine will. This conviction could be called religious worship or, Luzac revealingly added, natural law. The tendency of his whole argument was in fact to conflate the two notions: "the belief in a Divinity is as essential to natural law as that law is essential to the belief in a Divinity".[159] Contrary to materialist contentions, it was quite evident that human happiness and religious worship, in this restricted sense, were intimately linked.

Having exposed the weaknesses of both materialism and the broader conclusions derived from that doctrine, at the very end of his polemic Luzac once again cautioned his readers against overestimating the value of observation and experiment. First of all, he pointed out, following the Leiden Newtonian 's-Gravesande, the reliability of observation and experiment was not as unproblematic and self-evident as many nowadays seemed to suppose. Their use depended on subsequent reasoning by analogy, which presupposed the uniform operation of the laws of nature. The only basis for trusting in that uniformity, in turn, was a belief in God's goodness.[160] But even more important was the fact that observation and experiments were in themselves insufficient. They might help in discovering the truth, but only reason could finally establish it. "Without the art of reasoning *Newton*, *Boyle*, and *'s-Gravesande* would not have made much out of their experiments. This goes to show that he who leans entirely on the cane of experience can be no more than a miserable cripple".[161]

Although the refutation of materialism had been the main theme of *l'Homme plus que machine*, Luzac's interest in the problem of knowledge and in natural law had emerged as important subsidiary topics. Of these, the latter would come to dominate many of his later writings. In the long run, Luzac's preoccupations clearly were in the field of practical philosophy: ethics, economics, and politics. But the former also briefly deserves our attention, for in 1756 he published what would remain his only work

---

159. *Ibidem*, 138-161. The quotation is on 154-155 ("...la persuasion d'une Divinité est aussi essentielle au Droit Naturel, que ce Droit est essentiel à la conviction d'une Divinité.").

160. On the use of this argument by 's-Gravesande see Cassirer, *Philosophy of the Enlightenment*, 60-64 and De Pater, ed. *Willem Jacob 's-Gravesande*, 43-46.

161. *l'Homme plus que machine*, 174-176. The quotation is on 176 ("Sans l'art de raisonner, *Newton, Boyle, 's-Gravesande*, n'auroient pas fait grand chose de leurs expériences. On voit par là que celui, qui n'a que le bâton de l'expérience pour guide, ne peut qu'être un misérable boiteux."). *l'Homme plus que machine* is briefly discussed in Vartanian, *La Mettrie*, 105-106.

on epistemology, the *Recherches sur quelques principes des connoissances humaines*. Once again, this treatise showed Luzac's penchant for polemic, for it was occasioned by an attack on Leibnizian philosophy in the *Journal des Sçavans*.[162] The *Recherches* were partly authored by Luzac and partly consisted of the French translation of Antonius Brugmans's (1732-1789) doctoral dissertation *De Phaenomeno*. Luzac had met Brugmans, a professor at Franeker and later at Groningen University, through his friend Samuel Koenig, whose chief Dutch pupil Brugmans was.[163] Both Koenig and the young Brugmans, although heavily influenced by the German philosophy of Leibniz and Wolff, strongly believed that this mode of thought was compatible with Newtonian science. The new physics, they held, could very well be combined with a modern and systematically developed metaphysics. This had been the central message of, for instance, Koenig's voluminous 1746 Franeker inaugural lecture *De optimis Wolfiana et Newtoniana philosophandi methodis earumque amico consensu*.[164] A similar eclecticism, it might be added, also dominated the Berlin Academy of Sciences at the time.[165] It was in this same spirit that the *Recherches* were conceived.

Brugmans's contribution to the book was of a highly technical nature, with Luzac providing the more general observations. Constantly referring to the methodological writings of Christian Wolff, Luzac used this polemic to highlight the role of reason in human knowledge. It was reason's task, he argued at length, to order and analyze the utterly confused and frequently undependable deluge of material presented to our mind by experience. Reason had to separate reality from appearances. It performed the all-important function of developing ideas that were "clear", "distinct", "complete", "adequate", and "fixed".[166] Only such ideas constituted knowledge and, linked in a logical chain of argument, a

---

162. D.R. Boullier, "Mémoire sur les monades de Mr. Leibnitz", *Journal des Sçavans*, April 1753, 433-476. The polemic continued with a negative review of the *Recherches* in the *Bibliothèque des Sciences et des Beaux Arts*, vol.7, first part, January to March 1757, 223-231, followed by Luzac's response in vol.8, second part, October to December 1757, 464-468. The Francophone debate about Leibniz and Wolff has been reconstructed in great detail by Barber, *Leibniz in France*.

163. On Brugmans see Galama, *Wijsgerig Onderwijs*, 171-177.

164. *Ibidem*, 159-160.

165. Beck, *Early German Philosophy*, 314-317.

166. *Recherches*, 7-85. The quotations are on 20-21 ("...claires..."; "...distinctes..."; "...complettes..."; "...adequates..."; "...déterminées...").

science.[167] As Formey remarked in his favorable review of the *Recherches*, these views clearly made Luzac into an adherent of "the philosophy of Germany".[168] Yet it should be stressed that Luzac shared the eclecticism of Koenig, Brugmans and the Berlin Academy of Sciences. He did his utmost to convince his readers that the views he expressed were not incompatible with the procedures of Newtonian science, only with the vulgar brand of Newtonianism that reduced all knowledge to observation and experiment.[169] As W.H. Barber has observed, Luzac was in fact trying to argue that the metaphysical theories of Leibniz and Wolff were of the same nature as the hypotheses used by serious Newtonians. They were both no more than attempts to explain phenomena in terms of general principles.[170]

Having established his basic position, Luzac hastened to leave the realm of epistemology. For although, like many representatives of the Moderate Enlightenment, he was obsessed with the importance of the growth and spread of knowledge, he was more interested in its practical application than in its theoretical foundations. This preference, combined with the influence of the milieu he moved in, makes it unsurprising that he devoted most of his youthful energy to moral philosophy, a field he fervently desired to help develop in a systematic and scientific way. His 1753 treatise *Le bonheur ou nouveau système de jurisprudence naturelle* is the most interesting example of the earliest stage of what would become a lifelong endeavor, culminating in the posthumously published multi-volume *Du droit naturel, civil, et politique*. First published in Berlin, it was rapidly pirated in Paris and reprinted in the Netherlands as late as 1820.[171] Part of its fascination lies in the fact that it shows us Luzac still wrestling with the central concepts of moral science or natural law. About the proper method for studying this branch of knowledge, however, he had no doubts left. It was the Wolffian scientific, demonstrative, or mathematical method. In his 1749 *Disquisitio politico-moralis*

---

167. *Ibidem*, 10.

168. *Nouvelle Bibliothèque Germanique*, vol.21, second part, October to December 1757, 284 ("...la philosophie d'Allemagne...").

169. *Recherches*, 125-159. The distinction between these two kinds of Newtonianism can be found on 128-129.

170. Barber, *Leibniz in France*, 162-163. On the *Recherches* see also Cras, "Beredeneerd verslag", 24-35.

171. *Le bonheur* was published in Berlin in 1753 and reprinted there in 1754. On the Paris edition see *Corr. Formey*, Luzac to Formey, Leipzig, October 8, 1754. All references are to the 1820 Dutch edition.

he had already tried to show, as he later explained to Formey, that many questions in natural jurisprudence were being hotly disputed only because the wrong method of exposition was being followed. Certainty in this field, as in most others, could only be achieved by making use of "the method of the geometers": the clear definition of concepts and the construction of a logical chain of argument.[172]

It was this method that he now proposed to apply in constructing a new system of natural jurisprudence, with happiness as its central concept. Although it would continue to play an important role in his work, Luzac would later come to prefer the more abstract and comprehensive notions of perfection and harmony. Looking back on his earliest writings some years later, he remarked that his former preference for happiness had largely been inspired by the conviction that it was easy to understand: "the vulgar do not understand the concept of perfection. Speak of happiness, however, and everybody is suddenly fascinated".[173] Luzac may indeed consciously have emphasized the centrality of happiness for purely practical reasons. It is, however, far more likely that he was simply overwhelmed by its omnipresence in ethical debate at the time of his earliest writings. For although M. Pellisson has credited him with being the first author to give systematic form to "the new theory of happiness", Luzac was in fact encountering the concept everywhere.[174] Thus, for instance, he had been studying Maupertuis's *Essai de philosophie morale* (1749) and the manuscript of Formey's *Système du vrai bonheur* (1751) before he embarked on his own system.[175] The reviewer in the *Nouvelle Bibliothèque Germanique* was therefore entirely right to open his article with the words "this certainly is a highly fashionable topic".[176] Luzac's book was nonetheless remarkable, as R. Mauzi has rightly observed, for its "methodical and concise reasoning".[177] Its hundred and ninety-three paragraphs succinctly and systematically developed a complete system of

---

172. *Corr. Formey*, Luzac to Formey, Leiden, June 29, 1756 ("...la méthode des géomètres.").

173. "Solution", 228 ("...on ne seroit pas entendu si l'on parloit de perfection au vulgaire: parlez de bonheur, tout le monde accourt.").

174. Pellisson, "Bonheur", 491.

175. *Corr. Formey*, Luzac to Formey, Paris, December 1749 and Leiden, May 11, 1750.

176. *Nouvelle Bibliothèque Germanique*, vol.13, second part, July to September 1753, 163 ("C'est ici un sujet fort à la mode.").

177. Mauzi, *Idée du Bonheur*, 116. Mauzi's book provides an exhaustive treatment of the idea of happiness in eighteenth-century French thought. See also Hazard, *European Thought*, 14-25.

natural jurisprudence.

In *Le bonheur*, man was defined as an intelligent being, whose existence was a continuous process of transition from one state to another. These transitions were either happy, producing an "agreeable sentiment", or unhappy, producing the opposite effect.[178] By his intelligence, man was capable of evaluating the infinite variety of possible states of existence. He would necessarily prefer the one he thought would contribute most to his happiness. The will would then bring him to try and achieve that state. "In order to live happily and to enjoy a happy life one has to know what are happy and what are unhappy states. We are necessarily inclined to our happiness: that knowledge will therefore necessarily lead us to it. To enjoy happiness it is thus sufficient to know it".[179] The immutable and universal relations existing between human actions and human happiness were called moral or natural laws. They contained the reason why we should or should not do something and therefore constituted the basis of our duties and of our rights.[180] Natural jurisprudence could simply be defined as "the science of the relationship between the actions and the happiness of beings".[181] But man's happiness, Luzac pointed out after having laid this groundwork, could not be achieved in isolation. It was in fact totally dependent upon the cooperation of others. In order to augment his own happiness, man therefore had to make all others well disposed towards himself. His first absolute duty, in other words, was "constantly to act so as to increase the good disposition of others toward us".[182] And this could only be achieved by contributing with all his forces to the good of mankind in general.[183] The good of mankind as a whole should be the general goal of all our actions. From this general law, Luzac claimed, all other rights and duties between men could be derived.[184] He proceeded to do so in the remaining paragraphs

---

178. *Bonheur*, 1-11 ("...sentiment agréable...").

179. *Ibidem*, 41-46. The quotation is on 45-46 ("Pour vivre heureux, pour jouïr d'une vie heureuse, il faut...connoître quels sont les états heureux et quels sont les états malheureux. Nous sommes nécessairement déterminés vers notre bonheur: cette connoissance nous y portera donc nécessairement. Il n'y a donc qu'à connoître le bonheur pour en jouïr.").

180. *Ibidem*, 55-60.

181. *Ibidem*, 60-61 ("...la science des rapports que les actions ont avec le bonheur des Etres.").

182. *Ibidem*, 75 ("...agir constamment de manière à augmenter la bonne disposition des autres envers nous.").

183. *Ibidem*, 77. Luzac had argued the same point in his brief 1751 "Solution".

184. *Ibidem*, 78-79.

of *Le bonheur*, ascending from the family to civil and political society. The method of systematically arguing from well-defined general principles, Luzac remarked at the end of the treatise, not only brought greater clarity and certainty to the study of natural jurisprudence, but also cast doubt upon the usefulness of artificial constructs such as contract and consent in the analysis of our general rights and duties.[185] It was a point to which he would return in his later work.

The principles of natural jurisprudence that Luzac systematically unfolded in *Le bonheur* were, as he pointed out, ultimately founded on God's wise role as the creator of the universe. "His [i.e. God's] wisdom has determined his will to the existence of intelligent creatures, whose actions would in turn be determined by the resulting agreeableness or disagreeableness".[186] But having created the system, God apparently had no further active and direct role in it. In a move highly typical of the Moderate Enlightenment, Luzac was clearly replacing revealed religion with a rational system of morality. As Formey pointed out in his *Mélanges philosophiques*, it was in fact very hard to distinguish sharply between religion and morality: "Well understood and well explained, Christian religion is nothing but the perfect re-establishment of natural law".[187] But this conflation of religion and rational morality did, of course, raise the problem of the role of revelation. It was exactly this problem that Luzac addressed in his answer to the question raised by the *Legatum Stolpianum* in 1761: "How much has morality been improved by divine revelation?"[188]

Luzac's essay, systematically ordered in eighty one paragraphs, is highly interesting for the subtlety with which it ultimately dismisses, or at least severely reduces, the role of revelation in ethics. In order to answer the question posed, he remarked, it was sufficient to compare the ethics of the ancients to those of Holy Scripture. He thereby implicitly declined to comment on the relationship between biblical ethics and the, to his mind all important, modern *science des moeurs*. The moral thought of the

---

185. *Ibidem*, 118.

186. *Ibidem*, 62 ("Sa sagesse a déterminé sa volonté à l'existence des créatures intelligentes, dont les actions seroient déterminées par l'agrément et le désagrément, qui en sont les conséquences.").

187. Formey, *Mélanges*, vol.2, 135 ("La Religion Chrétienne, bien comprise et bien expliquée, n'est autre chose que le parfait rétablissement de la Loi naturelle.").

188. The *Legatum Stolpianum* was founded in Leiden after the death of J. Stolp in 1753. In his will Stolp had stipulated that part of his inheritance should be used for the organization of essay competitions in the fields of religion and ethics.

ancients, Luzac proceeded, had been highly sophisticated without the aid of revelation. The contempt with which it was frequently treated was completely unjustified. Although many of them were rather too fond of a vague concept of nature, the best ancient thinkers had sought the basis of morality in the existence of a perfect God. As the most important goal in human ethics they had identified happiness, by which they understood the satisfaction derived from the performance of virtuous deeds. They regarded the inborn desire for such happiness as the primary ethical motivation.[189] These were all perfectly respectable views, Luzac observed. But making it clear that his own thought on these matters had evolved in the years since he wrote *Le bonheur*, he immediately added that they lacked consistency, for to make God the basis of ethics had a number of logical implications. Since God was perfect, he must have created man and the universe with the goal of perfection in view. Man, as a part of creation, had therefore to take the perfection of the universe as the primary goal of his free actions and had to derive his motivation to do so from the knowledge that such behavior was in conformity with the will of God. Human happiness, far from being the completely independent ethical goal the ancients had taken it to be, was no more than the result of an attempt to contribute to the perfection of the universe.[190]

The ancients, Luzac stressed, should have been able to arrive at the same conclusion by the use of reason alone, but somehow they had failed to do so. Since the line of thought he had just sketched could easily be drawn from the Holy Scriptures, as he demonstrated with a wealth of quotations, it was clear that the ethics contained therein were superior to those of the ancients.[191] Biblical ethics also had another advantage, Luzac added almost as an afterthought. Its lessons were backed up by the promise of eternal rewards and the threat of eternal punishments, which would bring those not susceptible to abstract reasoning to obey them.[192] No doubt to the satisfaction of many of his readers, Luzac had thus established that the Holy Scriptures constituted a clear improvement over the ethics of the ancients. But he had also pointed out that the ancients could in theory have achieved the same improvement by making better use of their reason. The implicit conclusion could be none other than that revelation had no part to play in a modern and rational system of ethics

---

189. "Betoog", 89-116.
190. *Ibidem*, 116-120.
191. *Ibidem*, 121-134.
192. *Ibidem*, 134-135.

in which the flaws of ancient moral thought had been eliminated. Revelation, in short, was a subject perhaps best left to theologians.

CHAPTER II

ENLIGHTENMENT VERSUS ENLIGHTENMENT

"The power of reason is God's greatest gift to man", Christian Wolff observed in the preface to his German logic.[1] Luzac wholeheartedly agreed with this estimate. For although he never denied that the senses contributed to knowledge, it was the *mundus intelligibilis*, constituted by reason and logic, that was crucial.[2] In his early work, he had tried to establish the fundamental importance of systematic and logical reasoning from clear principles. The conviction that mankind had now learned to make a disciplined use of reason and was finally successfully applying it to the study of morality was an essential component of Luzac's youthful optimism. It was among the main reasons for his belief that he lived in an age superior to all previous ones.

Yet at the very moment that Luzac was beginning to enounce these principles of a rational and moderate Enlightenment, they were suddenly coming under heavy attack. It was with growing apprehension that he observed the triumphs of Lockean sensationalism and the development and increasing popularity of moral sense philosophy in England. But the gravest threat clearly came from France. In that country, the years around 1750 witnessed the breakthrough of the High Enlightenment with the publication of such works as Condillac's *Traité des systèmes* and d'Alembert's *Discours préliminaire* to the *Encyclopédie* (1751). These treatises were part of a campaign against metaphysics and oversystematization conducted by the *philosophes*, who distinguished a useful and flexible *esprit systématique* from a perverse *esprit de système*.[3] To Luzac, this change in intellectual climate could only appear as a malevolent destruction of knowledge and a triumph of frivolity. Surveying the state of European scholarship in 1760, he pointed out that the English, and even more the French, were totally ignorant of metaphysics. This ignorance, he added, resulted in a stream of French writings demonstrating the decline of ethical knowledge.[4] Some ten years later the French offensive seemed

---

1. Wolff, *Vernünftige Gedanken von den Kräften des menschlichen Verstandes*, Vorrede, 105.

2. On the *mundus intelligibilis* as superior to the *mundus sensibilis* see [Luzac and Vaster], *Briefwisseling*, 67.

3. Gay, *Enlightenment*, vol.1, 139-141.

4. *Nederlandsche Letter-Courant*, vol.3 (1760), 3.

to have succeeded on a European scale, for in the preface to his edition of Wolff Luzac bitterly complained that nowadays "anyone writing in an orderly way is accused of *esprit de système*".[5] In the course of his writing career, Luzac kept searching for explanations for this sudden and remarkable transformation of the Republic of Letters, which evidently, and understandably, obsessed him. In his later works, these explanations would take on strong political overtones. But when first confronted with this new mode of thought, posing such a threat to his own interpretation of Enlightenment, he put it down to experimental philosophy run wild.

Appalled by the nasty struggles and controversies the publication of the *Encyclopédie* gave rise to, Luzac, who had already critically discussed the *Discours préliminaire* in his review journal, decided in 1761 to examine briefly the reasons for the sad state the world of learning was in. Perhaps the best and most simple way to demonstrate the causes of the present degeneration of learning in France, he remarked, was to start with the great confrontation between Cartesians and Newtonians in the late seventeenth century. There could be no doubt whatsoever that in this battle Newtonian physics, rooted in experience and guided by mathematics, had vanquished Cartesian physics, based on reason alone. But by a fatal misunderstanding many had wrongly jumped to the conclusion that the triumph of Newtonian physics implied the superiority of its methods in all fields of knowledge. With metaphysics as the first casualty, the meaning of philosophy was henceforth increasingly narrowed down to experimental philosophy, a process greatly stimulated by the influence of Lockean sensationalism. Those wishing to use the work of Newton and Locke without limiting the whole of philosophy to it were hardly listened to and even less so as the century progressed.[6]

This transition in thought, Luzac admitted, was not completely without advantages, for it had dealt the final blow to the remnants of scholastic reasoning still present in philosophy. The triumph of experimental philosophy was, moreover, easy to understand. The new science had been the source of a great many important new discoveries. Even better, it frequently rewarded amateur practitioners with amazing and appealing results. The study of metaphysics, on the other hand, could not possibly provide such rewards. Instead, it required "deep modesty and the constant contemplation of abstract concepts, an activity exhausting to the mind and

---

5. Wolff, *Institutions*, vol.1, Dédicace, v ("...il suffit de procéder avec ordre dans un Ecrit, pour être taxé d'Esprit de Système...").

6. *Nederlandsche Letter-Courant*, vol.5 (1761), 7-8.

usually avoided by its habitual inertia".[7] Yet, Luzac insisted, invoking the names of Leibniz, 's-Gravesande, and Lulofs in his support, it remained an indisputable fact that experimental philosophy was but a part, and not even the most important part, of philosophy. The study of metaphysics, containing the important discipline of logic or "the art of making good use of one's reason", could not be ignored without disastrous consequences. The French, unloading their volumes of superficial nonsense on Europe, were the living proof of this simple truth.[8] Little did Luzac suspect that the worst was yet to come. For the author who took the tendencies he despised to their limits and added many new abominations, Jean-Jacques Rousseau, had still to publish his *Emile* and his *Contrat social*. In his book reviews, Luzac had been among the first to point to the dangerous aspects of Rousseau's thought. The appearance of these two new books so outraged him that he devoted a separate and lengthy treatise to each of them.

In writing about the products of the French High Enlightenment Luzac was playing a variety of roles. On the European scene, his battle with *philosophie* and his continued attempts to spread the blessings of the *science des moeurs* were clearly part of a concerted effort by the international liberal Protestant community to prevent the Moderate Enlightenment from being relegated to a marginal position in the Republic of Letters. Although their correspondence gradually petered out, Luzac faithfully kept Formey informed about his latest contributions to this struggle. Reporting his attack on the philosophy of d'Alembert, Luzac despondently observed: "I am outraged to find so much vanity combined with so little solid knowledge. Has the *century of style* arrived?"[9] Reading Rousseau, he confided to his friend while composing his treatises against that author, was among the most depressing experiences he had ever had.[10]

In the Dutch Republic Luzac's position was more complicated. There he found himself engaged in the delicate operation of simultaneously acquainting the Dutch audience with the French Enlightenment, attacking

---

7. *Ibidem*, 8-9. The quotation is on 9 ("...diepe ingetogenheid en aanhoudend gepeins over afgetrokken denkbeelden, daar de geest niet zelden door afgemat, en waar van dezelve in 't gemeen afgehouden wordt door een zekere logheid...").

8. *Ibidem*, 10-13. The quotation is on 13 ("...konst om van zyne reden een goed gebruik te maaken...").

9. *Corr. Formey*, Luzac to Formey, Leiden, May 26, 1760 ("Je suis indigné de voir tant de vanité avec si peu de connoissances solides. Sommes nous donc dans le *Siècle du Stile*?").

10. *Ibidem*, [Leiden], April 9, 1765.

philosophie, and defending the freedom of the press. It was, of course, a simple task to give wide publicity to the relatively uncontroversial works of the few French authors he admired. Thus Luzac, who was deeply impressed by Montesquieu's *Esprit des lois*, annotated a new Amsterdam edition of that work in 1759 and continuously used Montesquieu in his own writings. Refuting *philosophie*, too, should in theory have involved no more than adapting his international polemics for Dutch use. This, in fact, was one of the main functions of the *Nederlandsche Letter-Courant*. In his article on vulgar Newtonianism, for instance, Luzac emphatically warned against the perils of the increased support this superficial and flawed mode of thought was gaining in Dutch intellectual life.[11] Refuting *philosophie*, however, inevitably meant explaining it first. It was in this area that Luzac, who had been a controversial figure ever since the La Mettrie affair, had to tread carefully. In 1762, to give but one example, the States of Holland, acting on the advice of a committee of Walloon ministers, banned Rousseau's *Emile*.[12] The ban infuriated Luzac, for it prevented him from dealing with the book's content in the only way he considered acceptable: by rational argument. Yet he prudently refrained from reviewing it in the *Nederlandsche Letter-Courant*, albeit under protest.[13] Luzac's position, in short, was threatened from two sides. While on the international scene he was defending his rational Enlightenment against radical attacks, he was simultaneously still engaged in the attempt to establish its tolerant values in the Dutch Republic. In 1770 we therefore once again find him taking up his pen against clerical and governmental censorship.

1. *The Sublime Genius of France*

Montesquieu's *Esprit des lois* was, as P. Gay has observed, both the most disorderly and the most influential masterpiece of the eighteenth century.[14] Luzac's reaction to its appearance perfectly illustrated this dual characteristic. In his first mention of the book he remarked, while stressing its importance, that it certainly did not belong to the class of "sound books".[15] Montesquieu had clearly not developed his complex argument

---

11. *Nederlandsche Letter-Courant*, vol.5 (1761), 10-11.

12. Gobbers, *Rousseau in Holland*, 300-302.

13. *Nederlandsche Letter-Courant*, vol.9 (1763), 5.

14. Gay, *Enlightenment*, vol.2, 324-325.

15. *Corr. Formey*, Luzac to Formey, London, September 23, 1749 ("...livres solides...").

in the systematic way that Luzac was just coming to look upon as highly desirable. In his later comments, Luzac would keep returning to Montesquieu's many inconsistencies and to his excessive fondness for paradoxes. Reading and rereading the President's book, however, in the end brought him the conviction that, despite its methodological shortcomings, it was the work of a "sublime genius".[16] From the mid-1750s on Montesquieu figured prominently in most of Luzac's writings. In 1759 his commentary was added to a new edition of the *Esprit des lois*. It was soon reprinted and translated into Dutch at the end of the century.[17] In his preface Luzac remarked that whatever criticism one might have of the book, "it will always remain true that this is a book unique in its sort. It should be in the hands of anyone desirous to study public law, universal jurisprudence, and politics".[18] It would indeed be no exaggeration to say that, apart from the "modern moralists" from Grotius to Wolff, Montesquieu's *Esprit des lois* was the single most important book in shaping Luzac's outlook. It deeply influenced his thought on law, commerce, and politics. The two men shared a legal background, a great confidence in modern science, an interest in republicanism, a moderate temper, and a loathing of despotism. Yet it should be stressed that Luzac used the *Esprit des lois* for his own purposes and adapted its lessons to his own needs. His reception of Montesquieu was a clear case of "produktive Auseinandersetzung", not of "unkritische Übernahme".[19]

In books II through VIII of the *Esprit des lois* Montesquieu developed his well-known classification of the various types of government and their driving principles. The three main types of government he distinguished were despotism, monarchy and republic, the last being subdivided into an aristocratic and a democratic variety. The driving principles were, respectively, fear, honor, and virtue. This elaborate classification, still strongly

16. Wolff, *Institutions*, vol.1, §39, note b ("...Génie sublime...").

17. *De geest der wetten, door de heere baron De Montesquieu, etc.* 4 vols. and an index. Amsterdam, 1783-1787. The Dutch translation contains notes and an interesting reaction to Luzac's commentary by Dirk Hoola van Nooten, who also translated Condillac and Smith into Dutch.

18. *Esprit des loix*, vol.1, 12 ("...il sera toujours vrai, que c'est un Livre unique dans son espèce, qu'on ne peut guères se dispenser de lire et de posséder, pour peu que l'on veuille connoître la différente façon d'envisager les objets, relatifs au *Droit Public*, à la *Jurisprudence Universelle*, et à la *Politique*."). For Luzac's commentary on Montesquieu the 1763 edition has been used. Montesquieu himself is quoted from the modern *Oeuvres complètes*, ed. R. Caillois. For the English translation of passages from Montesquieu I have, in some cases, made use of Richter, *Political Theory of Montesquieu*.

19. For this distinction see Möller, *Vernunft und Kritik*, 20-21.

reminiscent of the classical division of governments into monarchies, aristocracies, and democracies, was parallelled and at times overshadowed by the more basic and simple distinction between despotism on the one hand and moderate government on the other.[20] Luzac severely criticized the first classification and highly approved of the second. The second, he contended, in fact made the first superfluous. The crucial distinction to be made was that between arbitrary and limited government. In limited governments the power of the state was restrained by fundamental laws and other devices, in arbitrary governments it was not. Despotism occurred as soon as an arbitrary will was exercised within the state. This could happen in republics as well as in monarchies. It was a dangerous error, Luzac warned, to suppose that only monarchies could easily degenerate into despotism.[21]

But Montesquieu's first classification not only obscured the most important differences between governments, it was also flawed. On the one hand, Montesquieu had been blind to the wealth of historical material proving that his rigid threefold classification highly simplified reality. On the other hand, he had been so obsessed with establishing the dominance of his driving principles that he ignored the very real similarities existing between various forms of moderate government. The purpose of Montesquieu's three principles, Luzac remarked, must have been to show either what makes different types of government work or what should make them work. If he intended to do the first, it was clear that experience contradicted his findings, for within one and the same form of government it was possible to find a multiplicity of driving passions and enormous changes over time. To claim otherwise was to obscure important historical differences, as Montequieu tended to do in his discussion of ancient and modern republics. Anyone studying the history and manifold aspects of a certain form of government would have to come to the conclusion that its essence, if any, could not be captured in one single driving principle.[22] As a normative theory Montesquieu's doctrine of principles was equally unsatisfactory, "because both theory and experience prove beyond a shade of doubt that *virtue*, by which term I understand all

---

20. Although now thirty years old, Shackleton's *Montesquieu* remains the standard work on this author. More recent general commentaries include Richter, *Political Theory of Montesquieu*; Cranston, *Philosophers and Pamphleteers*, 9-35 and Shklar, *Montesquieu*.

21. *Esprit des loix*, vol.1, 16-17 (book II, chapter 1).

22. *Ibidem*, 52-53 (book III, chapter 11); the remarks about Montesquieu's treatment of ancient and modern republics are on 186-187 (book VII, chapter 17) and 206 (book VIII, chapter 16).

the moral qualities leading us to perfection, is the only proper guide for all governments...and the sole basis for the flourishing of states".[23] Devotion to his artificial classification had also wrongly led Montesquieu to limit the importance of certain general mechanisms and institutions to one specific form of government. There was, for instance, no valid reason to discuss the fundamental role of *pouvoirs intermédiaires* in the sole context of monarchical government.[24]

Luzac's purpose in seizing upon the distinction between moderate and despotic government and in largely rejecting Montesquieu's emphasis on the essential differences between republics and monarchies had everything to do with his position in Dutch political debate. In that context, he was trying to formulate a modern and flexible definition of republicanism, free from the classical values and stern *vertu politique* still present in some of Montesquieu's passages and supporting his efforts to legitimate the presence of a Stadholder in the Dutch Republic. In his polemics with consecutive Dutch political opponents, first the *Staatsgezinden* and later the Patriots, Luzac in fact increasingly took the position that modern republicanism and moderate government were one and the same thing. Contrary to classical notions, Luzac came to argue that a republic was not primarily characterized by the absence of a single ruler or by the practice of political virtue by its citizens, but by the presence of a limited government guaranteeing the freedom of the individual inhabitants.[25]

In defining what exactly was to be understood by moderate and limited government, Luzac found Montesquieu's analysis of various constitutionalist mechanisms of great help. In his famous idealized treatment of the working of the English constitution Montesquieu had utilized four such mechanisms: the mixed constitution, the separation of powers, the balanced constitution, and the theory of checks and balances. None of this, of course, was entirely new.[26] Luzac was already familiar with the old doctrine of the mixed constitution. Although he repeatedly applied it to the Dutch Republic, he increasingly came to regard it as of dubious

---

23. *Ibidem*, 53-55 (book III, chapter 11). The quotation is on 53 ("...car la théorie et l'expérience ne laissent aucun doute à ce sujet; elles prouvent très-évidemment que la *vertu*, par laquelle j'entends toutes les qualités morales qui nous portent à la perfection, est le seul principe de conduite pour tous les gouvernemens...et l'unique qui ait fait fleurir et qui fera fleurir les états.").

24. *Ibidem*, 30-31 (book II, chapter 4). See also Wolff, *Institutions*, vol.2, 203-204.

25. For Luzac's political views in a Dutch context see Chapters IV and V.

26. Richter, *Political Theory of Montesquieu*, 84-97 offers a good discussion of these mechanisms. See also Vile, *Constitutionalism*, 76-97 and Granpré Molière, *Théorie de la Constitution anglaise*.

value. Most governments, he held, were mixed in one way or another, even those not very desirable.[27] The separation of powers however was an altogether different matter. Luzac clearly regarded Montesquieu as the first theorist to have convincingly pointed out its necessity to a free state. He discussed it at length and, combining it with a theory of checks and balances, applied it to the Dutch Republic, ascribing a key role to the Stadholder.[28] Montesquieu himself, it might be added, also considered the Stadholder an indispensable element in assuring the survival of a moderate and free government in the Dutch Republic.[29] In his general comments on the separation of powers Luzac denied the desirability of a legislative power consisting of separate houses for nobles and commoners. It was far better to unite these two bodies "to moderate the separate views and interests concerning the general good".[30] The executive power, he emphasized, should always be in the hands of one person, although not necessarily a monarch.[31] Finally, he wholeheartedly approved of the high status Montesquieu had conferred upon the third power, the judiciary.[32] An independent judiciary and the strictest adherence to the rules in all legal proceedings were, Luzac was convinced, among the hallmarks of a free state. His 1759 doctoral dissertation, which dealt with extraordinary procedures in criminal cases, fittingly carried a motto from the *Esprit des lois*.[33]

The purpose of these various constitutionalist mechanisms was to prevent despotism and to secure freedom. Luzac greatly admired Montesquieu's analysis of despotism and felt that he had convincingly and exhaustively treated the subject.[34] It was to Montesquieu's discussion of liberty in book XI that he would return over and over again. The short

---

27. *Esprit des loix*, vol.1, 102-103 (book V, chapter 12). See also Wolff, *Institutions*, vol.2, §993, note y.

28. For Luzac's views on the Stadholderate see 143-152.

29. Masterson, "Montesquieu's Stadholder".

30. *Esprit des loix*, vol.1, 266 (book XI, chapter 6) ("...pour modérer les vues et les intérêts séparés sur le bien général.").

31. *Ibidem*, 267.

32. It should be noted, however, that Luzac was opposed to the notion of trial by peers. *Ibidem*, 270-271.

33. *Specimen iuris inaugurale de modo extra ordinem procedendi in causis criminalibus*, 7. The motto is from book VI, chapter 2: "Mais, dans les États modérés, où la tête du moindre citoyen est considérable, on ne lui ôte son honneur et ses biens qu'après un long examen: on ne le prive de la vie que lorsque la Patrie elle-même l'attaque; et elle ne l'attaque qu'en lui laissant tous les moyens possibles de la défendre".

34. *Esprit des loix*, vol.1, 110-111 (book V, chapter 14).

chapter on "Divers significations données au mot de liberté" was in fact one of his favorite passages in political theory. He quoted it repeatedly and particularly liked the President's observation that certain people believed that wearing a beard was the height of freedom.[35] To this Luzac added: "I have read somewhere that some people think there is liberty when you wear a pair of bands, a long scarf, or a hat in the shape of a sugar loaf...".[36] But more important was the definition of liberty that Montesquieu provided in the next chapter. For despite the classical republican leanings that Luzac had discovered in some previous books of the *Esprit des lois*, Montesquieu here unambiguously defined liberty in a negative way as the rule of law.[37] And that, of course, was exactly in line with the views Luzac was absorbing from his study of the exponents of modern natural law.

The originality of Montesquieu's *Esprit des lois* derived to a large extent from the fact that the work immensely broadened the study of positive law. By the spirit of the laws Montesquieu understood, as he explained in book I, much more than the relation between the laws and the form and principle of a government. It consisted of "the various relationships that laws may have to things".[38] The climate and size of a country, the *moeurs* and *manières* of its inhabitants, the means of existence - all these factors were highly relevant to the study of the laws. This comprehensive and complex approach greatly appealed to Luzac and, in a general way, taught him several enduring lessons. First of all, it made him realize that the universalist abstractions of natural jurisprudence could not always be applied directly to existing societies. Secondly, it contributed to his view that, given the extraordinary complexity and the interrelatedness of existing arrangements in any given society, frequently the product of centuries of history, the potential for change was always limited. Finally, it convinced him that a broadening of scope was not only salutary in the study of law, but also highly desirable in the study of history. Having ignored this was, in Luzac's view, one of the main shortcomings of Jan Wagenaar's immense *Vaderlandsche historie*, published in twenty-one volumes between 1749 and 1759.[39]

---

35. Montesquieu, *Oeuvres complètes*, vol.2, 394 (book XI, chapter 2).

36. *Zugt*, 90 ("...ik heb ievers geleezen dat'er zyn die de *Vryheid* stellen in het draagen van een uitgestreeken bef, van een langen das, van een hoed in de gedaante van eenen brood-suiker, enz."). See also *Holland's rijkdom*, vol.3, 212.

37. Montesquieu, *Oeuvres complètes*, vol.2, 395 (book XI, chapter 3 and 4).

38. *Ibidem*, 238 (book I, chapter 3).

39. For Luzac's views on Wagenaar see 133-134.

In his more specific comments on Montesquieu's treatment of the larger contexts in which positive law was to be understood, Luzac stressed the fact that too much was being made of physical causes in the *Esprit des lois*. With his usual imperviousness to the commonplaces of his age, David Hume had already declared in 1748 that "physical causes have no discernible operation on the human mind".[40] Luzac tended to agree with him. While not entirely denying the importance of climate, he completely rejected the central role Montesquieu ascribed to it. Upbringing, education and laws were much more important in shaping the behavior of a people. Anyone paying attention to history, Luzac remarked repeating an argument he had previously used in criticizing Montesquieu's doctrine of principles, could see this: "History is full of changes in the *moeurs* of peoples, to such an extent that sometimes one generation is completely different from the next. Surely it would be wrong to attribute this to the influence of climate".[41] The importance of the size and nature of the territory, too, was always subordinate to moral causes.[42] Given this preference for moral causes, it is unsurprising that Book XIX, on the relations between the laws and the *esprit général*, *moeurs*, and *manières* of a nation was highly appreciated by Luzac.[43]

But it was the next section, the discussion of the relationship between the laws and commerce in books XX and XXI, that drew Luzac's attention to a whole new area of inquiry. Montesquieu, who never entirely relinquished the austere ideals of classical republicanism, held curiously ambiguous opinions about the effects of commerce.[44] Some aspects of commercial society he clearly loathed. When he visited the Dutch Republic in 1729 he came to the conclusion that "the heart of people living in commercial countries is entirely corrupted", an opinion he later repeated in his *Esprit des lois*: "Commerce corrupts pure *moeurs*".[45] Yet he realized that the spirit of commerce had come to dominate modern

---

40. Hume, *Essays moral, political, and literary*, 203 ("Of national characters").

41. *Esprit des loix*, vol.2, 86-87 (book XIV, chapter 15). The quotation is on 87 ("L'histoire est remplie de changemens arrivés dans les moeurs des peuples, au point qu'une génération ne ressemble en rien à une autre. Personne ne sera assez mal-avisé pour les attribuer à l'influence du climat.").

42. *Ibidem*, 152-153 (book XVIII, chapter 3).

43. *Ibidem*, 188-189 (book XIX, chapter 3) and 196-199 (book XIX, chapter 14).

44. Montesquieu's penchant for classical values is emphasized by Keohane, *Philosophy and the State in France*, 392-419.

45. Montesquieu, *Oeuvres complètes*, vol.1, 864 (*Voyage de Gratz à La Haye*) and vol.2, 585 (*Esprit des lois*, book XX, chapter 1).

Europe and, despite some remaining doubts, his final verdict was that this development had been for the good. He even became a great exponent of the doctrine of *doux commerce*. Commerce had a civilizing effect, it promoted peace between the nations, and it sometimes even provided an alternative to *vertu politique* in preventing the corruption and decline of republics.[46] Luzac avidly absorbed these views and frequently returned to them in his many subsequent discussions of the nature of commercial society. The brief history of commerce that Montequieu provided in Book XXI, although not quite satisfactory in Luzac's opinion, helped to convince him that the history of Dutch commerce needed to be written. The final product of this new interest was to be *Holland's Wealth*, published some twenty years later.[47]

2. D'Alembert and the Decline of Philosophy

While Luzac was still working on his annotated edition of Montesquieu, attention in France turned to the *Encyclopédie*. The years between 1758 and 1762 were in fact to a large extent dominated by the struggles surrounding its publication. Not only was its privilege revoked in 1759, the whole undertaking was also constantly attacked by such writers as Charles Palissot. One of the results of all this was that the *philosophes* increasingly came to be viewed, and came to view themselves, as a coherent group.[48] Luzac, too, during these years became convinced that a well-organized army of *philosophes* was fighting for dominance in the French and eventually the European world of learning. His own role, unique in the Dutch Republic, was both to keep the Dutch audience informed about events surrounding the publication of the *Encyclopédie* and to criticize the work itself.

From a twentieth-century perspective it is highly tempting to tell the story of the *Encyclopédie* as that of the heroic struggle of a tiny group of *philosophes*, devoted to reason and to the principle of criticism, against the massive forces of an obscurantist Catholic church and an authoritarian

---

46. *Ibidem*, vol.2, 585-586 (book XX, chapters 1 and 2) and 280 (book V, chapter 6). Montesquieu's views on commerce are discussed by Pangle, *Montesquieu's Philosophy of Liberalism*, 200-248; Hirschman, *The Passions and the Interests*, 70-81; Pocock, *Machiavellian Moment*, 490-493; Hutchison, *Before Adam Smith*, 220-224.

47. *Esprit des loix*, vol.2, 322-325 (book XXI, chapter 23). For Luzac's views on commerce see Chapter IV. Unfortunately, the Dutch reception of Montesquieu has not been adequately studied. The two existing brief articles on the subject by S.J. Fockema Andreae and J.W. Bosch are both unsatisfactory.

48. Wade, *Structure and Form*, vol.2, 184-186.

absolute monarchy. But although both appealing and partially true such a rendering is, to say the least, incomplete. Its main deficiency is that it fails to explain why such representatives of a Moderate Enlightenment as Luzac and Formey came to oppose the French High Enlightenment. It tends to obscure the fact, in other words, that there existed an enlightened opposition to *philosophie*. It is, of course, perfectly true that the *En-cyclopédistes* favored a free exchange of intellectual opinions and viewed this as a precondition for the growth of knowledge. "Everything should be examined, without exception or reserve, everything should be questioned", in the well-known words of Diderot.[49] But the very same position had, as we have seen, already been defended by Luzac in 1749. It was there-fore not the critical spirit of the *philosophes*, of which P. Gay has made so much, that drove Luzac into opposition.[50] And if the radicalism of the *Encyclopédie* had solely consisted, as R. Darnton has maintained, in the attempt "to map the world of knowledge according to new boundaries, determined by reason and reason alone", Luzac would equally not have found grounds for a major quarrel.[51] In his own work revealed religion certainly no longer functioned as the trunk of the tree of knowledge. Even before the *Encyclopédie* started to appear, the principles of open discus-sion and rational analysis were warmly admired and constantly defended by Luzac. The whole point of his opposition to the *Encyclopédie* was that he did not see it as furthering the cause of reason and Enlightenment. To Luzac, *philosophie* represented an assault on reason and a regrettable decline in knowledge. In its Rousseauist guise, it even constituted a dangerous relapse into primitivism.

The purpose of the *Nederlandsche Letter-Courant*, Luzac always emphasized, was to announce and briefly discuss scholarly publications from all over Europe. Something truly exceptional was required to deviate from this fixed formula. The appearance of an Amsterdam reprint of Jean Le Rond d'Alembert, *Mélanges de littérature, d'histoire, et de philo-sophie*, coinciding with the intense French debate about the *Encyclopédie*, clearly was such a special occasion. In 1760, Luzac discussed d'Alem-bert's essays in no less than eight issues of his journal, devoting more space to them than to any other publication.[52] This unusually lengthy polemic, he pointed out, was more than warranted by the threat posed by

49. *Encyclopédie*, vol.2, 60.

50. Gay, *Enlightenment*, vol.1, 127-159.

51. Darnton, *Business of Enlightenment*, 9.

52. *Nederlandsche Letter-Courant*, vol.3 (1760), 308-310, 315-318, 322-325, 334-336, 339-343, 350-351, 355-359 and vol.4 (1760), 106-112.

d'Alembert's thought, as exemplified particularly in the *Discours prélimi-naire* to the *Encyclopédie*, reprinted in the first volume of the *Mélanges*. In combatting *philosophie*, Luzac remarked in his favorable review of Palissot's comedy *Les philosophes*, ridicule could be a deadly weapon.[53] Yet in matters of such great importance he himself preferred rational argument.

There was no denying, Luzac admitted, that the *Discours préliminaire* was brilliantly written. It was in fact precisely the elegance of its lan-guage and the fluency of its style that tended to overwhelm the reader and to obscure the fact that the text was packed with dubious doctrine.[54] According to Luzac, the root cause of all the flaws in the *Discours* was to be found in the simplistic and wrongheaded sensationalist epistemology it defended. At the very beginning of the *Discours*, d'Alembert ascribed a decisive role to sensation in the formation of knowledge. All our knowl-edge, he stated, is either direct (*connaissances directes*) or reflective (*connaissances réfléchies*). Direct knowledge we immediately receive from the senses, reflective knowledge we acquire by unifying and com-bining the elements of direct knowledge. It was therefore clear, he concluded, that "it is to our sensations that we owe all our ideas".[55] Luzac completely disagreed. Since all our knowledge presupposes reflec-tion, he remarked, there is no such thing as direct knowledge. As to reflective knowledge, to limit this to a simple combination of so-called direct knowledge was an absurd reduction of the role of reason and the understanding. The conclusion that all our ideas were ultimately based on sensation, moreover, did not follow from the previous analysis and was therefore unfounded. "The existence of the senses can certainly not be doubted; but to conclude from their existence that they are *the basis of ALL our knowledge* not only is a logically flawed argument, it also means bizarrely preferring our least important property as a thinking being to that property which rightly gives man the name of a reasonable ani-mal".[56] It would seem, Luzac added at this point, that d'Alembert had

53. *Ibidem*, vol.4 (1760), 20-24. On Palissot's comedy see Wilson, *Diderot*, 393-395.

54. *Nederlandsche Letter-Courant*, vol.3 (1760), 342-343.

55. *Encyclopédie*, vol.1, 77.

56. *Nederlandsche Letter-Courant*, vol.3 (1760), 315-318. The quotation is on 318 ("Het bestaan der zinnen kan zekerlyk niet in twyffel getrokken worden; maar van hun bestaan te besluiten tot de hoedaanigheid die dezelven maakt *tot het grondbeginsel ALLE onzer kundigheeden*, is niet alleen zeer wyd gesprongen, maar zelfs aan de minste onzer hoe-daanigheeden als denkende wezens eene zonderlinge voorkeur gegeeven boven die, welken den mensch eigentlyk den naam van redelyk dier doen erlangen.").

only read Locke on this subject and had misunderstood him to boot. He might certainly profit from a consultation of the works of 's-Gravesande, who had clearly explained the limited role of the senses many years ago.[57]

D'Alembert continued his *Discours* by explaining that man's need to protect himself from pain and destruction had led to the formation of societies. The extreme inequality and oppression reigning in these early societies had, in turn, given birth to a sense of injustice and to notions of moral good and evil. The basis of human morality was, in short, to be found in feeling or "the cry of nature".[58] Luzac totally rejected this analysis, including d'Alembert's later contention that the rules of morality were grounded in inspiration. To base morality on feeling, inspiration, or the cry of nature, he replied, was to reduce man to the level of the lowest beings, driven by instinct. Feelings, widely different in every individual, could clearly never serve as the foundation of any coherent, systematic, and universal theory of morality.[59] D'Alembert did little better in his treatment of religion, the next subject he touched upon. The human mind and the human body, he suddenly remarked, were completely different, yet worked together harmoniously. Awareness of this fact was sufficient to convince man of the existence of God.[60] It was unnecessary, Luzac observed in return, to prove God's existence by means of such an involved argument. The simple fact that what existed had to have been created out of nothing combined with the contemplation of the wonders of creation should be sufficient to convince every reasonable being of the existence of a wise and perfect God.[61] But apart from being inadequate, d'Alembert's view of religion was also inconsistent, for in later parts of the *Mélanges* he referred to religion as a sixth sense. "Wonderful maxims! Although they do not enlighten the mind, they do at least show us that Mr. d'Alembert, in full conformity with his love for knowledge based on the unclear and muddled thoughts occasioned by the senses, is very eager to base religion and belief exclusively on a certain feeling, on a certain urge or drive, in which reason plays as little part as it does in the

57. *Ibidem*, 317-318.

58. *Encyclopédie*, vol.1, 80-82.

59. *Nederlandsche Letter-Courant*, vol.3 (1760), 322-324 and 355-356.

60. *Encyclopédie*, vol.1, 82-83.

61. *Nederlandsche Letter-Courant*, vol.3 (1760), 325.

stupidest of animals...".[62]

Modern commentators have interpreted d'Alembert's disorderly and somewhat clumsy manner of proceeding in the early parts of the *Discours* as the result of both a conscious subversive strategy and a very real intellectual confusion.[63] To Luzac, this lack of clarity was far from puzzling. It was, on the contrary, exactly what was to be expected from an author trying to reduce every variety of knowledge to sensation. D'Alembert's brief history of learning confirmed him in this judgment. Luzac certainly did not disagree with d'Alembert's view that philosophers were the real heroes of human history, nor did he object to the important role accorded to Bacon, Descartes, and Newton. But d'Alembert had misunderstood Leibniz and, unsurprisingly, greatly exaggerated the role of Locke.[64] How could anyone seriously maintain that Locke had created metaphysics almost as Newton had created physics? Locke had indeed been important, but among seventeenth-century philosophers he could not be compared to either Descartes or Leibniz. In the course of the eighteenth century, moreover, the study of metaphysics had been greatly improved by the refinements of the demonstrative method. The fact that d'Alembert, basing himself on Condillac's *Traité des systèmes*, dismissed this very real progress as a manifestation of the harmful *esprit de système* only proved how backward the French were in all subjects metaphysical.[65]

Having finished his discussion of the *Discours préliminaire*, Luzac briefly commented on d'Alembert's *Tableau de l'esprit humain au milieu du XVIIIe siècle*. He condemned the piece as containing "even less truth, if possible, than Voltaire's *Siècle de Louis XIV*" and as exhibiting a disgusting intellectual arrogance in its depiction of the *Encyclopédie* as

---

62. *Ibidem*, 356 ("Heerlyke spreuken! verlichten ze het verstand niet veel, zy toonen ten minste, dat gelyk de Hr. d'Alembert alle weetenschappen doet rusten op de onklaare en duistere denkbeelden, door de zintuigen verwekt, hy niet minder yverig is, om den godsdienst en 't geloof enkelyk te doen afhangen van een zeker gevoel, eene zekere aandoening, eene zekere aandryving of drift; daar de reden alzo weinig in te stade komt, als dezelve schynt plaats te hebben in de allerdomste dieren...").

63. R. Darnton, "Philosophers Trim the Tree of Knowledge: the Epistemological Strategy of the *Encyclopédie*" in: Darnton, *Great Cat Massacre*, 202-204.

64. For d'Alembert's views on Leibniz see Barber, *Leibniz in France*, 156-158.

65. The *Encyclopédistes'* views on seventeenth-century thought are discussed by Wade, *Structure and Form*, vol.1, 53-84 and Braun, *Philosophiegeschichte*, 161-167. For d'Alembert on Locke and on the *esprit de système* see *Encyclopédie*, vol.1, 145-147 and 155-156. Luzac's reply is in the *Nederlandsche Letter-Courant*, vol.3 (1760), 341-342.

the culmination of human knowledge.[66] Even apart from content, as Luzac remarked elsewhere in discussing the craze for dictionaries and encyclopedias of all sorts brought about by the *Encyclopédie*, encyclopedism in itself was a step backward and a sign of intellectual decline, for this form of presentation obscured the interdependence of all human knowledge.[67] In the final analysis, d'Alembert's views differed little from those of the growing army of vulgar Newtonians. What they amounted to was an arbitrary narrowing down of the province of reason. By his exaggerated sensationalism and his emphasis on feeling in matters of religion and morality, d'Alembert was contributing to the destruction of large areas of rational and valuable human knowledge. Should his views prevail, all books ever written on morality, the laws of nature, and natural theology might as well be committed to the flames and be burned to ashes.[68] Yet despite all his glaring faults, d'Alembert had at least not dismissed all knowledge as useless and the whole of existing civilization as corrupt. That noble task had been left to his fellow *philosophe* Jean-Jacques Rousseau.

3. *Rousseau Rejected*

It was not until Rousseau's works were translated into Dutch at the very end of the eighteenth century that they started to receive widespread attention in the Dutch Republic. Until that time, even though they were printed by Marc-Michel Rey and Jean Néaulme and repeatedly banned by the authorities, very few Dutchmen seemed to realize their enormous importance.[69] Among the exceptions was Luzac, who more than any of his compatriots regarded Rousseau as somebody to be reckoned with. Rousseau, of course, is notoriously hard to classify. Even his fellow *philosophes* hardly knew what to make of this highly unconventional figure. Although they clearly thought of him as one of theirs, very few of them actually remained on speaking terms with the quarrelsome citizen of Geneva. Diderot detested his views on the theater and Voltaire, to give but two well-known examples, accused him of writing books against the human race.[70] Apart from being sharply divided over whether he be-

---

66. *Nederlandsche Letter-Courant*, vol.3 (1760), 355 ("...waarin misschien nog minder waerheid in te vinden is dan in de *Siècle de Louis XIV van Voltaire*...").

67. *Ibidem*, vol.1 (1759), 82-83.

68. *Ibidem*, vol.3 (1760), 355-356.

69. Gobbers, *Rousseau in Holland*, *passim*.

70. Gay, *Enlightenment*, vol.2, 258-259; Cranston, *Jean-Jacques*, 306-307.

longed to the Enlightenment or to Romanticism, modern commentators have detected Rousseau at the origin of almost every twentieth-century current of thought from psychoanalysis to totalitarianism.[71] Luzac, however, had no doubts whatsoever as to Rousseau's place. To him, Rousseau's writings represented the full results of the systematic destruction of knowledge the French called *philosophie*. Rousseau exemplified everything that Luzac loathed and dreaded.

Despite his fundamental disagreement with *philosophes* such as Voltaire and d'Alembert, Luzac still shared some common ground with them. He clearly sympathized with their views on religious toleration and the freedom of expression and he shared their reverence for intellectual progress and scientific knowledge, although he held very different views on what these last notions meant. Rousseau's thought, however, seemed totally devoid of even potentially attractive features. To start with, Rousseau's writings were to Luzac the best possible proof of his contention that the French neglect of metaphysics, including logic, had deprived the *philosophes* of the ability to reason coherently and systematically. Rousseau, he admitted, was an unsurpassed master of "the art of persuading". His specialty was to hide the utter absence of proof for his various extreme statements in streams of eloquence.[72] Luzac was not even going to try to rival Rousseau in this skilled manipulation of language. That would indeed be both impossible and unfitting for a "a small shoot of the French, transplanted to the Batavian marshes".[73] Fortunately, it was also unnecessary and undesirable, for it was not style and the tricks of classical oratory that counted in a process of rational intellectual exchange, but "the art of convincing", the unadorned presentation of convincing arguments.[74] In this last art, Rousseau was a dismal failure. There was not a single rule he did not break. He failed to define the words he used and he relied on assertion more than on argument.[75] Where he tried to argue, he showed complete ignorance of the most basic rules of logic.[76] His treatises, moreover, lacked clear principles and were very poorly organized.[77] Rousseau, in short, committed blunders "unfor-

---

71. On modern interpretations of Rousseau see Gay, *Party of Humanity*, 211-261.

72. *Seconde lettre*, xii ("...l'art de persuader...").

73. "Examen et critique", 102 ("...un petit rejetton de François, transplanté dans les marais Bataves...").

74. *Seconde lettre*, xii ("...l'art de convaincre...").

75. *Lettre d'un anonime*, 80 and 85.

76. *Ibidem*, 29; *Seconde lettre*, 26.

77. *Lettre d'un anonime*, 83-84 and 248-249.

givable even in second-rate writers".[78] Luzac mercilessly exposed them and convinced many contemporary critics, one of whom opened his review of Luzac's attack on *Emile* with the words: "There is no greater scourge for an orator than a philosopher, especially a Wolffian philosopher!"[79]

The content of Rousseau's writings posed even bigger problems than the form. Rousseau's depiction of a largely instinctive human happiness in the pre-social state of nature was abhorrent to Luzac, who regarded man as first and foremost a reasonable being. Given this starting point, it was hardly surprising that Rousseau should choose to dismiss contemporary high culture, to Luzac the culmination of a long and fruitful development in the arts and sciences, as totally corrupt. The alternatives he presented, ranging from praise for the most brutal aspects of life in the classical republics to the idealization of rural democracy, seemed both regressive and unrealistic to Luzac.[80] Possibly even more alarming was the fact that Rousseau vigorously attacked the very tradition that Luzac was trying to carry on, that of modern natural law from Grotius onwards. Luzac attached great importance to exposing Rousseau's fallacies in interpreting Grotius, Pufendorf, and Barbeyrac. Rousseau, he claimed, was doing much more than willfully misrepresenting these theorists. He was engaged in subverting the generally accepted meaning of words, using them as empty shells to create a new vocabulary suiting his own political purposes. This complaint about the abuse of words and language would in due course become one of the staples of counterrevolutionary argument, used by such conservatives as Burke in England, La Harpe in France, and Luzac and Kluit in the Dutch Republic.[81] Its appearance at this relatively early point in Luzac's work strongly suggests that he was seriously beginning to worry about the direct political aims and consequences of French radical thought. This interpretation finds further support in the fact that he emphatically pointed out that Rousseau's theories delegitimized every single existing government in Europe.

---

78. *Ibidem*, 41 ("...impardonnables dans un écrivain même de la plus basse classe.").

79. *Bibliothèque des Sciences et des Beaux Arts*, vol.26, second part, 1766, 607 ("Quel fléau pour un Orateur, qu'un Philosophe, et un Philosophe Wolfien!").

80. Good discussions of the alternative political orders idealized by Rousseau may be found in Shklar, *Men and Citizens*, 1-32 and Keohane, *Philosophy and the State in France*, 420-449.

81. Blakemore, *Burke and the Fall of Language*, *passim*; Hunt, *Politics, Culture, and Class*, 19 and 25; Reichardt and Schmitt, ed. *Handbuch politisch-sozialer Grundbegriffe*, vol.1/2, 2-12.

But even quite apart from these explicit differences between the thought of Rousseau and Luzac, there was something less easy to grasp that separated the two men. In typical early Enlightenment fashion Luzac always tried to appear in his publications as the rational, objective, and somewhat distant commentator. He was therefore revolted by the explicitly subjective and highly emotional tone Rousseau affected. Contrary to thousands of readers deeply moved by this novel mode of presentation, Luzac judged it to be tasteless, insincere, and demagogic.[82] It positively infuriated him. What, for instance, was all this sentimental drivel about the great instinctive humanity of "the savage man", nowadays only to be found in the common people? It would certainly do Rousseau a great deal of good to attend a public execution, where he would not find the reasonable men he so despised, but his beloved and goodhearted common people thoroughly enjoying "the inhuman pleasure of seeing a poor wretch suffer".[83]

Luzac's first response to Rousseau was occasioned by the appearance of the *Discours sur l'origine et les fondemens de l'inégalité parmi les hommes* in 1755. He immediately summarized the treatise in the *Bibliothèque Impartiale* and in 1756 he subjected it to an *Examen et critique desintéressée* in that same journal.[84] In the *Discours*, Rousseau offered a hypothetical account of man's gradual emergence from a pre-social state of nature. Natural man, he claimed, lived a largely isolated yet happy life. He knew few passions, had no moral notions except an instinctive feeling of pity, and did not even possess the gift of language. Man distinguished himself from the beasts by his freedom and his capacity for self-improvement, not by his reason. For a variety of reasons, the economic shortages caused by population growth among them, mankind slowly began to form societies. Through the rather idyllic state of "nascent society", in which they lived like brothers, the early inhabitants of the earth passed to pre-political and finally to political society. Rousseau described this process to a large extent as that of the corruption of natural man. The development of ever more sophisticated forms of sociability not only transformed man himself, giving him an artificial *amour propre*, but also greatly increased inequality by the introduction of such new features as the division of labor and private property. These changes were made

---

82. On readers' response to Rousseau see Darnton, *Great Cat Massacre*, 215-256.

83. Rousseau, *Oeuvres complètes*, vol.3, 156; "Examen et critique", 446 ("...le plaisir inhumain de voir souffrir un malheureux.").

84. *Bibliothèque Impartiale*, vol.12 (1755), 213-238 and vol.14 (1756), 101-124 and 434-451.

permanent by the introduction of a grossly unfair system of law, foisted upon the poor by the rich with the sole purpose of perpetuating their newly acquired dominance. Such, according to Rousseau, had been the road to the "the fatal enlightenment of civilized man".[85]

Luzac first of all stressed the fact that Rousseau's entire treatise was pure speculation, a castle in the clouds, or - less friendly - "a fiction spawned by one of the darkest recesses of his misanthropical brain".[86] Secondly, he deplored the general drift of the *Discours*. It was filled with thoughts contrary to common sense, human happiness, and the respect for God. As a professed enemy of the "development of the mind", Rousseau was out to persuade man to extinguish this "divine torch". He blamed all evils on society, the product of man's industry and knowledge, preferring instead an imagined state of brute stupidity and considering man's capacity to improve himself a "fatal gift of God to man".[87] Having condemned Rousseau's general thesis, Luzac in the third place offered detailed comments on the first part of the *Discours*. The whole problem of human inequality only posed itself, he observed, if one insisted on contrasting man's social life, always marked by inequality, with an imaginary egalitarian state of nature.[88] But since Rousseau had obviously chosen to do so, it would be instructive to take a close look at his argument. While not entirely denying the uses of the concept of a state of nature, Luzac insisted that it was wrong to regard this state as radically different from civil society. Both Rousseau and Hobbes had made a fatal mistake in supposing it to be so. "Both Hobbes and Rousseau, equally intent upon destroying the distinction between moral good and moral evil, build their arguments on false principles. The former wrongly presumes that the state of nature is a state of war and that therefore laws are necessary to suppress injustice and violence. The latter mistakenly views the state of nature as a state of peace in which man's lack of passions and

---

85. On Rousseau's *Discours* see Cranston, *Jean-Jacques*, 292-309 and *Philosophers and Pamphleteers*, 64-83. The quotation is in Rousseau, *Oeuvres complètes*, vol.3, 170. In the text, I have used M. Cranston's translations of Rousseau: *A Discourse on Inequality* (Harmondsworth, 1984) and *The Social Contract* (Harmondsworth, 1968).

86. "Discours", 218 and "Examen et critique", 109 ("...un Roman enfanté dans un des reduits les plus ténébreux de son cerveau misantrope.").

87. "Examen et critique", 103-105 ("...culture de l'esprit..."; "...divin flambeau..."; "...funeste présent que Dieu a fait aux hommes...").

88. *Ibidem*, 110.

stupidity render all laws superfluous".[89] But although both men were wrong, Rousseau's version of the state of nature was by far the more unlikely.

To depict natural man, Luzac believed, Rousseau had simply stripped civilized man of all the qualities that made him human. He held Rousseau's contention that it was not reason, but freedom and the capacity for self-improvement that distinguished man from the beasts to be thoroughly flawed, for both qualities in fact presupposed the capacity to reason.[90] Even worse, however, was the fact that Rousseau described his natural man as perfectly happy and content with the simple pleasures of food, sleep, and casual sex. Such a conception of happiness Luzac could only regard as a shocking assault on human dignity. It was inconceivable to him that man could be, or had ever been content without the least desire "to enrich his mind, to adorn it, to fill it with the sublime knowledge of which it is capable".[91] Rousseau's outrageous views were crowned by his insistence that man had achieved this state of savage happiness in almost complete isolation. This repellent vision of "a generation of totally isolated and mute human beings" struck Luzac as utterly unrealistic, for it could not be doubted that man always had been a social being.[92] To suppose that it had taken mankind many centuries to develop even the most basic forms of communication was a thought that could only have occurred to a misanthrope. But that, Luzac concluded his review of the *Discours*, was exactly what Rousseau was. "To suggest that in order to fulfill their true nature and to live happily men have to turn themselves into veritable monsters testifies to a regrettable lack of respect for mankind".[93]

After his first attempts at cultural criticism, Rousseau set out to sketch

---

89. *Ibidem*, 441-442 ("Hobbes et Mr. Rousseau, tous deux dans les mêmes vuës et pour parvenir au même but, qui est d'anéantir la distinction du bien et du mal moral, bâtissent sur des principes également faux. Le premier en supposant que l'Etat de Nature est un Etat de Guerre qui a rendu les loix nécessaires pour reprimer l'injustice et la violence; et le second en supposant que c'est un Etat de Paix, où les Hommes, entièrement exempts de passions parce qu'ils étoient stupides, n'avoient pas besoin par conséquent de Loix pour les reprimer.").

90. *Ibidem*, 117-119.

91. *Ibidem*, 122 ("...d'étendre ses lumières, d'orner son esprit, de l'occuper des connoissances sublimes dont ses facultés le rendent susceptible.").

92. *Ibidem*, 436-437 ("...une génération d'Hommes entièrement isolés et muets.").

93. *Ibidem*, 449 ("Il faut bien peu respecter les Hommes, pour oser leur dire que c'est en vrai monstres qu'ils doivent vivre, s'ils veulent rentrer dans l'Etat auquel la Nature les avoit destinés, et vivre heureux.").

the ways in which the corruption of civilized society might be remedied. He did so in a series of works appearing in 1761 and 1762: *La Nouvelle Heloïse*, the *Contrat social*, and *Emile*. Luzac had little to say about the first of these, although he briefly announced the book's appearance in the *Nederlandsche Letter-Courant*.[94] The *Contrat social*, however, he judged worthy of an immediate review and a separate lengthy refutation. Only weeks after its original publication Luzac attacked the treatise in his journal, thereby providing what very probably was the first review of the *Contrat social* in Europe.[95] Dissatisfied with the limited possibilities inherent in the review genre and convinced that Rousseau was widely recognized as an important political theorist, he subsequently decided to expand his polemic. "I am presently composing a letter to Mr. J.J.R.. My aim is to show that his reasoning is bad, that he is no philosopher, and that he is ignorant of the subjects he discusses. I hope to convince the public that its enthusiasm for Rousseau is unwarranted. I am not yet sure whether I'll have it printed", he wrote to Formey in January 1765. In the end, he decided to have the letter printed. It appeared in 1766 as *Lettre d'un anonime à Monsieur J.J. Rousseau*.[96]

The discussion of the "principles of political right" that Rousseau presented in the *Contrat social* to a large extent consisted of an attack on the most eminent representatives of modern natural law.[97] Grotius, in particular, was one of his main targets. He was put in the company of Hobbes as a proponent of slavery and boundless tyranny, accused of establishing right by fact and represented, together with Barbeyrac, as a

---

94. *Nederlandsche Letter-Courant*, vol.5 (1761), 117-119.

95. *Ibidem*, vol.8 (1762), 52-54, 60-62, 67-69, 75-78, 84-86. It is a contested matter who wrote the first extended critical review of the *Contrat social*. In his "Réfutations du 'Contrat Social'" R. Derathé claimed that P.L. de Bauclair's *Anti-Contract social* (1764) and Luzac's *Lettre d'un anonime* were the first two published reactions. J. Lough, however, has found an earlier one. It appeared between September and November 1763 in a French periodical entitled *La Religion vengée ou Réfutation des auteurs impies*. See Lough, "Earliest refutation". Luzac's review in *Nederlandsche Letter-Courant* predates all of these.

96. *Corr. Formey*, Luzac to Formey, Leiden, January 21, 1765 ("Je suis à composer une Lettre à Mons. J.J.R. Mon but est de faire voir qu'il raisonne mal, qu'il n'est point philosophe, qu'il ignore ce qu'il devroit savoir sur les sujets qu'il traitte, le tout pour faire revenir le Public, plus ou moins, de l'enthousiasme dans lequel il le jette. Je ne sai, si je la ferai imprimer."). The exact publishing date of the *Lettre d'un anonime* is uncertain. The book's title page says 1766, but it was reviewed in 1765 by both the *Bibliothèque des Sciences et des Beaux Arts* (vol.23, second part, 1765, 569-573) and the *Journal Encyclopédique* (1765, vol.6, first part, 18-30).

97. This has been demonstrated in great detail by R. Derathé in his excellent *Jean-Jacques Rousseau et la Science Politique de son Temps*.

repulsive and venal flatterer of princes.[98] Luzac was thrown into par-
oxysms of rage by this assault on the man he regarded as the founder of
the modern *science des moeurs*.[99] The demonstration that Rousseau
simply did not know what he was talking about formed an important part
of his response. "To censure Grotius one should first understand him", he
snapped at Rousseau and proceeded to explain the writings of the master.[100] Thus, to give but one example, he refuted Rousseau's claim that
Grotius saw war as establishing a right to slavery by pointing out that
Grotius in fact only explained the content of *ius gentium* and, moreover,
particularly stressed the difference between *ius gentium* and natural law
on the subject of slavery.[101] "Could we now ask you, Sir, what the
purpose of your feeble attempts against Grotius is?"[102] Much the same
was true for Rousseau's treatment of Pufendorf and Barbeyrac.[103] But to
prove that Rousseau's attack on these giants was misconceived and
unjustified was not enough, for the real danger of the *Contrat social* lay
in the fact that it substituted an incoherent and subversive doctrine for the
teachings it rejected.

   "Man was born free, and he is everywhere in chains" ran the famous
opening sentence of the first chapter of the *Contrat social*.[104] Luzac
seized upon it to make the point that Rousseau's treatise largely consisted
of inflated rhetoric. It was utter nonsense, he claimed, to conceive of man
as born entirely free. He was, on the contrary, born in "an extreme
dependence" and the very fact of his birth created a large number of
obligations, for instance to his direct family.[105] Since Rousseau, by
positing that man in the state of nature was an amoral being guided by
instinct, denied the validity of natural law, it was hardly surprising that he
held this view.[106] But it was, Luzac continued, equally untrue that man
was now everywhere in chains, for even the most despotic rulers allowed

98. Rousseau, *Oeuvres complètes*, vol.3, 352-353 and 370-371.

99. For Luzac's views on Grotius's role in the history of the *science des moeurs* see 92-94.

100. *Lettre d'un anonime*, 44 ("Pour censurer Grotius il faudroit commencer par l'en-
tendre.").

101. *Ibidem*, 44-55.

102. *Ibidem*, 55 ("Pourroit-on maintenant vous demander, Monsieur, à quoi bon vos efforts
contre Grotius?").

103. For Luzac's efforts to defend Grotius, Pufendorf, and Barbeyrac against Rousseau see
also Derathé, "Réfutations du 'Contrat Social'", 33-45.

104. Rousseau, *Oeuvres complètes*, vol.3, 351.

105. *Lettre d'un anonime*, 6 ("...une extrême dépendance...").

106. *Ibidem*, 70.

their subjects a measure of liberty in at least some areas of life. On close inspection Rousseau's resounding opening statement turned out to be entirely devoid of meaning.[107] Yet he cheerfully proceeded to pile one unproven assertion on top of another and to attach wholly new and arbitrary meanings to words such as liberty, sovereignty, and government. Luzac was particularly distressed by Rousseau's unprecedented insistence that sovereignty could not be alienated and always remained in the hands of the people. Not only did Rousseau fail to explain satisfactorily why the normal rules of contract did not apply to the transfer of sovereignty, his extreme position also widely opened the door to "those inclining to revolt and rebellion".[108]

What made matters worse, however, was the fact that this arbitrary manipulation of the terms of political discourse contributed very little to the solution of the *Contrat social*'s central problem. "How to find a form of association which will defend the person and goods of each member with the collective force of all, and under which each individual, while uniting himself with the others, obeys no one but himself, and remains as free as before" had been Rousseau's problem and the formation of a political society based on inalienable popular sovereignty had been his solution.[109] Luzac pointed out in response that the problem was by definition unsolvable and that the solution proposed did not in fact meet Rousseau's own requirements. "If you believe, Sir, that the form of association in which each member is a part of the sovereign solves your problem, you are evidently mistaken. To be obliged to follow a will in the determination of which one has participated is certainly not the same thing as following one's own will. According to me, doing as one pleases in everything and being forced to conform to the will of the multitude will always remain two quite different and distinct things".[110]

In failing to provide an answer to his own misconceived central question, Rousseau had clearly demonstrated his inability to reason. His subsequent more factual discussion of Roman politics hardly improved his

---

107. *Ibidem*, 6-7.

108. *Ibidem*, 90-97 and 104 ("...ceux qui ont l'esprit porté à la révolte et à la rebellion...").

109. Rousseau, *Oeuvres complètes*, vol.3, 360.

110. *Lettre d'un anonime*, 73-74 ("Si vous croyez, Monsieur, que la forme d'association, par laquelle chaque membre fait partie du Souverain, y satisfasse pleinement, vous vous trompez; car devoir suivre la détermination d'une volonté à laquelle on a concoûru, n'est certainement pas suivre celle de la sienne propre; et selon moi, agir de son propre mouvement en tout, et ne pouvoir agir en certaines occasions que conformément au gré de la multitude; sont deux modifications très-distinctes, de quelque manière que vous les envisagiez.").

performance in Luzac's view, for it combined a lack of historical accuracy with a regressive preference for classical republican politics. Liberally quoting from Vertot's *Histoire des révolutions arrivées dans le gouvernement de la république Romaine* and Montesquieu's *Considérations sur les causes de la grandeur des Romains et de leur décadence*, Luzac pointed out that Rousseau had committed a regrettable error in discussing the history of the Roman Republic as if it were a unity. In reality, it had undergone "constant revolutions and changes".[111] More serious, however, was the fact that Rousseau, so innovative in many of his other views, now turned out to be a representative of that widespread idealization of classical antiquity that Luzac so detested. In the *Contrat social*, Rousseau favorably contrasted "the simple habits of the early Romans, their taste for agriculture, and their contempt alike for commerce and for the pursuit of profit" with the "devouring greed, unsettled hearts, intrigue, continual movement and constant reversals of fortune" prevalent in modern times.[112] To Luzac, such a view was both misleading and unacceptable. The history of Rome, he contended, contained no salutary lessons for the modern age. Should Rousseau ever take the trouble to study it in depth, he would soon find out that the glory of Rome was entirely based on slavery and conquest, two phenomena he had so vociferously rejected in the earlier parts of his treatise.[113] Indeed, it should be clear to all but the most stubborn primitivists that modern commerce had led to a state of affairs vastly superior to the inhuman cruelty continuously displayed in the history of Rome. "I simply do not see to what purpose the Romans are always paraded before us as an example to follow. I vastly prefer a republic that is content with its possessions and with the task of providing its inhabitants with a quiet and peaceful life. If good sense prevails, it will be seen that such a commercial republic is neither less honorable nor less honored. It is time to discard those ancient prejudices whereby honor is solely thought to consist in killing one's neighbor and in depopulating the earth".[114]

111. *Ibidem*, 204 ("...des révolutions et des altérations continuelles.").

112. Rousseau, *Oeuvres complètes*, vol.3, 448.

113. *Lettre d'un anonime*, 235-241.

114. *Ibidem*, 246 ("Je ne vois point quel avantage il y a de nous donner éternellement les Romains pour modèle. J'aime bien mieux une République, contente de ses possessions, ne cherchant qu'à les conserver, et à procurer à ses habitans une vie tranquile et paisible. Passée dans les affaires de commerce, elle n'en sera ni moins honorable ni moins honorée, si le bon sens reprenant ses droits nous fait perdre ces prejugés anciens, qui attachent l'honneur uniquement à l'art de tuer le prochain et de dépeupler la terre.").

After his futile attempt to redefine the principles of politics, Rousseau had unfortunately still felt the need to round off his attack on civilization with an assault on the role of reason in both education and religion. Such, at least, was Luzac's opinion of the content of *Emile*. To substantiate his verdict, he wrote a *Seconde lettre d'un anonime à Monsieur J.J. Rousseau*, published in 1767. Having been accused by a critic of the use of somewhat harsh terms in his first letter to Rousseau, Luzac admitted that he had been severe. But the truth had to be told and he was not out to please but to argue and to convince.[115] The theory of education developed in *Emile*, he continued, was a most singular one. First of all, it was of a remarkably elitist nature. Rousseau, the champion of equality, here unfolded a plan of education that was only suitable for well-born, rich, strong, and healthy children. Who but the most affluent, to give but one example, could afford a governor for years?[116]

But quite apart from the extraordinary circumstances required for the implementation of Rousseau's educational ideas, they were in themselves unsound. They had, in fact, very little to do with education at all, for Rousseau's views could be summed up in the statement that "the education of man consists almost entirely in preventing the development of his intellectual capacities".[117] The whole of *Emile* was but one more example of Rousseau's rabid anti-intellectualism. But what else could one expect from an author who wrote: "I hate books. All they do is teach you to speak about things you do not know"?[118] While Luzac was fully convinced that a child should not be treated like a miniature grown-up, he insisted that the capacity for rational thought should be trained and developed from an early age on, "because for the happiness of mankind one cannot cultivate the understanding soon enough".[119] To let a child simply roam through nature, to postpone teaching it to read until adolescence and yet to expect it to develop into a sensible human being was absurd. But it was also fatal, for by the time Rousseau proposed to

115. What has been said about the publication date of the *Lettre d'un anonime* (note 96) is also true for that of the *Seconde lettre*. Although the title page says 1767, it was reviewed in the *Bibliothèque des Sciences et des Beaux Arts* in the previous year (vol.26, second part, 1766, 607-612). The review Luzac referred to in the *Seconde lettre* (v) was probably that in the *Bibliothèque des Sciences* mentioned in note 96.

116. *Seconde lettre*, 9-11.

117. *Ibidem*, 2 ("...l'éducation de l'homme consiste presqu'entièrement dans le soin d'empêcher que les facultés intellectuelles ne se perfectionnent.").

118. Rousseau, *Oeuvres complètes*, vol.4, 454.

119. *Seconde lettre*, 3 ("...parce que...pour le bonheur du genre humain on ne puisse trop tôt cultiver l'entendement...").

introduce the child to the more sophisticated intellectual, moral, and social skills, it would already be too old to acquire them in full.[120]

The ideas on religious instruction contained in the *Profession du foi du vicaire Savoyard*, finally, were "pure gibberish".[121] They seemed to amount to the glorification of a highly individual conscience and of sentiment and emotion in matters of religious belief. This, of course, was an extremely dangerous position to take, for "to *surrender oneself to sentiment* is in fact to abandon oneself to the torrent of those emotions which render man irrational and unreasonable".[122] Rousseau, moreover, once more launched a gratuitous attack on a great scholar. This time it was Locke. While Luzac freely admitted that he disagreed with Locke on a number of issues, he held Rousseau's suggestion that the English philosopher was "a sophist of bad faith" for having speculated on the possibility of thinking matter to be totally unfounded.[123] It was as distasteful as his earlier insinuations about Grotius and Barbeyrac had been.[124] The *Profession*, however, was not only dangerous and slanderous, it was also inconsistent, for in its final part Rousseau suddenly claimed that mankind's greatest ideas about God stemmed from reason.[125] It was too much for Luzac. But for the general decline in knowledge brought about by *philosophie*, it was impossible to understand how any reader could take Rousseau seriously. Having tried every argument at his disposal against him, the exasperated Luzac offered one final piece of advice. Rousseau, he suggested, would do both himself and mankind a great favor by putting down his pen and henceforth devoting himself to that activity which he so justly praised: agriculture.[126]

4. *A Battle on Two Fronts*

The greatest threat to Luzac's rational Enlightenment clearly came from France. The writers of that country, always given to extremes, were

---

120. *Ibidem*, 156-207.

121. *Ibidem*, 234 ("...pur galimathias...").

122. *Ibidem*, 210 ("...se *livrer au sentiment,* c'est proprement s'abandonner au torrent de ces impressions, qui rendent l'homme irraisonnable et déraisonnable.").

123. Rousseau, *Oeuvres complètes*, vol.4, 585.

124. *Seconde lettre*, 224-227.

125. *Ibidem*, 239.

126. *Nederlandsche Letter-Courant*, vol.8 (1762), 86. Brief discussions not mentioned so far of Luzac's writings against Rousseau include Valkhoff, "Luzac", 106-113 and Trousson, "Deux lecteurs de Rousseau", 196-202.

carrying the destruction of knowledge to such lengths that the very survival of civilized society was beginning to be seriously threatened. The same could obviously not be said of Britain. Yet there, too, the triumph of sensationalism was giving rise to dubious developments in the field of moral philosophy. Increasing numbers of British theorists, Luzac observed, were embracing the flawed view that the foundation of ethics was to be sought in sentiment rather than in the understanding. He first commented on this tendency in British thought when reviewing Adam Smith's *Theory of moral sentiments* in 1759, the year of its publication. While praising Smith's efforts to develop the science of morals, Luzac rejected his central contention that it ought to revolve around sympathy. Experience, he remarked, did not show that all people were equally moved by sympathy. But even supposing this sentiment to be effective in all human beings, it could still be remarked that it was too narrow in scope to serve as a general principle. It explained far less than, for instance, the desire for happiness did. Most important, however, was the fact that sympathy was a mere subjective feeling. It was therefore by definition too confused and unclear to serve as the first principle in a system of morality.[127]

More than a decade passed before Luzac returned to this theme at some length. His renewed interest was caused by the growing popularity of moral sense philosophy in the Dutch Republic. The publication of his views on the subject was, as H.C. Cras relates, the result of the efforts of Johannes Petsch (1711-1796), the Dutch translator and defender of Leibniz. Having criticized the Amsterdam Baptist minister A. Hulshoff for extolling the moral sense in an essay that was crowned by the *Legatum Stolpianum* in 1765, Petsch found himself under attack from an anonymous author in 1770.[128] In that same year, it came to his attention that Luzac was informally corresponding about the theory of moral sense with Frederik Vaster, a learned civil servant of Wolffian persuasion.[129] Petsch obtained permission from the two men to publish their exchange of letters and did so in 1771, adding his own commentary. The result was the *Correspondence between Philagathos and Philalethes on the theory of moral sense*.[130] It was a pamphlet in which, as one reviewer noted, "the

127. *Nederlandsche Letter-Courant*, vol.1 (1759), 402-403.

128. *De leer van het zedelyk gevoel, opgeheldert en verdedigt in eenen brief aan een geleerd man.* Groningen, 1770. On Petsch see *Biografisch lexicon*, vol.1, 249-250.

129. Cras, "Beredeneerd verslag", 61-70.

130. *Briefwisseling van Philagathos en Philalethes over de leer van het zedelyk gevoel, etc.*

doctrine of moral sense is more strongly attacked than ever before".[131]

Although Petsch's rather rambling comments took up more than half of the pamphlet, its centerpiece was constituted by Luzac's sustained attack on all doctrines of moral sense. Luzac first of all pointed out that nobody, prominent theorists such as Francis Hutcheson not excepted, had succeeded in giving a clear and convincing definition of the moral sense. There were, it seemed, as many different opinions as there were followers of this elusive doctrine.[132] All adherents of moral sense theory, however, seemed in one form or another to share the view that morals depended not on reason and the understanding, but on sentiment and feeling.[133] This, therefore, was the point that needed to be discussed. Experience showed, Luzac continued, that human beings did indeed have a sort of primary, semi-instinctive moral reaction in many situations. But since this reaction was clearly unrelated to the direct or indirect influence of physical objects on the mind, it was a matter of the understanding. What was frequently called moral sense, in other words, was nothing but an unclear and muddled first understanding of ethics. It was perfectly true, Luzac admitted, that such an imperfect immediate understanding was sufficient to deal with most ethical problems arising in the course of daily life. But since it was different in every single human being and since it was by definition confused, it was unable to provide certainty in moral matters.[134]

Having reduced the moral sense to, at best, a confused form of ethical understanding, Luzac proceeded to sketch the rudiments of a system of morality based on the more developed use of our understanding. Morality, he pointed out, could be defined as the relationship between our actions and our duties. A fully fledged system of morals should therefore start with an explanation of our duties. Such an explanation should be systematically developed from a single, universal, clear, and objective principle, preferably that of perfection. Luzac, it is obvious, had arrived where he wanted to be: knowledge, not feelings, constituted the basis of morality.[135] Feelings, he once again emphasized at the end of his contribution to the *Correspondence*, could be invoked to justify every

---

131. *Bibliothèque des Sciences et des Beaux Arts*, vol.35, second part, April-June 1771, 336 ("...la Doctrine du Sens Moral est plus fortement attaquée qu'elle ne l'avoit encore été jusques ici.").

132. *Briefwisseling*, 43-55.

133. *Ibidem*, 55-58.

134. *Ibidem*, 63-72.

135. *Ibidem*, 73-83.

possible kind of abominable behavior. The reliance on sentiment in matters susceptible to rational analysis paved the way for all kinds of emotional excesses, as the history of religion amply demonstrated. The theory of moral sense, in fact, was nothing but enthusiasm in a new guise. It was, indeed, hardly surprising to find a Baptist minister among its most prominent Dutch supporters.[136]

Even before Luzac warned against this new form of enthusiasm, however, an old form of fanaticism had once again reared its head in the Dutch Republic. In the *Nederlandsche Letter-Courant* Luzac, as was noted above, repeatedly complained that he was not at liberty to discuss all the things he wished. Restrictions on the freedom of expression eventually contributed to his decision to terminate the journal's publication in 1763. Before he did so, he bitterly accused theologians of stigmatizing everything they happened to dislike as freethinking or even atheism.[137] He also, once again, emphatically rejected the imposition of forced silence in intellectual matters.[138] But his impassioned pleas went unheard. The 1760s, in fact, witnessed a marked increase in the number of attempts to curtail the freedom of expression in Holland. Worried by the growing tide of radical publications, the authorities issued bans against a number of philosophical writings, Rousseau's *Contrat social* and *Emile* and Voltaire's *Dictionnaire philosophique* among them.[139] Persecution increasingly threatened both publishers and authors. In 1760, J. Baroen was imprisoned and subsequently banished for having published Pieter Bakker's *Religion without superstition*.[140] In 1766 the Amsterdam Walloon Consistory saw to it that Vincenzio Gaudio was sentenced to no less than thirty years of imprisonment for having written an article about Rousseau containing strongly anti-clerical passages.[141] Luzac, of course, had seen it all before and operated with the utmost caution. He used all the tactics of evasion he had learned to perfection since the La Mettrie affair to remain anonymous as the author of two treatises about Rousseau. He deliberately but indirectly insulted the clergy by hardly mentioning Rousseau's views on civil religion in his otherwise quite exhaustive discussion of the *Contrat social*. By the late 1760s, however, things were

---

136. *Ibidem*, 91-92.

137. *Nederlandsche Letter-Courant*, vol.3 (1760), 164-165.

138. *Ibidem*, vol.10 (1763), 212-213.

139. Zwager, *Nederland en de Verlichting*, 58.

140. Evenhuis, *Ook dat was Amsterdam*, 190-198.

141. *Ibidem*, 252-253.

beginning to look so serious that he decided openly to confront the enemy.

On September 7, 1769, the Court of Holland, acting on the advice of a group of Dutch Reformed ministers, urged the States of Holland to appoint *Censores Librorum*, entrusted with the general task of preventing the publication of undesirable books.[142] The plan was rejected on the grounds that it presented too many practical difficulties, but early in 1770 the States seriously considered issuing a decree forbidding "the production, printing, and publishing of all books in which the foundations of Christian Religion are attacked, or the Holy Writ and the true Reformed Religion are ridiculed, as well as all books and writings tending to corrupt good manners and to ruin the young by their obscene content, the penalty being a fine, banishment, or imprisonment".[143] The concept of this decree, stipulating an unprecedented range of controls on publishers and booksellers, became widely known and provoked a stream of reactions. The Amsterdam guild of booksellers and publishers addressed a written protest to the city government, begging it to prevent the decree from being adopted by the States.[144] A number of Leiden booksellers undertook a similar action. Wishing to present their case as forcefully as possible, they asked Luzac to support their request with a thoroughly argued statement. It was the opportunity he had been waiting for.

In his 1749 *Essai sur la liberté de produire ses sentimens* Luzac had defended the freedom of expression at a relatively high level of abstraction. His 1770 *Memorie*, intended to stop a specific measure, was of quite a different nature. It was a step by step argument against the concept of the decree of the States of Holland as it circulated early in 1770. The *Memorie*'s main focus was on technical legal matters and on the consequences the decree's promulgation would have for Holland. Yet despite these differences between the *Essai* and the *Memorie*, the main thrust of both pieces was identical. The rise of *philosophie* had not caused Luzac to change his mind on the freedom of debate. The concept of the decree,

---

142. The complete plan for the appointment of *Censores Librorum* is printed in Kruseman, *Boekhandel van Noord-Nederland*, 390-395.

143. Bodel Nyenhuis, *Wetgeving op Drukpers en Boekhandel*, 169 ("...het maken, drukken en uitgeven van alle zoodanige boeken, waarbij de gronden van den Christelijken Godsdienst aangetast, of de H. Schrift, als mede de ware Gereformeerde Religie, op eene spotachtige wyze behandeld worden, gelijk ook alle boeken en geschriften, door hunnen obscoenen inhoud geschikt om inbreuk te doen op de goede zeden, en strekkende tot bederf der jeugd: onder bedreiging van geldboete, ban of gevangenis...").

144. *Ibidem*, 170. The Amsterdam protest is printed in *Nieuwe Nederlandsche Jaerboeken*, vol.5, second part, July 1770, 788-807.

Luzac first of all remarked, did not meet the basic requirements for any criminal law. It was a well-known fact that a criminal law in which the punishable act was not unambiguously defined was unsound and dangerous, for it could easily develop into an instrument of despotism. Yet the concept vaguely referred to blasphemy and obscenity, ignoring the fact that no two people actually agreed on what these notions meant. This objection was equally valid for those passages in which a higher degree of precision was attempted. It would indeed be quite instructive, Luzac observed, to hear the legislators explain what exactly was to be understood by "true Reformed Religion". But not only did the concept give no satisfactory definitions, it also failed to provide details about the nature of the punishments to be meted out. As a result of this double omission, the judges would in practice have to take on the role of legislators. How undesirable such a situation was had already been demonstrated by Montesquieu in his *Esprit des lois*. "When the judge presumes, judgments become arbitrary" was a remark not to be taken lightly.[145]

After this brief lesson in the proper techniques of legislation, Luzac explained that the measures proposed would bring about the total ruin of Holland's book trade.[146] Even more important, however, was the fact that all arguments advanced to legitimate the imposition of these disastrous controls on the freedom of expression were invalid. It was perfectly true, Luzac admitted, that sovereigns were allowed and even obliged to defend themselves against the violation of their rights. But the publication of religious views, whatever their nature, could not possibly be regarded as an attack on the rights of the sovereign. The expression of religious opinions, in fact, could not be regarded as a violation of anybody's rights and it could therefore not be subject to prohibition under positive law at all.[147] The position that sovereigns could simply limit any freedom they judged to be harmful to society was equally unacceptable. Those who invoked this argument should realize that its adoption made it impossible to criticize any sovereign, however arbitrary his measures.[148] Governments, Luzac continued, certainly held a measure of responsibility for everybody's welfare, but this did not mean that they

---

145. "Memorie", 813-845. Luzac's Montesquieu quotation may be found in Montesquieu, *Oeuvres complètes*, vol.2, 880 (*Esprit des lois*, Book XXIX, chapter 16). In writing the *Memorie* Luzac was assisted by his younger brother Isaac Elias. From its style and content, however, it is clear that Elie was the main author.

146. "Memorie", 845-855.

147. *Ibidem*, 860-863.

148. *Ibidem*, 863-866.

were free to stunt the intellectual development of their citizens by decree. They should, instead, follow the natural and positive route of rewarding virtue and of providing their citizens with a solid education.[149] These general truths all applied to Holland, but in addition, Luzac emphasized, it should be realized that freedom of religious expression had always been considered an integral part of Holland's constitution. That it had been judged prudential to adopt one dominant religion had until now never been taken to mean that those not belonging to it should be deprived of the freedom to express their views.[150] Indeed, was not the free search for religious truth supposed to be one of the main differences between Protestantism and Catholicism?[151] The conclusion to be drawn from this barrage of arguments was clear. "Neither the care for the general good, nor vigilance for religion, nor the supervision of the young can...justify an act which deprives the citizens of that which the highest wisdom wishes them to enjoy".[152]

The adoption of the concept would, moreover, destroy Holland's commerce and culture in general. "The experience of all countries in all times", Luzac observed, "confirms the truth that learning and commerce flourish where there is liberty and languish where liberty is suppressed".[153] Holland would certainly not be an exception to this rule. The measures proposed would definitely put an end to Holland's position as an intellectual staple market, a position already precarious because of the increasing liberty in other parts of Europe.[154] They would also turn the province into an intellectual desert. Scholarship would wither, old superstitions would resurface, and the clergy would once again seize its chance to impose its reign on an ignorant population.[155] Not only would the decree ruin much, Luzac finally added, it would also fail to achieve its objectives. First of all, it greatly exaggerated the influence of books on their readers. A well-bred person would not suddenly be corrupted by the

149. *Ibidem*, 866-868.

150. *Ibidem*, 868-870.

151. *Ibidem*, 871-872.

152. *Ibidem*, 872 ("Geen zorg voor 't algemeen nut; geen waekzaemheid voor den Godsdienst; geen toezicht voor de Jongelingschap kan...eene daed wettigen, welke aen Burgers beneemt dat geene, 't welk de opperste Wysheid wil dat zy genieten zullen.").

153. *Ibidem*, 873 ("Van alle oude tyden heeft de ondervinding in alle Landen de waerheid bevestigd, dat de Wetenschappen en Commercie floreeren daer vryheid is, en te niet loopen daer dezelve bedwongen worden.").

154. *Ibidem*, 873-874.

155. *Ibidem*, 874-883.

perusal of an obscene publication; a debauchee would hardly sink any further by reading yet another lurid tract.[156] It was, furthermore, impossible to tell what means of gratification, perhaps of a much more harmful nature, devotees of pornography would turn to if deprived of their relatively innocent reading pleasures. The possible bad effects of a book should, in other words, be weighed against the good it could do. That, after all, was common practice in many other areas. To ban obscene books and at the same time to tolerate brothels was the height of legislative inconsistency.[157]

Prohibiting a book, Luzac continued, was moreover probably the most effective way to draw the general public's attention to it. Once people were determined to read it, nothing would be able to stop them. If not legally available, they would get it from another country, from another province, or through a clandestine bookseller. The decree, in short, would never work.[158] Even in terms of its own objectives it was completely superfluous, for the existence of a clear link between the freedom of expression and blasphemous or obscene behavior had never been established. On the contrary: "The whole of human history does not provide us with one single example proving that the curtailment of the freedom of expression, the freedom to speak, to write, to paint, or to print, has ever led to a less blasphemous and obscene manner of living than that which prevails where complete freedom of the press has been granted".[159]

Luzac's powerful statement, together with the other protests, succeeded in preventing the adoption of the decree by the States of Holland. But the triumph was short-lived, for in 1773 the violent polemics about Marmontel's *Bélisaire* led to the imposition of a general prohibition of all books ridiculing the foundations of Christian religion.[160] This time, however, Luzac remained silent. He had, as he wrote to Formey in July 1770, withdrawn himself from the daily affairs and struggles of bookselling and publishing in order to be able to pursue his interest in legal

---

156. *Ibidem*, 884-886.

157. *Ibidem*, 886-887.

158. *Ibidem*, 888-889.

159. *Ibidem*, 891 ("Men doorloope alle Historien van alle tyden, men wyze een enkele stip op den Aerdkloot aen, alwaer de vryheid van zyne gevoelens uit te brengen, van spreken, schryven, schilderen, of drukken, beteugeld zynde, minder godslasterlyk, minder obscoen is geleefd, dan alwaer de vryheid van de Pers volstrekt is vry gelaten.").

160. Bodel Nyenhuis, *Wetgeving op Drukpers en Boekhandel*, 174-175; Kruseman, *Boekhandel van Noord-Nederland*, 398-399. On the so-called Socratic war Marmontel's *Bélisaire* gave rise to in the Dutch Republic see De Bie, *Petrus Hofstede*, 177-241.

scholarship.[161] In his modest countryhouse in Koudekerk, close to Leiden, he was now quietly devoting himself to the preparation of his French edition of Christian Wolff's *Institutiones iuris naturae et gentium*.[162] When the book appeared in 1772, it definitively established Luzac's reputation as a scholar in the field of natural law.

161. *Corr. Formey*, Luzac to Formey, Leiden, July 3, 1770.
162. Cras, "Beredeneerd verslag", 74.

CHAPTER III

MORAL SCIENCE VINDICATED

In retrospect, there seems to be more than a little truth in the observation that natural law represented the common framework of thought of the educated part of the world in the eighteenth century.[1] To contemporary adherents of natural law, however, such a claim would doubtlessly have seemed distinctly odd. What they saw was not so much consensus as struggle and disagreement. They were, first of all, well aware of the fact that the receptivity to modern natural law was very slight in many Catholic countries, with France as the prime example. Natural juris-prudence was and remained, as R. Tuck has recently stressed, an embat-tled and polemical movement.[2] This was even true for those countries where it was accepted on a wider scale, for that acceptance never came without prolonged wrangles with the exponents of various Protestant orthodoxies. Thus in the Dutch Republic professor F.A. van der Marck (1719-1800), one of Luzac's many correspondents, was expelled from Groningen University as late as 1773 for having undermined the doctrines of the Dutch Reformed Church with his Wolffian natural law teachings.[3] It was, as Luzac wrote to Herman Cannegieter, one more example of the constant threat posed by an intolerant *furor theologicus*.[4]

In the second half of the century, to make matters worse, the orthodox resistance against modern natural law was overtaken by the secular phil-osophical attacks of such major theorists as Hume and Rousseau. Finally, the followers of natural law frequently disagreed among themselves. As so often happens, differences that may seem relatively minor in retrospect tended to obscure fundamental shared values. Indeed, instead of em-phasizing the existence of a consensus, the eighteenth-century adherents of natural law dwelled with what almost seems delight on the infinite variety of systems. They went to extraordinary lengths to specify in detail what exactly they accepted or rejected, as may be illustrated by Van der Marck's self-description: "I am strongly anti-Hobbesian, and somewhat

---

1. J.B. Schneewind, "The Divine Corporation and the history of ethics" in: Rorty, et al., ed. *Philosophy in History*, 184.

2. Tuck, "Moral Science", 4.

3. Lindeboom, *Frederik Adolf van der Marck*, 49-101.

4. Provinciale Bibliotheek Leeuwarden, Hs 1152, no.21, Luzac to Herman Cannegieter [undated, but probably 1773].

more Grotian than Pufendorfian, but as to the scope and perfection of the laws of nature I reject Grotius for a broadly Wolffian position. In some branches of this science I am somewhat Wielingian...I have never been a Thomasian in natural law, but I esteemed this clever man highly in church law, and therefore I am rather more quasi-Erastian than Voetian".[5]

If the above observations are correct, it would seem worthwhile to try and write the history of modern natural law not as the abstract story of the universal triumph and subsequent rapid decline of a certain mode of thought, but as the story of constant external struggles and internal disagreements in the context of specific historical circumstances. In this chapter, an attempt will be made to analyze Luzac's thought on natural law along such lines. After a first section providing the necessary contextual information, the second section will explore Luzac's perception of his own historical position by reconstructing his account (scattered throughout his later writings) of the history of the science of morals. This will be followed, in section three, by a discussion of his substantive contribution to natural law, which mainly took the form of a constructive and critical commentary on the system of Christian Wolff. The fourth section, finally, will look at Luzac's views on the relationship between natural and Roman law.

1. *The Background to Luzac's Legal Scholarship*

It was during the 1740s, as a student at Leiden University, that Luzac was first introduced to the study of both Roman law and natural jurisprudence. To judge by his *Disquisitio politico-moralis* Luzac, who was not to obtain his doctorate in law until 1759, was already an accomplished jurist by 1749. Leiden University's reputation in legal studies was primarily based on its leading role in "elegant jurisprudence", the Dutch continuation of the humanistic mode of legal study known as *mos gallicus*.[6] Luzac greatly admired the work of one of the foremost representatives of the

5. Quoted in Duynstee, *Geschiedenis van het natuurrecht*, 55-56 ("Namelijk ik ben sterk anti-Hobbesiaansch gezind, en wat meer Grotiaansch als Pufendorffiaansch, doch omtrent de uitgestrektheid en volmaaktheid der natuurwetten gaa ik af van Grotius en ben daar in wat ruim Wolffiaansch. Ja, in verscheidene deelen dezer wetenschap loopt er zomtijds bij mij wat Wielingiaansch tusschen...Voorts ben ik in het natuurrecht nooit Thomasiaansch geweest, maar wel een weinigje in het kerkelijk recht, waar ik dezen schranderen man hoog schatte, dus ik hierin liever wat semi-Erastiaansch, als Voetiaansch ben.").

6. On Leiden as an important center of Roman law see e.g. Wieacker, *Privatrechtsgeschichte der Neuzeit*, 168-169; Feenstra and Waal, *Seventeenth-Century Leyden Law Professors*; Schneppen, *Niederländische Universitäten und deutsches Geistesleben*, 98-105.

elegant school, Gerard Noodt (1647-1725), who had taught at Leiden University from 1686 until his death.[7] In 1760, he published an edition of Noodt's complete works, including Barbeyrac's biography of the legal scholar.[8] Luzac received his own training in Roman law from J.C. Rücker (1691-1778), a professor of civil law at Leiden University between 1734 and 1769 who worked in the tradition of Noodt.[9] Ultimately, however, Luzac, who developed a strong interest in the study of Roman law, rejected the strongly antiquarian approach to the subject favored by the elegant school. Nor, it should be added, did he fully share the views of the adherents of the *usus modernus pandectarum*, who advocated an adaptation of Roman law to modern circumstances and legal practice, or did he follow those who proposed to discard Roman law altogether in favor of natural law.[10]

Luzac, in fact, came to occupy a unique middle ground in the contemporary Dutch debate about Roman law. On the one hand, he was well aware of the fact that Roman law could not always be easily applied as subsidiary law in a modern commercial republic. It was evident, he remarked, "that Roman law is not the only source to be consulted in all cases, but only in those where it is applicable".[11] On the other hand, he kept insisting that Roman law was of enormous and permanent worth. To suggest that it should be discarded altogether, as F.A. van der Marck and W. Schorer were beginning to do in the second half of the century, was simply unacceptable. The solution to the problem, Luzac insisted, was neither to adapt Roman law on an *ad hoc* basis nor to reject it completely. It was, instead, the creation of a synthesis of Roman and natural law. On the basis of the truths of a developed system of natural law, Luzac maintained, the wisdom of many clauses in Roman law could easily be demonstrated. To do exactly this was, indeed, the principal purpose of his 1772 commentary on Christian Wolff's *Institutiones iuris naturae et gentium*. "The main aim of my commentary", he wrote to the

---

7. On Noodt see Van den Bergh, *Gerard Noodt*.

8. Gerardi Noodt, *Opera omnia, recognita, aucta, emendata, multis in locis, atque in duos tomos distributa. Accessit V.Cl. Joannis Barbeyracii historica vitae auctoris narratio. Editio novissima, etc.* Lugduni Batavorum, apud Eliam Luzac, 1760.

9. On Rücker see *Nieuw Nederlandsch Biografisch Woordenboek*, vol.2, 1240-1241 and Ahsmann and Feenstra, *Bibliografie*, 203-205.

10. The Dutch eighteenth-century debate on Roman law has recently been the subject of Jansen's excellent monograph *Natuurrecht of Romeins recht*.

11. *Droit naturel*, vol.2, 259 ("...que le Droit Romain ne doit pas être consulté uniquement et dans tous les cas, mais dans celui où il permet l'application.").

Franeker legal scholar Cannegieter in 1769, "is to make it clear how philosophical principles can be applied to the law; this allows me to demonstrate in a large number of places that the *Iurisconsulti Romani*, although they have generally failed to indicate the grounds of their decisions, have thought and reasoned more accurately and consistently than many modern Philosophers. This work will, I hope, present the *Ius Romanum* in a more favorable and useful perspective to those who have rejected its study as unhelpful and superfluous; nobody until now, as far as I know, has shown how Roman law is compatible with the real foundations of true philosophy".[12]

Leiden University, of course, had more to offer than a first introduction to the intricacies of Roman law. The formal introduction of chairs in natural law took place at a relatively late date in the Dutch Republic, certainly compared to the Holy Roman Empire. It was not until 1746, at Utrecht University, that the first such chair was instituted in a legal faculty.[13] But professors had been teaching the subject privately for many decades. Gerard Noodt, for instance, taught Grotius, and it has already been noted that Johan Lulofs, Luzac's most important Leiden preceptor, discussed Pufendorf's *De officio hominis et civis* in his private lectures.[14] In 1747 Andreas Weiss (1713-1792), whom Luzac mentioned as one of his teachers and whom he kept seeing after he formally left the university in 1750, joined the Leiden law faculty as a *professor ordinarius iuris publici ac privati*. In that capacity he lectured on Grotius's natural jurisprudence on a regular basis.[15] Luzac, it is clear, had ample opportunity to acquaint himself with the rudiments of natural law as a student. His very strong preference for Wolffian natural law, however, probably

12. Provinciale Bibliotheek Leeuwarden, Hs 1152, no.130, Luzac to Herman Cannegieter, Leiden, October 18, 1769 ("Het voornaamste doelwit van myne aantekeningen is om te doen zien, hoe men de philosophische principes op het recht kan appliceeren, en dit geeft my gelegenheid om op veelvuldige plaatsen aan te toonen, dat de Jurisconsulti Romani, accurater en consequenter gedagt en geraisonneerd hebben dan onze moderne Philosophen, ofschoon zy de gronden van hunne decisien weinig hebben geexprimeerd. Dit werk zal, zoo ik my verbeelde, het Jus Romanum eenigzins favorabeler en nuttiger doen voorkomen aan die geenen, welke de studie van hetzelve, als onnoodig en ondienstig afkeuren, als tot nu toe geschied is; en voor zo veel ik weet heeft niemand zich nog toegelegd om te toonen hoe de dispositie van 't R.R. quadreert met de echte gronden van de waare philosophie."). For another such statement see *Corr. Formey*, Luzac to Formey, Leiden, August 22, 1768.

13. Van den Bergh, *Gerard Noodt*, 231.

14. For further examples see Jansen, *Natuurrecht of Romeins recht*, 146-147.

15. *Disquisitio politico-moralis*, Dedication and *Corr. Formey*, Luzac to Formey, Leiden, March 3, 1756. On Weiss see Ahsmann and Feenstra, *Bibliografie*, 358-359 and Kundert, "Andreas Weiss".

owed most to his international connections. The liberal Protestant community in which Luzac started to play such an active role from the late 1740s on was positively saturated with Wolffian natural law. The importance of Koenig, Des Champs and especially Formey in this context has already been discussed. The intellectual outlook that Luzac acquired through these contacts made him into one of the first Dutch adherents of Wolffian natural law.[16]

It was, indeed, not until well into the second half of the eighteenth century that this variety of natural jurisprudence came to hold a dominant position in the Dutch universities. In Groningen, F.A. van der Marck, who in 1771 remarked that "before Wolff a truly complete system of natural law has never existed in the world of letters", supervised a large number of Wolffian legal dissertations from 1758 on.[17] In 1773 he was succeeded by L.C. Schroeder, another Wolffian.[18] Meanwhile in Leiden the Wolffian F.W. Pestel (1724-1805) had been appointed as Weiss's successor in 1763. He rapidly acquired a prominent reputation with his textbooks. In 1789, honorably resigning from a term as president (*rector magnificus*) of the university, he summarized his optimistic view on the influence of Wolffian natural law in a farewell address *On the fruits the European peoples have derived from a more perfect jurisprudence in the XVIIIth century.*[19] In 1771, finally, Luzac's protégé H.C. Cras, whom he had personally trained in Wolffian doctrine, was appointed professor at the Amsterdam *Athenaeum.*[20] Luzac's early enthusiasm for Wolffian natural law was, it is evident, by no means an isolated phenomenon. It foreshadowed a development that would make Wolff, as W.J.A.J. Duynstee has put it in his brief survey of Dutch natural law, into "the most fashionable philosopher of the second half of the century" in the Dutch

16. There is no thorough study of Dutch Wolffianism in any field, but see Sassen, *Geschiedenis van de wijsbegeerte*, 217-268 and, on the Dutch translation of Wolff's German works, Wielema, "Christian Wolff in het Nederlands".

17. Quoted in Duynstee, *Geschiedenis van het natuurrecht*, 57 ("...ante Wolffium completum Iuris naturae systema veri nominis in toto litterarum orbe numquam exstiterit.").

18. *Ibidem*, 62-63.

19. *Oratio de fructibus qui ex jurisprudentia perfectiori ad populos Europaeos saeculo XVIII pervenerunt.* Lugduni Batavorum, 1789. On Pestel most recently Worst, "Staat, constitutie, en politieke wil".

20. Cras has described his conversations with Luzac about Wolff in "Beredeneerd verslag", 74-75. On Cras see P.C. Kop, "Hendrik Constantijn Cras (1739-1820)" in: Veen and Kop, ed. *Zestig juristen*, 190-195.

Republic.[21]

In Leiden, it can furthermore be established on the basis of the limited information available, the printing and publishing of natural law texts remained a profitable business throughout the second half of the eighteenth century. Barbeyrac's Grotius translation, *Le droit de la guerre et de la paix*, went through Leiden editions in 1759 and 1768.[22] His Pufendorf translation, *Le droit de la nature et des gens*, was printed there in 1759 and 1771.[23] Pufendorf's *De officio hominis et civis* came from the Leiden presses in 1769, including commentaries by Otto, Treuer, Titius, Carmichael, and Barbeyrac.[24] There was not only a continuing strong demand for these standard texts, but also for new expositions of natural law, as evidenced by the success of F.W. Pestel's work. His *Fundamenta jurisprudentiae naturalis* were first published in Leiden in 1772, went through four subsequent Latin editions (1774, 1777, 1788, 1806) and were translated into French (1774, second edition 1775) and Dutch (1783-1785).[25] Thus Luzac's 1772 publication of a sequel to Barbeyrac's projects, an annotated edition of Wolff's *Institutions du droit de la nature et des gens*, took place in a lively natural law market. The two simultaneously produced editions of the work completely sold out.[26]

Critics, both in the Dutch Republic and elsewhere, immediately hailed Luzac's Wolff as a masterpiece. The reviewer in the *Bibliothèque des Sciences et des Beaux Arts*, correctly identifying the book's descent and intention, described Luzac's notes as "excellent and more than worthy to be compared to those of Barbeyrac on Grotius and Pufendorf". He proceeded to discuss them for no less than fifty pages, finally concluding that Wolff could not possibly have found a more worthy commentator.[27] In the *Göttingische Anzeigen von Gelehrten Sachen* A.G. Kästner equally praised Luzac's commentary "full of philosophical insight and juridical

---

21. Duynstee, *Geschiedenis van het natuurrecht*, 56. See also Jansen, "Docenten natuurrecht".

22. Ter Meulen, "Liste bibliographique", 189-190.

23. Othmer, *Berlin und die Verbreitung des Naturrechts*, 202.

24. *Ibidem*, 206.

25. Ahsmann and Feenstra, *Bibliografie*, 194-195. On the natural law texts used in the Dutch universities see Jansen, "Docenten natuurrecht".

26. *Droit naturel, Programme*, 29.

27. *Bibliothèque des Sciences et des Beaux Arts*, vol.37, second part, April to June 1772, 283-305 (the quotation is on 289: "...excellentes, et très dignes d'être comparées à celles de Barbeyrac sur Grotius et sur Puffendorff") and vol.38, second part, October to December 1772, 294-326.

erudition".[28] The *Encyclopédie d'Yverdon*, F.B. de Félice's Protestant competitor to the French *Encyclopédie*, highly recommended the book as "an outstanding work for those wishing to learn the principles of natural law".[29] Finally, the most important Dutch-language review journal, the *Hedendaagsche Vaderlandsche Letter-Oefeningen*, explicitly discussed the appearance of Luzac's Wolff in the context of the Dutch debate about the relative merits of Roman and natural law. Luzac's synthesis of the two, the reviewer observed, constituted the only possible path towards a perfect jurisprudence. Luzac, he added, had put the whole learned world in his debt.[30] Looking back on the book's publication some twenty-five years later, Luzac could truthfully write "I have had the pleasure to see my work well received".[31] Despite increasing signs of an international onslaught against sound philosophy, it was apparently still worthwhile to keep up the attempt to perfect the *science des moeurs*. Luzac's continued effort was to result in the massive *Du droit naturel, civil, et politique*, part of which was posthumously published in 1802.

2. *The Rise and Fall of Morality*

The lengthy *Historical and critical account of the science of morality* that Jean Barbeyrac affixed to his French translation of Pufendorf's *De iure naturae et gentium* was but one, albeit an extremely influential, example of the new genre of the history of morality that began to flourish in the early eighteenth century.[32] From that time on, most exponents of natural law thought it proper to comment on the history of their field of endeavor before they made their own specific contribution. They usually started with classical antiquity, continued with the resurrection of moral science in modern times by Grotius, and ended with tracing the further development of the *science des moeurs* until their own time. Luzac, who had clearly been inspired by the work of Barbeyrac and was attempting to continue it, was no exception. Unfortunately, however, his account of the

---

28. *Göttingische Anzeigen von Gelehrten Sachen*, 1772, vol.2, 1075 ("...voll philosophischer Einsicht und juristischer Gelehrsamkeit...").

29. *Encyclopédie, ou dictionnaire universel raisonné des connoissances humaines*, vol.42, 711 ("...un excellent ouvrage pour...apprendre les élémens du *Droit Naturel*."). On this *Encyclopédie d'Yverdon* see Darnton, *Business of Enlightenment*, 19-21.

30. *Hedendaagsche Vaderlandsche Letter-Oefeningen, etc.*, vol.1, part one, 1772, 399-402.

31. *Droit naturel, Programme*, 29 ("J'ai eu l'agrément de voir que mon travail a été accueilli.").

32. Tuck, *Natural Rights Theories*, 174-177.

history of morality was not as orderly as Barbeyrac's had been. It has to be reconstructed from digressions spread through the entire body of his later writings.

Barbeyrac, at the beginning of the century, had defined the science of morals in a comprehensive way: "By that, and by the term morality, I understand not only what is normally thereby understood, but also natural law and politics, in short everything necessary to know how to behave properly...".[33] Luzac, too, favored a broad definition and used the terms *science des moeurs, morale,* and *droit naturel* interchangeably.[34] His account of the development of the science of morals not only included ethics, law, and politics, but also touched upon epistemology, logic, and mathematics. He used the term metaphysics for everything related to the study of intelligent beings.[35] Luzac was entirely convinced that the scientific study of morality had never come so close to perfection as in the first half of the eighteenth century.[36] This firmly held view gave his history of morality a peculiar slant. He was, in fact, not so much writing a history as reconstructing the genealogy of his own position. Possessed of true insights into epistemology, method, and principles, he measured the accomplishments of the various historical schools (or "sects", as the eighteenth century would have it) with these standards. In the resulting Whiggish account everybody became either a precursor or a misguided fool. What saved Luzac from complacency was his awareness of the fact that this intellectual battle between light and darkness was not necessarily destined to have a happy ending. Indeed, in the end it was impossible to avoid the bitter conclusion that, despite its undoubted intellectual superiority, the modern science of morals was losing ground. Truth in itself was apparently not enough.

Luzac started his historical overview in classical antiquity. He certainly did not belong, as has already been observed, to those eighteenth-century theorists who still uncritically admired many aspects of ancient history. On the contrary. If, as J. Shklar has suggested, the battle between the ancients and the moderns lasted until after the French Revolution,

---

33. Barbeyrac, "Préface", ii, note b ("J'entens par là, et par le nom de *Morale,* non seulement ce que l'on appelle ordinairement ainsi, mais encore le *Droit Naturel,* et la *Politique,* en un mot tout ce qui est nécessaire pour savoir de quelle manière chacun doit se conduire...").

34. E.g. *Droit naturel,* vol.1, 7.

35. *Droit naturel, Programme,* 10; *Droit naturel,* vol.1, 300.

36. E.g. Wolff, *Institutions,* vol.1, Dédicace, *passim.*

Luzac firmly belonged in the camp of the moderns.[37] Too great an
admiration for the intellectual achievements of classical antiquity, he
maintained, led to the replacement of thought by erudition.[38] Ancient
thinkers, moreover, had almost without exception been obsessed with
eloquence, a predilection that had frequently led them to be obscure and
to indulge in meaningless rhetoric. They had failed to define the concepts
they used and had mistakenly preferred "the art of persuading" over "the
art of convincing". Even an otherwise excellent book such as Cicero's *De
officiis* had not been free from these flaws.[39] Yet Luzac refused to trade
one extreme for another. To replace the worship of the ancients as unsurpassed authorities by the total neglect of their valuable insights seemed
absurd to him. He openly and repeatedly praised their intellectual accomplishments. It has already been noted, for instance, how he lauded
them for having developed a respectable, if ultimately unsatisfactory,
system of ethics. The moderns were indeed superior, but only because
they could stand on the shoulders of the ancients.[40] It was simply undeniable that the works of the classical sages were "filled with enlightenment, knowledge, and wisdom" and that many important issues had first
been addressed there.[41]

In Luzac's rendering (though he did mention Stoicism and Epi-
cureanism) the main debate in Greece had been between Platonism and
intellectual Pyrrhonism, an early version of the modern opposition
between Cartesian and experimental philosophy, or rationalism and sensationalism. Plato, a "profound philosopher", had been the first to recognize the superiority of the mind over the senses. "Studying the source of
our errors and illusions, and having recognized that the senses do not take
us beyond appearances and that it is only the understanding which is
capable of the knowledge of beings and of the causes of their preservation, he devoted himself to metaphysics, the science which studies
intelligent beings and their attributes".[42] Unfortunately, Plato had been

37. Shklar, *Men and Citizens*, 225.

38. *Droit naturel, Programme*, 15.

39. *Seconde lettre*, xii-xiii ("...l'art de persuader..."; "...l'art de convaincre..."); *Droit naturel*,
vol.1, 20-22 and 129.

40. *Nederlandsche Letter-Courant*, vol.5 (1761), 161-162.

41. *Droit naturel, Programme*, 13-14 ("...remplis de lumières, de connoissances et de
sagesse...").

42. *Ibidem*, 10 ("...Philosophe profond..."; "Recherchant la source de nos erreurs et de nos
illusions, et ayant reconnu que les sens ne nous font appercevoir que des apparences, que
c'est par l'entendement que l'on parvient à la connoissance des êtres, à celle des causes de

misunderstood by those who claimed that he was an unrealistic dreamer, who left experience out of his constructs.[43] It was therefore not surprising that an anti-Platonist Pyrrhonism had gained a widespread acceptance in Greece. In its extreme form it had only been a short-lived success, since it was absurd and impossible to doubt for long one's own existence and the existence of the things the senses indicated.[44] But in the form of intellectual Pyrrhonism, the conviction that only the senses are trustworthy, it had turned out to be a powerful doctrine, both in antiquity and in modern times.[45]

The main contribution of the Romans, generally content to take the Greeks as their models in the arts and sciences, had of course been Roman law. This was, as we have seen, a topic of absorbing interest to Luzac, not only because it was directly relevant to debates being conducted in the Dutch Republic, but also because he realized that the material content of all the major systems of natural law was largely derived from Roman law.[46] In his Wolff edition, he brought this out in lengthy technical essays on points of Roman law such as imputation, injury, possession, promises, mandates, and the law of proof. The history of the *science des moeurs*, however, called for a general evaluation of Roman law. Having first of all once more pointed out that it was utterly ridiculous to discard the rich store of experience contained in Roman law, Luzac did not hesitate to make some critical remarks about it. Roman law's first and most obvious weakness was a lack of unity. "Roman

leur conservation, il s'est singulièrement appliqué à l'étude de la science, que l'on nomme métaphysique, et qui a pour objet celle des Etres intelligens et de leurs attributs.").

43. *Ibidem*, 13. In the *Seconde lettre*, 1-2, Luzac described Descartes's importance in almost exactly the same terms: "Le plus grand présent, le présent le plus utile que *Descartes* aît fait au genre humain, sont, si je ne me trompe pas, ses *Méditations*. C'est là qu'il nous a tracé la route que nous devons tenir, pour parvenir à la découverte et à la connoissance de la Vérité; c'est là que nous voyons combien il importe d'en écarter les illusions, auxquelles un usage non-réfléchi de nos sens nous expose sans cesse; c'est là enfin que nous apprenons à donner un juste prix aux vérités, que les sens nous présentent, et à celles que nous dévélope une force supérieure aux sens, cette faculté de démêler et de saisir le vrai, que nous nommons Raison". But unfortunately "les méditations de Descartes eurent le sort de celles de Platon" (*Droit naturel, Programme*, 16).

44. *Droit naturel, Programme*, 12.

45. *Ibidem*, 13.

46. As M. Stolleis points out, there is much to be said for the view that "das Naturrecht sei der Sache nach im wesentlichen Gemeines (römisches) Recht, dem 'more geometrico' ein zeitgemäßes sprachliches Gewand gegeben worden sei". M. Stolleis, "Reichspublizistik - Politik - Naturrecht im 17. und 18. Jahrhundert" in: Stolleis, ed., *Staatsdenker im 17. und 18. Jahrhundert*, 20.

legislation, as transmitted to us through the Digest and the Code, is really a compilation of specific cases and their outcomes; it is largely a body of opinions on particular cases, with very few general principles".[47] The principles the Roman jurisconsults did use, moreover, were incompatible and resulted in internal contradictions.[48] They furthermore had never realized the importance of a clear and unambiguous system of concepts, not even bothering to define the notion of right in general. But the central problem of Roman law, to which the others were related, was its lack of an adequate notion of natural law. The Romans had, it is true, recognized that there are rights and duties inherent in human nature, but their development of this insight had been very deficient: "their understanding of that truth was not so profound as to allow them to turn it into the basis of a principle of natural law".[49] Instead, they had been convinced that "what man has in common with the brutes and what is generally accepted in civilized nations would sufficiently indicate the duties and rights inherent in the nature of man".[50] Clearly this would not do. For what man has in common with animals is instinct, and instinct cannot possibly be the basis for rights and duties, which suppose the presence of a "a moral faculty wholly absent in animals".[51] This failure to understand rights and duties as attributes of moral beings also explained the constant confusion of moral and physical power in Roman law.[52] As to the second principle, what civilized nations accept varies widely and even if it does not it may very well be based on the wrong principles.[53] Thus Luzac, who in passing pointed out that Wolff had never fully understood these flaws in the Roman notion of natural law, clearly demarcated the line separating classical from modern natural law.

47. Wolff, *Institutions*, vol.1, Dédicace, xix ("La Législation Romaine, telle qu'elle nous a été transmise dans les Digestes et dans le Code, est, il est vrai, proprement une compilation de cas particuliers avec leurs décisions, et en grande partie un assemblage de sentimens et d'opinions sur des cas qui peuvent exister: nous n'y voyons que très-peu de principes généraux...").

48. E.g. *Droit naturel*, vol.2, 286-287.

49. Wolff, *Institutions*, vol.1, §56, note h ("...ils n'ont...pas assez approfondi cette vérité, pour en déduire un principe du droit naturel...").

50. *Ibidem* ("...ce que l'homme a de commun avec les brutes et ce qui se trouve généralement adopté chez les Nations policiées, leur indiqueroient suffisamment les devoirs et les droits, auxquels la nature et l'essence de l'homme donnent lieu.").

51. *Ibidem* ("...une faculté morale, dont on n'a jamais prétendu que les animaux fussent doués...").

52. E.g. *Ibidem*, vol.2, §713, note y.

53. *Ibidem*, vol.1, §56, note h; vol.2, §1088, note a.

Luzac hardly discussed the millennium between the *Corpus Iuris* and the Reformation, except as an age of barbarous sentiments and bigoted religion. The crucial turning point had been the early seventeenth century. Everything had changed for the better "since Grotius has published his work on war and peace, a work that has been followed by a number of others in the same genre, all intended to teach man his rights and duties".[54] This was, of course, a highly familiar periodization in the history of morality. Barbeyrac, who also jumped from antiquity to the seventeenth century in his account of the *science des moeurs*, had designated Grotius "as the one who broke the ice".[55] To Christian Wolff Grotius's book obviously was a landmark. He lectured on it and even edited it in 1734, because it had been buried under too many layers of commentary.[56] Although he disapproved of Grotius's method, he also pointed out "how similar Grotius's tenets are to my philosophical theses and how much our thought has in common".[57] Luzac's contemporary Van der Marck, writing about the history of natural jurisprudence, equally attributed a decisive importance to Grotius.[58] And even today, although we have learned to read Grotius's text in its scholastic and other contexts, *De iure belli ac pacis* is still viewed as an original work and a beginning of sorts.[59]

To Luzac Grotius, although clearly heavily indebted to the writings of the ancients and to Roman law, had been the first to perceive that "the only way to make people more moderate and just was to create a consensus on what was to be considered just and unjust. This in turn could only be accomplished by means of a methodical work in which this extremely important subject was expounded with order and proof".[60] Grotius had

---

54. *Droit naturel*, vol.1, 186-187 ("...depuis que Grotius a publié son ouvrage *de la Guerre et de la Paix*, ouvrage, qui a été suivi par nombre d'autres de ce genre, destinés à apprendre aux hommes, leurs droits et leurs devoirs...").

55. Barbeyrac, "Préface", civ ("...comme celui qui a rompu la glace...").

56. *Hugonis Grotii de iure belli ac pacis libri tres. Editio nova cum annotatis et prefatione Christiani Wolfii*. Marburgi, 1734. On Grotius-commentaries as a growth industry in Germany see Reibstein, "Deutsche Grotius-Kommentatoren".

57. Wolff, *Gesammelte kleine philosophische Schriften*, vol.3, 338-339. This is the German translation of Wolff's preface to Grotius (see note 56).

58. Van der Marck, *Lectiones academicae*, 142.

59. See recently Haakonssen, "Hugo Grotius".

60. *Seconde lettre*, xxxiii-xxxiv ("...pour rendre les hommes plus modérés et plus justes, il n'y avoit d'autre moyen que celui de les mettre d'accord sur les idées du juste et de l'injuste: et que la seule voye de parvenir à ce but, seroit un ouvrage méthodique, dans lequel on verroit exposé dans un certain ordre, et avec une certaine évidence tout ce qui peut

tried to form a coherent system, based on the most general principles of morality. But precisely because he had been the first author to attempt this, his work showed a number of deficiencies. First of all, he had been too eclectic in his designation of the sources of our knowledge of human rights and duties. To observations drawn from the nature of man, he had added others from a wide variety of sources, "such as the received customs of nations, the opinions of the most famous authors of antiquity, and the precepts to be found in the Holy Scriptures and the most esteemed profane writings".[61] By taking "the natural penchant for society, the necessity of sociability, and right judgment, which makes us see the equity or the iniquity of an action" as the foundations of natural law he had, moreover, failed to lay bare the highest principle under which these things could be subsumed.[62] Finally, Grotius had not been quite as exact as desirable, both in his definitions and in the development of his argument: "...had Grotius's mind been formed by geometry instead of belles-lettres, he would no doubt have given us a work less filled with erudition and more methodical in its deduction of consequences from principles".[63] This last point echoed Wolff's pompously self-assured criticism: "He [Grotius] wrote his book in the ordinary manner because he was unfamiliar with the proper way to present the sciences (*methodus scientifica*), as indeed everybody was before my time".[64]

Having listed these various shortcomings of Grotius's masterpiece, Luzac spent considerable time defending it against misinterpretation and unjustified attacks. First, it was important to realize that Grotius had employed a literary rather than a strictly demonstrative mode of arguing in order not to make himself incomprehensible to his contemporaries.[65] Secondly, it was essential to recognize that Grotius's goal in *De iure belli ac pacis* had been to describe man's duties as "sociable beings", as

convaincre l'esprit sur un objet si important.").

61. *Droit naturel*, vol.1, 237 ("...tels que les coutûmes reçuës par les nations: les sentiments des plus célèbres auteurs de l'antiquité, les préceptes répandus dans les saintes écritures et dans les ouvrages profanes les plus estimés.").

62. *Seconde lettre*, xxxv ("Le penchant naturel à la société, la nécessité de la socialité et le jugement droit, qui nous fait d'abord apercevoir l'équité ou l'iniquité d'une action...").

63. *Ibidem*, xxix ("...si Grotius eut eu l'esprit formé par la Géométrie, comme il l'a été par la belle Litterature, peut-être nous eût-il donné un ouvrage moins rempli d'érudition, et où les conséquences eussent été déduites plus méthodiquement de leurs principes.").

64. Wolff, *Kleine Schriften*, 696-697. The quotation is from the German translation of chapter eight of the 1735 *Ratio praelectionum*: "De praelectionibus privatis in libres Grotii de iure belli ac pacis".

65. *Lettre d'un anonime*, 60-61.

Christians, and as "members of the political body of our globe".[66] Since his treatise had not simply been about natural law, it was a mistake to reject Grotius's prudential *ius gentium*, based on a conformity of opinions, without even trying to understand its purpose, as Wolff had done.[67] But Wolff's misinterpretation was trivial compared to the abominable treatment Grotius received at the hands of Rousseau and of an increasing number of other radical authors. Luzac, as has already been noted, energetically tried to protect the writings of the founder of modern moral science from this unprecedented onslaught, particularly in his lengthy polemics against Rousseau.

In continuing the story of the development of the *science des moeurs*, Luzac rapidly moved from Grotius, the first modern moralist, to Wolff, who would solve most of the problems left by the great pioneer. He repeatedly touched upon the scientific revolution of the seventeenth century, praising the sublime Newton for having brought about a breakthrough in the study of physics. He never did so, however, without simultaneously condemning the subsequent popular misapplication of Newtonianism by the *philosophes*, who had used it to make the study of metaphysics suspect "as a vain and uncertain science, consisting of frivolous speculation".[68] The two seventeenth-century moralists after Grotius that Luzac singled out for special discussion were Hobbes and Pufendorf. Hobbes, although certainly a profound genius, had made the mistake of confounding the factual and the legitimate. Observing that man's behavior was dominated by the passions, Hobbes had concluded that humankind was in a perpetual state of war (*homo homini lupus*; *bellum omnium contra omnes*). As a pure statement of fact, Luzac admitted, this was not entirely untrue. "As to the facts this writer has certainly not been wholly wrong: we can see every day that people's behavior owes more to a sentiment of malevolence than to its opposite".[69] But Hobbes had mistakenly taken this to imply that man should only be considered "as a being that needs to avoid the effects of the passion and malice of others" and had therefore failed to establish

---

66. *Seconde lettre*, xl ("...Etres sociables..."; "...membres du corps politique de notre globe.").

67. Wolff, *Institutions*, vol.2, §1088, note a; *Seconde lettre*, xl-xlv.

68. *Droit naturel, Programme*, 17 ("...comme étant une science vaine, incertaine et consistant en spéculations frivoles...").

69. *Droit naturel*, vol.1, 124 ("Quant au fait, cet écrivain n'a pas eu grand tort; car nous voyons tous les jours, que les hommes se conduisent les uns envers les autres plus par un sentiment de malveillance que par le sentiment contraire...").

rules for legitimate conduct, "because it is evident that the passions, be they our own or those of others, will never provide us with a rule of conduct or even indicate such a rule".[70] Hobbes had not recognized that although they are frequently totally disregarded, the principles of natural law nevertheless always retain their validity, because they do not refer to the facts.[71]

Luzac's attitude towards Pufendorf was somewhat ambivalent. On the one hand he regarded him as one of the modern moralists who had carried on the work that had been started by Grotius. Pufendorf, with whose work he was thoroughly familiar, was the author he quoted most after Grotius and Wolff. On the other hand, he criticized Pufendorf severely. His work suffered from the same defaults that marked all pre-Wolffian writing on morals. They were "less a system than a compilation of vague reasonings".[72] To support this judgment, Luzac approvingly quoted Leibniz' *Opinion on the principles of Pufendorf.*[73] Pufendorf's books were "better suited to instruct the multitude than to satisfy these who demand to be convinced".[74] He had failed to improve upon Grotius's principle of sociability and had been wrong in many particulars, for instance in his views on the division of authority in the family, the primitive community of property, and the reasons for leaving the state of nature.[75]

It was Christian Wolff who would bring the *science des moeurs* to an unprecedented height. By designating perfection as the most general

70. Wolff, *Institutions*, vol.1, §99, note d ("...comme un être qui doit éviter tous les effets de la passion et de la malice des hommes..."; "...car il est évident que les passions considérées, soit par rapport à nous-mêmes, soit par rapport aux autres, ne peuvent en aucune façon nous fournir, ou même nous indiquer une règle de conduite...").

71. *Droit naturel*, vol.3, 48.

72. *Ibidem*, vol.1, 238 ("...moins un systhème, qu'un assemblage de raisonnemens vagues...").

73. *Ibidem.* About Pufendorf's *De officio* Leibniz wrote: "I could wish...that something more solid and effective existed, which would give clear and fruitful definitions, which would draw its conclusions from correct principles as if by a thread (of logic), which would establish in order the fundamental principles and exceptions valid by nature, which would, finally, afford students of the science (of natural law) a sure way to supply for themselves that which is left out, and to decide the questions which are submitted to them by a fixed method". Riley, ed. *Political Writings of Leibniz*, 65.

74. *Droit naturel*, vol.1, 243 ("...plutôt propres à instruire la multitude, qu'à satisfaire ceux, qui demandent à être convaincus...").

75. *Droit naturel*, vol.1, 237. 270, 279-281, 381; *Lettre d'un anonime*, 76-77.

principle, Wolff had greatly improved the study of morals.[76] But even more important was the fact that he had dispelled all doubt about the certainty of moral knowledge by applying the mathematical or demonstrative method to it. Before Wolff, no author had given "precise definitions, just principles, sustained reasoning characterized by that coherence of ideas, that chain of propositions, that thread of arguments that is indispensable to make us grasp the all-important combination of truths".[77] Luzac closely followed Wolff in pointing out the essential elements of the mathematical method.[78] First of all, the words to be used should be defined in a completely unambiguous way. "Words are arbitrary, but in order to treat a matter demonstratively it is absolutely necessary to determine their meaning".[79] Secondly, every step of the argument, starting from the most general principle, should be proven. Thirdly, all statements should be linked together by a solid and unbreakable chain of arguments. They should be "like branches and twigs, which must remain connected to their first origin, to the common stem which serves them as a basis and from which they should never separate themselves".[80] In order to avoid mistakes in this whole procedure, a knowledge of logic was indispensable.[81] The proper use of syllogisms formed part of that, but logic in the broadest sense simply was the art of right thinking.[82] With the help of this scientific, demonstrative, or math-

---

76. *Droit naturel*, vol.1, 145-146. In the first thesis attached to his 1759 *Specimen iuris inaugurale* Luzac had already observed: "Perfectio est fundamentum totius Iuris Universi".

77. Wolff, *Institutions*, vol.1, Dédicace, v ("...des définitions exactes, des principes justes, des raisonnemens suivis, et dans lesquels on trouve cette liaison d'idées, cette chaine de propositions, ce fil de démonstrations, qui seul peut nous faire appercevoir et saisir la combinaison de toutes les vérités qu'il nous importe si fort de connoitre.").

78. Wolff, *Ausführliche Nachricht*, 61-62: "Wenn ich alles auf das genaueste überlege, was in der mathematischen Lehr-Art vorkommet, so finde ich diese drey Haupt-Stücke, 1. dasz alle Wörter, dadurch die Sachen angedeutet werden, davon man etwas erweiset durch deutliche und ausführliche Begriffe erkläret werden; 2. dasz alle Sätze durch ordentlich an einander hangende Schlüsse erwiesen werden; 3. dasz kein Förder-Satz angenommen wird, der nicht vorher wäre ausgemachet worden und solcher-gestalt die folgenden Sätze mit dem vorhergehenden verknüpft werden...". For discussions of this method see Frängsmyr, "Wolff's mathematical method" and Röd, *Geometrischer Geist*, 117-128.

79. *Bonheur*, 7 ("Les mots sont arbitraires, mais lorsqu'il s'agit de traiter une matière démonstrativement, on ne peut apporter trop de soins pour en fixer le sens.").

80. *Droit naturel*, vol.1, 162 ("...comme des branches et des rameaux, qui doivent tous se rapporter à leur première origine, comme à un tige commune, qui leur sert de base, et de laquelle ils ne doivent jamais s'écarter.").

81. *Ibidem*, 286-315 ("Sur l'utilité de la logique").

82. *Ibidem*, 298.

ematical method, the *science des moeurs* could reach its ultimate perfection. It was Wolff's great merit to have been the first one to show this, although he had not been completely successful in practice. "Nobody fully succeeds in the first attempt and it would surely be less than generous to judge our author on the basis of his errors. The important thing is that his method allows us to correct him. This unique fact should in itself be enough to make us prefer him to all others".[83]

But just now that Luzac himself was preparing to step in and help the science of morals reach its apogee, the whole elaborate structure suddenly threatened to come down. At mid-century, Wolff himself had already sensed an impending crisis. "The love of serious and solid knowledge is rapidly declining. It is being replaced by a superficial mixture of so-called Newtonian philosophy and French flippancy", he wrote to J.D. Schumacher in 1748.[84] More than two decades later A.G. Kästner opened his highly favorable review of Luzac's Wolff edition in the *Göttingische Anzeigen von Gelehrten Sachen* with the sad question "who will read the dry Wolff these days, even in French? Everything, including metaphysics, is nowadays expected to be amusing and entertaining".[85]

It has already been noted that this profound change in intellectual climate was one of Luzac's central preoccupations and that, at first, he simply ascribed it to the dominance of a misinterpreted Newtonianism, as Wolff had done. As the century progressed, however, he became more and more convinced that the crisis in the science of morality was of a political nature. This interpretation started to play an increasingly important role in his work from the moment that he was confronted with Rousseau's single-minded campaign to destroy "all generally accepted and practiced moral ideas and sentiments".[86] What he was witnessing, Luzac came to believe, was the willful perversion of an established vocabulary, spreading from France to the rest of Europe, and ultimately motivated by the political self-interest of a fanatical group of men of letters intent on

---

83. Wolff, *Institutions*, vol.1, Dédicace, xvi ("S'il n'est pas donné à l'homme de réussir dès le premier essai, ce seroit méconnoître l'humanité, que de juger de notre Auteur sur les méprises qui peuvent lui être échappées: la méthode qu'il a suivie, nous met sur les voies de pouvoir le corriger; c'est un avantage...qui lui est particulier, et qui suffiroit seul pour lui donner la préférence sur tous les autres.").

84. Wolff, *Briefe aus den Jahren 1719-1753*, 142-143.

85. *Göttingische Anzeigen von Gelehrten Sachen*, 1772, vol.2, 1074 ("...wer wird zu unsern Zeiten, da Alles, selbst Metaphysik nur Ergötzung und Zeitvertreib seyn soll, den trocknen Wolff, sogar französisch lesen?").

86. *Droit naturel*, vol.1, 189 ("...toutes les idées et tous les sentimens de la Morale généralement réçus et suivis...").

destroying existing civilization. He thus linked the crisis in the *science des moeurs* to the rise of a radical revolutionary politics. From being implicitly political all along, Luzac's account at this point became explicitly so. By effectively blackening all serious knowledge with their admittedly elegant rhetoric, Rousseau and his *philosophe* companions had managed to establish themselves as leaders within the Republic of Letters, first in France and then in the whole of Europe.[87] From the top, Luzac observed at the end of his life with the *ancien régime* coming down around him, the *philosophes* had spread their ideas to the bottom and had succeeded in poisoning the masses: "people have drunk in the poison contained in their productions, opinions, and sentiments. They have acquired a taste for their manner of thinking, reflecting, and reasoning. That is the cause of the present corruption of morals. That is the source of the abominations perpetrated in several countries".[88]

It was evident to Luzac that the very same poisoning had also spread to the Dutch Republic. The disastrous consequences could be seen everywhere, but nowhere more clearly than in the work of Joan Derk van der Capellen (1741-1784), the leader of the Dutch Patriot movement. Indeed, it was Van der Capellen who, in a revealing letter to M. Tydeman, made it abundantly clear that what Luzac suspected was perfectly true: radical Patriot politics was based on the total rejection of the sources and foundations of the *science des moeurs*. "The only excuse for his [Grotius] writings that I can think of", Van der Capellen wrote in 1776, "is that he lived and wrote in a time when the science of government hardly existed and the rights of man were largely unknown. Grotius's thought was corrupted by Roman law, that stinking source of despotism, military jurisdiction, passive obedience, *crimen majestatis*, and other such great blessings. I would gladly sacrifice Grotius and Roman law to liberty!"[89]

---

87. Wolff, *Institutions*, Dédicace, IV.

88. *Droit naturel*, vol.1, 190 ("...on a avalé à long traits le poison répandu dans leurs productions, leurs opinions et leurs sentimens; on a pris goût à leur manière de penser, de réfléchir et de raisonner: Voilà comment les idées Morales se sont corrompues de nos jours: voilà la source des abominations qui se commettent en plusieurs pays.").

89. Universiteitsbibliotheek Leiden, BPL 945, J.D. van der Capellen to M. Tydeman, July 20, 1776 ("Het eenige dat ik tot 's mans verschooning weet is dat hy in een tyd leefde en schreef, toen de regeerkunde noch in haare kindschheid was en men de rechten van 't menschdom nog niet kende. Grotius had zyne wyze van denken bedorven door 't Roomsche regt die stinkende bron van despotisme, militaire jurisdictie, lijdelijke gehoorzaamheid, crimen majestatis, en meer zulke fraaiigheden. Geerne offerde ik en Grotius en 't Roomsche Regt aan de vryheid!"). Several months later, sending Tydeman a copy of his translation of Richard Price, Van der Capellen observed that Grotius, Pufendorf, and Roman law had totally corrupted Dutch political thought (Universiteitsbibliotheek Leiden, Ltk. 997, January

There was, Luzac realized, very little that could be done against this
international triumph of revolutionary sentiments based on ignorance and
self-interest. One could only keep spreading the truth, try to reconquer the
audience, and hope for the eventual restoration of sanity in moral science
and politics.

3. *Christian Wolff Adapted*

In Luzac's historical account the science of morals had, despite hesitant
beginnings in the ancient world, only grown into full maturity from the
early seventeenth century onwards and had culminated in the meth-
odologically flawless work of Christian Wolff. Its crisis starting at mid-
century was an unmitigated disaster for several reasons. First of all, man's
unassisted common sense was ultimately insufficient to arrive at the
proper rules of behavior.[90] Whereas the verities of disciplines such as
mathematics were of a somewhat remote utility, those of the science of
morals were directly relevant to daily life. It clearly was crucial to every
individual to learn how to avoid vice and pursue virtue.[91] But the systematic study of morality was equally important to society as a whole. To
Luzac, the blossoming of the *science des moeurs* since Grotius had coincided with and partly caused the progress of civilization that could be
observed in Europe. He strongly believed that the works of the modern
moralists had greatly helped "to polish and refine the barbarous *moeurs*
and sentiments still prevalent in Europe three centuries ago".[92] Violent
conquest, slavery, and religious persecution had all declined since the
modern moralists had started to spread their truths.[93] The reverse, as
Luzac found out at the end of the century, was equally true. As soon as a
people became convinced that it could dispense with a "scientific morality", there was a rapid decline in *moeurs*, followed by such "terrible
lawlessness, abominable excesses, and disgusting obscenities" as could be
witnessed in, for instance, the French Revolution.[94]

Since the science of morals was of such paramount importance both to

26, 1777).

90. Wolff, *Institutions*, vol.1, Dédicace, vii-ix.

91. *Seconde lettre*, xxiv-xxv; *Droit naturel*, vol.1, 11.

92. *Droit naturel*, vol.1, 186 ("...adoucir les moeurs et les sentimens barbares, qui pré-
valoient encore en Europe, il y a trois siècles...").

93. *Ibidem*, 186-188.

94. *Ibidem*, 83-84 ("...Morale scientifique...") and 190 ("...des déréglemens affreux, des
débauches exécrables, des obscénités dégoutantes...").

the individual and to society and since its decline caused such disasters, Luzac did his utmost to clarify its principles. Like Barbeyrac, who had specifically aimed his translations and commentaries at "young people aspiring to ecclesiastical and political occupations" and "ordinary un-scholarly people", Luzac wrote for more than a scholarly audience.[95] Although, like Wolff, he did not believe that the multitude was capable of fully mastering the subtleties of morality, this still left a wide group that could potentially profit from his publications.[96] In the preface to his Wolff edition he pointed out that while he was admittedly not writing for those "who desire to be no more than unskilled workers", most people could nonetheless read his work.[97] In *Du droit naturel*, his final work on natural law, he claimed that everybody should know the science he proposed to discuss, although it would be particularly useful to "young people desiring to study and practice sound politics or the law".[98]

To make his instructions more agreeable, he consciously avoided Wolff's imitation of the geometry textbook, with its constant cross-referencing, and adopted the popular dialogue form, although he strictly adhered to the demonstrative method as to the content.[99] But this con-cession was as far as he would go, for he refused to accept the view that a loose collection of maxims could ever be a viable substitute for sys-tematic understanding, even for the simple-minded.[100] At one level or another, everybody ultimately had to try and understand the fundamental principles of the science of morality. Having experimented with a wide variety of fundamental notions ranging from happiness to perfection in his early writings, Luzac had come to embrace his definitive views on natural law by the time he published his Wolff edition in 1772. At the very end of his life he would once more explain this mature vision in his post-humously published *Du droit naturel*. Although his version of natural law was evidently strongly inspired by the work of Christian Wolff, Luzac never slavishly followed the German philosopher. Indeed, he funda-mentally criticized a number of philosophical, religious, and political

---

95. Barbeyrac, "Préface", cxii-cxiii ("...les Jeunes Gens, qui se destinent aux Emplois, tant Ecclésiastiques, que Politiques."; "...les Gens sans Lettres, ou les Gens du Commun...").

96. On this problem in Wolff's work see Schneewind, ed. *Moral Philosophy*, vol.1, 333.

97. Wolff, *Institutions*, vol.1, Dédicace, vi ("...qui veulent se borner à l'état de simples ouvriers.").

98. *Droit naturel*, vol.1, Epitre Dédicatoire ("...jeunes gens destinés à l'Etude et à la pratique de la saine politique ou à celle du Barreau.").

99. *Droit naturel, Programme*, 28.

100. *Droit naturel*, vol.1, 168-184.

aspects of Wolff's natural jurisprudence. The purpose of the remaining part of this section is to demonstrate how Luzac deviated from and adapted the teachings of his German example.[101]

Luzac started his explanation of natural law with the observation that human nature was characterized by a desire for self-preservation. This was a general impulse, the "the original moving force of all our actions".[102] But not only did man want to preserve himself, he also wanted to live in the most agreeable way possible and to avoid disagreeable situations.[103] The basis of all human action was, in short, "the penchant to preserve ourselves and to lead an agreeable life" and happiness was the situation of the person who attained these things: "that person is called *happy* who enjoys self-preservation and an agreeable life".[104] Luzac proceeded to indicate his intellectualist position by pointing out that happiness could not be achieved under the guidance of the passions, but only through knowledge.[105] Human knowledge, he hastened to add, was far from perfect or complete. On the contrary, both reason and the senses had their limitations.[106] But this need not lead to a sceptical attitude, for Pyrrhonism rested on the *non sequitur* that "perfect knowledge is impossible, therefore we are unable to acquire any certainty".[107] A measure of certainty could be derived from the experiential *datum* that the representations of external objects and the operations of the mind showed a certain order and regularity and were thus presumably regulated by constant and unchanging laws.[108] On the basis of this experienced uniformity and order of the created universe man could arrive at a knowledge that was sufficient to fulfill his needs.

Thus even our imperfect knowledge of the structure of the universe indicated with sufficient clarity that the most general behavioral principle to be followed in order to achieve happiness was harmony. "Everything the universe presents to our contemplation makes us discover a harmony,

---

101. The best recent overview of all aspects of Wolff's philosophy is Schneiders, ed. *Christian Wolff*.

102. *Droit naturel*, vol.1, 59 ("...le mobile primitif de toutes nos actions...").

103. *Ibidem*, 112-114.

104. *Ibidem*, 114 ("...le penchant de se conserver et vivre agréablement.") and 118 ("...l'on nomme *heureux*, celui, qui jouit de la conservation de soi-même et d'une vie agréable...").

105. *Ibidem*, 65.

106. *Ibidem*, 41 and 110.

107. *Ibidem*, 44 ("...nous ne pouvons rien connoitre parfaitement: par conséquent nous ne pouvons acquérir aucune certitude.").

108. *Ibidem*, 42-44 and 106-107.

that is to say not only a merging of the forces and movements of all its parts, but also a cooperation which preserves its ever-changing existence. We observe a similar preserving harmony in each particular species and individual. We notice that as soon as this harmony is altered or destroyed in objects, they tend to their destruction. From this we conclude that it is this harmony which preserves the universe and its changing parts. We also conclude that the divine will, which has created the existing universe, has established harmony as the means of its preservation and therefore as the first law of nature. That law is general both for the universe as a whole and for its individual parts, mankind in particular. From this it follows that harmony must be the basis for the preservation of mankind and of all individuals".[109] Harmony by its very nature supposed order, sociability, and perfection and could therefore serve as the principle from which all subsequent rules of conduct, all duties and rights, could be derived in a continuous chain of demonstration.[110] Luzac was now ready to sum up the foundations of his system in one simple sentence: "Happiness is the goal to which we tend; the desire to obtain it is the motive of our actions; the way to get there is to take harmony as the general principle of these actions".[111]

This line of argument served as the basis for Luzac's first major criticism of Wolff's system. First of all, the German philosopher had not correctly established the validity of his otherwise exceptionally fruitful principle of perfection. According to Luzac, Wolff's argument amounted to the following. What tends to perfection is called good, what tends to

---

109. *Ibidem*, 160-161 ("Tout ce que l'Univers présente à notre contemplation nous y fait découvrir une harmonie; c'est-à-dire non-seulement un concours de forces, et de mouvemens, de la part de toutes ses parties; mais encore une coöpération, qui en conserve l'existence avec les changemens qui s'y opèrent: nous remarquons une pareille harmonie dans chaque espèce et dans chaque individu pour sa conservation particulière: nous nous appercevons, qu'à mésure que cette harmonie est altérée ou détruite dans quelques objets, ils tendent à leur déstruction: nous inférons delà que c'est cette harmonie qui conserve l'Univers, les parties, qui le constituent et les changemens, qui y tendent; nous concluons en outre, que la volonté Divine, qui a donné l'existence à l'univers, tel qu'il est, a effectivement établi l'harmonie comme moyen de sa conservation; qu'ainsi il en a fait la première loi de la Nature: que cette loi est générale tant pour l'Univers, dans son ensemble, que pour ses parties individuelles, et notamment pour le genre humain: d'ou il s'ensuit, que l'harmonie doit être la baze de la conservation du genre humain, ainsi que des individus qui le composent.").

110. *Ibidem*, 165-167.

111. *Ibidem*, 162 ("En un mot notre bonheur est le but auquel nous tendons; le désir de se le procurer est le motif qui nous fait agir; le moyen d'y parvenir c'est de prendre l'harmonie pour principe général de nos actions.").

the opposite is called bad. Perfection is desirable and man in fact by nature desires it. Perfection therefore is a general, natural, invariable, and necessary rule or law, obliging all.[112] By arguing thus, Wolff had failed to show the source of man's supposed desire for the good defined as perfection and had simply jumped from what was desirable to what was desired. His argument was insufficiently related to man's natural penchants, which should be taken into account in any effective system of morality.[113] He should have started from the impulse to self-preservation as the *motive* for human actions and should then have proceeded to show that the most rational *means* to be successful in self-preservation was to adopt the idea of perfection as a general behavioral principle. That way, he would have succeeded in establishing a connection between natural impulse and intellectual imperative. He would also have shown the difference between the desired and the desirable, which was necessary to account for the fact that in practice many people did not adopt the principle of perfection at all, although clearly they should. "He could therefore have used the following argument: by a natural impulse people tend to preserve themselves; to a large extent their preservation depends on their perfection: if therefore they wish to preserve themselves, they *must* adopt perfection as one of the first principles of their duties. In this manner he would equally have arrived at the system of natural law and of the law of nations he has authored and published".[114]

But quite apart from the fact that his argument to establish it was unsound, Wolff's general principle of natural law itself - "to do those things that contribute to the perfection of man and of his situation; to refrain from doing the opposite" - seemed overly narrow and individualistic to Luzac.[115] It was better and more comprehensive to take man's place in a harmonious universe as the basis of his duties: "According to the author's doctrine it would seem that, in the end, it is sufficient to try to maximize our own perfection. This, however, is to offer a very problematic and limited theory concerning our duties to others and even to ourselves. It is much better to posit that man has to strive for his own

---

112. *Ibidem*, 145-148.

113. Wolff, *Institutions*, vol.1, §118, note n.

114. *Droit naturel*, vol.1, 151 ("Il auroit donc pu faire ce raisonnement-ci: les hommes tendent, par une impulsion naturelle, à se conserver; leur conservation dépend en grande partie de leur perfection: ils *doivent* donc, s'ils veulent se conserver, adopter pour un des premiers principes de leurs devoirs, celui de se perfectionner: de cette manière il seroit également venu au système du Droit de la Nature et des Gens, qu'il a fait et publié.").

115. Wolff, *Grundsätze des Natur- und Völckerrechts*, §43.

perfection and that of his neighbor because he is part of a larger whole toward the perfection of which he has to contribute as much as possible".[116] The consequence of Wolff's principle was that man in the end always had to give himself preferential treatment and that charity and generosity were relegated to a marginal position.[117] It meant treating the duties of humanity as imperfect in all cases.[118] The principle of harmony, on the other hand, sometimes demanded the sacrifice of one's own interest for the good of others.[119]

The second way in which Luzac modified Wolff's teachings was by reducing God's role in natural law even further than the German had already done.[120] Luzac thoroughly approved of Wolff's efforts to establish the doctrine that actions were intrinsically good or bad, "that they do not first have to be made so by a command or by a prohibition".[121] According to Wolff the obligation to do good, that is to strive for perfection, was contained in the nature of man. It was therefore a law of nature from which natural rights could be derived as the moral power to do what one was obliged to do by the law of nature. Luzac took this whole line of argument to imply that it was possible to develop a truly naturalistic system of natural law, in which God was absolutely no more than the original creator of the universe and its principles. If natural duties could be derived from the nature and essence of man and creation, it was both superfluous and wrong to have recourse to particular acts of will or characteristics of the Supreme Being. "For although it is true that God, as the first being and the creator of mankind, has willed these duties to exist, it is equally true that this will is solely based on the nature and essence of things, resulting from the divine will, as a consequence of which mankind exists. So that once the divine will has had its effect through the creation, the duties and rights resulting from human nature are immutable and

---

116. Wolff, *Institutions*, vol.1, §44, note e ("...suivant la doctrine de l'Auteur, il sembleroit qu'on ne doit travailler à sa propre perfection et à celle du prochain, qu'autant que la nôtre l'exige et en est une conséquence; ce qui donne une théorie très chancelante et limitée par rapport à nos devoirs envers les autres et même envers nous-mêmes: là où elle devient très étendue, lorsque l'on considere que l'homme doit travailler à sa propre perfection et à celle du prochain, parce qu'il fait partie d'un tout, à la perfection duquel, il doit contribuer autant qu'est en lui.").

117. *Ibidem*, §64, note l.

118. *Ibidem*, §78/79, note p.

119. *Ibidem*, §64, note l.

120. For Wolff's contemporary reputation as a secularizer see T.P. Saine, "Who's Afraid of Christian Wolff?" in: Kors and Korshin, ed. *Anticipations of the Enlightenment*, 102-133.

121. Wolff, *Grundsätze des Natur- und Völkerrechts*, §14.

unvarying".[122] This was also what Wolff had seemed to be saying and Luzac was therefore astonished to find that same author contending that man should determine his actions by motives drawn from the divine attributes. "It is certain that the attributes of the Divinity can be deduced from the way in which the natural actions of man and of all things in the world are determined. Since free actions are determined in the same way as natural actions, and since these actions stem from the will of man, which must in turn be determined by motives, it is evident that man has to determine all his free actions on the basis of motives taken from the attributes of the Divinity. From that it is clear that human perfection consists in the ability to represent God, as a mirror of divine perfection".[123]

Wolff here, Luzac pointed out, first of all contradicted his previous demonstration that actions tending towards perfection contained a motive of volition in themselves. Secondly, it was improper to say that man should mirror the divine perfection "since a created being cannot represent a being existing in virtue of its own essence". But even accepting Wolff's premises for the moment, the argument was flawed. For Wolff contended that natural actions are so determined that one *can* deduce the divine attributes from them and that man therefore should determine his free actions according to motives taken from the divine attributes. This was to say nothing, however, because to prove the conclusion Wolff should have demonstrated that man's free actions have *no other* "final cause" than to conform to the divine attributes.[124] Refusing to entangle himself in similar contradictions and ambiguities, Luzac not only avoided all but the most general references to the original Creator, but also radically eliminated the customary section on man's duties towards God from his system. Those duties, he maintained, did not belong to natural law. They were the object of "a separate science known as theology".[125]

Luzac's most striking and wide-ranging modification of Wolffian

---

122. Wolff, *Institutions*, vol.1, §38, note a ("Car quoiqu'il soit vrai que Dieu, comme premier Etre et Créateur des hommes, a voulu que ces devoirs eussent lieu, il n'en est pas moins vrai, que cette volonté est uniquement appuyée sur la nature et l'essence des choses, résultant de la volonté divine, en conséquence de laquelle le genre humain existe. De sorte que la volonté divine ayant eu son effet par la création, les devoirs et les droits qui résultent de la nature de l'homme sont immuables et invariables."). See also *Droit naturel*, vol.1, 123, 134-135, 239-240.

123. Wolff, *Grundsätze des Natur- und Völckerrechts*, §160.

124. Wolff, *Institutions*, vol.1, §160, note e ("...raison finale..."; "...attendu qu'un Etre créé ne peut représenter l'Etre qui existe en vertu de sa propre essence...").

125. *Droit naturel*, vol.1, 199 ("...une science particulière, que l'on nomme *Théologie*...").

natural jurisprudence, however, was his attempt to discard its individualistic, egalitarian, and contractarian elements. Following countless predecessors, Wolff had started his account of society and the state with free and equal individuals as bearers of duties and rights in the state of nature, which was a state of primitive community of property. From this beginning, the individuals developed private property in things. They also engaged in a variety of social and political relations based on mutual consent. Luzac had already implicitly shown his disapproval of this scheme by substituting a comprehensive harmony for an individualistic perfection as the highest principle of natural law. He now proceeded to draw the consequences from this point of view. Wolff's individualistic approach, he observed, had led him to treat humans as isolated beings, instead of as the social beings they naturally were. It was a mistake to rigidly separate pre-social, independent man from social man. Born completely helpless, man could in fact only survive within a protective configuration of relations.[126] Wolff had completely disregarded this, "he has abstracted man from all those relationships in which he finds himself from the very first moment of his existence".[127] Wolff's abstract line of argument could clearly not be applied to man "as the order of nature gives birth to him".[128] All previous writers on natural law had made this same mistake of developing their accounts from the hypothesis of free, equal, and independent individuals. They should, instead, have started from the "successive creation of beings". That was the only way to arrive at a mode of analysis in accordance with the order of nature and constituting "the only proper way to envisage mankind if one wishes to discover and establish its rights and duties as accorded or dictated by nature".[129]

Starting from this simple but basic criticism of Wolff's atomistic perspective, Luzac discarded many of natural law's most treasured concepts and arguments. The first thing that had to go was the concept of natural equality, used with such ambiguity by Pufendorf, Heineccius, and

---

126. *Lettre d'un anonime*, 6; *Droit naturel*, vol.1, 381-382.

127. Wolff, *Institutions*, vol.1, §36, note y ("...il a considéré l'homme, abstraction fait de tous les rapports, dans lesquels il se trouve dès le moment de son existence...").

128. *Ibidem*, §76/77, note o ("...tel que l'ordre de la nature le fait naître.").

129. *Droit naturel*, vol.1, 346 ("...création successive des Etres..."; "...le véritable point de vue sous lequel les hommes, ou pour mieux dire, le genre humain doit être envisagé lorsqu'on veut rechercher les droits et les devoirs, que la nature établit entre eux, auxquels elle les assujettit d'une part, et qu'elle leur accorde d'une autre côté.").

Wolff.[130] It was incompatible with man's "successive existence" and could only be maintained in a completely unrealistic theory. "Differences in temperament, genius, powers and capacities - all evident from birth - produce a natural inequality that is impossible to deny or ignore".[131] Once man's natural inequality was admitted, it was no longer necessary to explain inequalities in property by resorting to the elaborate construction of a primitive community of property that was subsequently given up. As Luzac explained at length, there was no reason in either nature or history to suppose that such a state had ever existed.[132] Man's basic needs had driven him to appropriate things from the very beginning.[133] Given natural inequality, some had been rather more successful than others in acquiring the things they needed to fulfil their natural duties, the first of which was to survive by taking care of the body. This was so simple that savages could understand it.[134] Even on the basis of his own principles, Wolff should have arrived at the same conclusion. "I do not see how, even on the basis of our author's own principles, it is possible to deny man in the state of nature the right to appropriate the things nature offers him freely and of which he believes he can make use for his needs or pleasure".[135] It was clear, in short, that man had always had the right to the things he needed "in order to live in a harmonious way" and that the concept of a primitive community of property had therefore been introduced in natural law "without foundation, without benefit, and even more without necessity".[136]

A further exploration of the natural *rapports* and *relations* in which man was born revealed that it was unnecessary and wrong to reduce all human relations to contract and consent. Taking the family as an example, Luzac contended that it was superfluous to deduce the father's

---

130. *Ibidem*, 381.

131. *Ibidem*, 381 ("....existence successive...") and 382 ("La différence de leur tempérament, de leur génie, de leurs forces, de leurs facultés en tout genre, qu'on leur remarque dès leur naissance, produit une inégalité naturelle qu'on ne peut desavouer.").

132. Wolff, *Institutions*, vol.1, §194, note h; *Droit naturel*, vol.1, 273-286, 316-350, 360-382.

133. *Droit naturel*, vol.1, 361-362.

134. *Ibidem*, 341.

135. Wolff, *Institutions*, vol.1, §186, note b ("Je ne vois point que dans les principes-mêmes de notre Auteur on puisse refuser à l'homme, supposé dans l'état de la nature, le droit de s'approprier ce que la nature lui offre à saisir, et dont il croit pouvoir faire usage, soit pour ses besoins, soit pour son utilité, soit pour son agrément.").

136. *Droit naturel*, vol.1, 382 ("...pour vivre d'une manière convenable à l'harmonie.") and 361 ("...sans fondement, sans utilité, et encore plus sans nécessité.").

right to govern his children from tacit consent, as Locke, Wolff, and many others had done, since in fact it flowed from "the necessity to maintain harmony in the family, which could not survive if the children had the right to be disobedient".[137] Wolff had been equally mistaken in his treatment of the other forms of *imperium*. Thus he had repeated the same argument in explaining the origin of civil society and the state, because his flawed hypothesis of human equality made him suppose that no form of rule or dependence could exist without consent or contract. But in fact history showed us very few contracts indeed and reason could equally well dispense with them, for the following argument was a much more satisfactory, simple, and natural basis for civil society: "People must strive for their perfection as the source of their happiness: the perfection of human society results from the harmony of its parts: the more those parts are united and linked, the better they can contribute to the perfection of human society and to people's happiness which results from it: now since civil society is a means which particularly unites and links the members of human society, people have an interest to make use of it and thereby to make their situation more perfect and thus more happy".[138]

Luzac's adaptation of Wolffian natural law came at a time when the vocabulary of natural jurisprudence, which could be used to legitimate a wide variety of political arrangements, was increasingly being re-interpreted to support theories of popular sovereignty and inalienable natural rights. Rousseau's political writings were one example of this development, the rise of Lockean radicalism, more important in the Dutch context, was another. But this process was even apparent within Wolffian natural law itself, both in the Holy Roman Empire and in the Dutch Republic, as demonstrated by Van der Marck's interpretation of Wolff, in

---

137. *Ibidem*, 269 ("...la nécessité d'entretenir l'harmonie dans la famille, laquelle ne pourroit subsister, si les enfants avoient le droit d'être rénitans."). See also Wolff, *Institutions*, vol.2, §887/888, note a.

138. Wolff, *Institutions*, vol.2, §972, note h ("Les hommes doivent tendre à leur perfection comme source de leur bonheur: la perfection de la société humaine resulte de l'harmonie des parties: plus ces parties sont unies et liées, plus elles peuvent contribuer à la perfection de la société humaine, et au bonheur des hommes, qui doit s'ensuivre: or comme la société civile est un moyen, qui unit et lie plus particulièrement les membres de la société humaine, les hommes sont intéressés à s'en servir, pour rendre par là leur état plus parfait, et conséquemment plus heureux..."). Luzac had experimenté avec similar views as early as 1749, in chapter one of his *Disquisitio politico-moralis*: "De variis sententiis circa originem civitatum".

which the permanent validity of Wolff's *iura connata* was emphasized.[139] By depicting a hierarchical and harmonious society as man's true state of nature and thereby emptying that notion of its subversive potential, Luzac clearly tried to close the door to such radical uses of natural jurisprudence. But this should not be taken to mean that he was simply overtaking Christian Wolff on the political right, to use an anachronism. Luzac's adaptation of Wolffian natural law, on the contrary, was not only intended to put a stop to radical natural rights theories, but also, paradoxically, to eliminate the potentially authoritarian implications of Wolff's system.

In Wolff's doctrine, as E. Hellmuth has recently demonstrated, concepts such as the state of nature, natural equality, and natural liberty only served as the theoretical starting point for the legitimation of an authoritarian and paternalistic state, exercising an enormous power over its subjects.[140] Whereas Wolff's *iura connata*, losing their significance as soon as the *status originarius* was left, were no more than a purely analytical construct, Luzac ascribed a permanent validity to his structure of natural duties and rights. It served to limit the power of the state over individuals. This essential difference with Wolff was brought out well in Luzac's criticism of the German's views on sovereignty. Wolff's definition of sovereignty as the right to determine the free actions of others at will, Luzac remarked, was so wide-ranging as to be totally unacceptable. Clearly nobody could legitimately exercise such an unlimited power over another person "because on the one hand no man can so completely renounce his rights and his duties to himself as to make himself completely dependent on a strange will, possibly of a highly capricious nature; on the other hand no man can acquire such an unlimited and arbitrary power over the free actions of another person".[141] Luzac was

---

139. On Van der Marck's Wolff-interpretation see Jansen, *Natuurrecht of Romeins recht*, 85-113; on changes in German natural law in the second half of the eighteenth century see Klippel, "Naturrecht als politische Theorie" and, by the same author, "The True Concept of Liberty. Political Theory in Germany in the Second Half of the Eighteenth Century" in: Hellmuth, ed. *Transformation of Political Culture*, 447-466.

140. Hellmuth, *Naturrechtsphilosophie und bürokratischer Werthorizont*, 27-110. Other important recent discussions of Wolff's natural law and politics include Bachmann, *Naturrechtliche Staatslehre Christian Wolffs* and C. Link, "Die Staatstheorie Christian Wolffs" in: Schneiders, ed. *Christian Wolff*, 171-192.

141. Wolff, *Institutions*, vol.2, §833, note a ("...parce que d'un côté aucun homme ne peut se dépouiller de ses droits, jusqu'au point de renoncer entièrement à ce qu'il se doit à lui-même, et de se rendre entièrement dépendant d'une volonté étrangère, quelque capricieuse qu'elle fut; et que de l'autre côté, nul homme ne peut acquérir un pouvoir si illimité sur les actions libres d'un autre, au point de pouvoir le traiter arbitrairement.").

sharply aware of the fact that Wolff, by making the state entirely responsible for the welfare of all citizens, had greatly expanded its role. For
Wolff, he observed, "there is nothing the sovereign is not allowed to
decide, even to the point of ordering his citizens what to eat and what to
drink".[142] In Wolffian political discourse the state appeared as the active
creator of happiness, providing guidance in all aspects of human life. In
Luzac's writings it never did. Instead, the main function of the state was
to provide the security within which social happiness and harmony could
be achieved. A sovereign, Luzac emphasized, should constantly ask
himself "to what degree he may dispose of the liberty of his citizens".[143] While firmly opposing the radical threat, it is clear that Luzac
had no intention to join the authoritarian and paternalist camp.

4. *The Laws of Nature and the Laws of Rome*

Since well before the emergence of the Dutch Republic in the sixteenth
century, Roman law had been regarded as subsidiary law in the Low
Countries, as was the case elsewhere on the European continent. When
local laws, written or unwritten, were silent, Roman law was the first and
most authoritative source to be consulted. It was the customary *ius
commune* and was defined as such in widely circulating and frequently
reprinted textbooks such as Grotius's *Introduction to the jurisprudence of
Holland* (1631) and Simon van Leeuwen's *Roman-Dutch law* (1664).[144]
In academic teaching, internationally oriented because of the large number
of foreign students, Roman law almost completely dominated the legal
curriculum for a long time.[145] It was during the eighteenth century, as
C.J.H. Jansen has recently demonstrated, that this situation slowly began
to change. In the legal faculties, the study of Roman law was gradually
supplemented with that of natural and Dutch law. In legal practice, the
relevance of Roman law increasingly began to be questioned.[146] These

142. *Ibidem*, §1021, note o ("...il n'est point d'arrangement ni de disposition que le
Souverain ne puisse prendre; jusqu'a ordonner même ce que les citoyens mangeront et
boiront.").

143. *Ibidem* ("...jusques à quel degré il lui est permis de disposer de la liberté des Citoyens.").

144. Grotius, *Inleidinge*, book I, part 2, §22; Van Leeuwen, *Rooms-Hollands-Regt*, book I,
part I, §11.

145. On the Dutch legal system and Dutch legal education in general in the early modern
period see De Monté Ver Loren and Spruit, *Hoofdlijnen*, 184-225; Lokin and Zwalve,
Inleiding in de rechtsgeschiedenis, 343-375; Veen and Kop, ed. *Zestig juristen*, 9-20.

146. Jansen, *Natuurrecht of Romeins recht*, *passim*.

developments gave rise to lively debates and forced every Dutch legal scholar to formulate clearly his opinion on the status of Roman law. Luzac, as we already briefly indicated at the beginning of this chapter, came to occupy a middle ground in this confrontation between those who rejected Roman law altogether and those who desired to cling to it with as little change as possible. Adopting one of his favorite strategies, Luzac embraced modernity without discarding the erudition and accomplishments of the past.

As one of the leading Dutch propagandists of modern moral science, Luzac evidently was aware of the many shortcomings of Roman law. In his historical account of the development of the *science des moeurs* he had exposed its glaring philosophical deficiencies. The principles of natural law, not those of Roman law, were the ultimate basis of all jurisprudence to Luzac.[147] It was completely wrong, he insisted, to regard Roman law as the universal *ratio scripta* or the "civil law of the universe".[148] It had obviously been written in a certain time and place and had to be modified and supplemented in the light of modern circumstances. Commerce, for instance, was a subject treated very inadequately in Roman law. Thus the Roman prohibition of compound interest might have had its uses in antiquity, but it was most harmful in a country "whose wealth is founded on the use and circulation of money".[149] Similarly, the Romans had been unable to understand the concept and practice of commission selling, as evidenced by their restrictive interpretation of mandates.[150] All this was hardly surprising, since modern commerce had been unknown to the ancient world. It only served to show that laws and regulations should always be adapted to local circumstances, to "the genius, the *moeurs*, the uses and customs" of the nation that adopted them.[151] So should legal scholarship. It was absurd that a commercial country's legal faculties were dominated by professors steeped in Roman law, but unable to answer the most simple questions "about insurance, general average, or bills of exchange".[152] The exclusive aca-

---

147. Wolff, *Institutions*, vol.2, §928, note h.

148. *Ibidem*, vol.1, Dédicace, xvi ("...le Droit Civil de l'Univers...").

149. *Ibidem*, §651, note p ("...dont la richesse est fondée sur l'usage et la circulation de l'argent.").

150. *Droit naturel*, vol.2, 237-264 ("Sur l'application de la doctrine concernant le mandat dans le droit Romain, et sur ce que l'on appelle commission en stile de commerce.").

151. Wolff, *Institutions*, vol.2, §1068, note r ("...le genie, les moeurs, et les us et coutumes...").

152. *Ibidem*, vol.1, Dédicace, xvii ("...d'assurance, de grosse avarie, de lettres de change...").

demic obsession with Roman law furthermore had a pernicious effect on the students, since it did not adequatly prepare them for the social reality that awaited them in their later professional lives.[153]

What then, given these criticisms, was the use of Roman law, or at least of those parts of it that were of enduring value? Abstract truth, Luzac pointed out, was only one of the goals of the human quest for knowledge. At least as important was the capacity to apply that truth in practice. In jurisprudence, abstract truth was largely provided by Wolff's system of natural law, containing "the most general principles of universal jurisprudence". The richest store of practical and concrete legal decisions, however, was embodied in the ancient corpus of Roman law. A synthesis of the two, in which the principles of natural law would be linked to and serve to elucidate the often excellent practical decisions contained in Roman law, would lead to a perfect jurisprudence.[154] But although this was Luzac's most important argument in favor of the continued use of an adapted version of Roman law, it was not the only one. The exclusive focus on Roman law could, it is true, render students unfit to confront the modern world. But properly used, Roman law habituated the mind "to exactitude, clarity, and precision" and thereby provided a unique intellectual training.[155] Roman law, moreover, was codified. To Luzac, who as we have seen did not wish the judiciary to take on a legislative role, this was a major and substantial advantage. There could be no doubt about the abstract truths of natural law, but they did not limit the judge's interpretative freedom by providing an authoritative written text that could not be ignored. Excessive reliance on natural law in legal practice could easily degenerate into the subjective *iurisprudentia cerebrina* that had, early in the century, already been dreaded by the great Cornelis van Bynkershoek (1673-1743).[156]

Luzac's attempt to bring about the synthesis of natural and Roman law in his 1772 Wolff edition was, as we have noted, hailed by many a critic. Frederik Adolf van der Marck, however, would hear of no such compromises. In the years after his appointment in 1758 the pugnacious Groningen professor launched a series of vehement attacks on Roman

---

153. *Ibidem*. See also *Vryaart*, vol.3, part 9, 3-18.

154. Wolff, *Institutions*, vol.1, Dédicace, xx-xxii. The quotation is on xx ("...les principes les plus généraux de la Jurisprudence Universelle...").

155. *Ibidem*, xxii ("...à l'exactitude, à la netteté, à la précision.").

156. *Nederlandsche Letter-Courant*, vol.6 (1761), 61-62. On Van Bynkershoek see Star Numan, *Cornelis van Bynkershoek* and A. Krikke and S. Faber, "Cornelis van Bynkershoek (1673-1743)" in: Veen and Kop, ed. *Zestig juristen*, 141-149.

law. He proposed to discard it altogether and to replace it with natural law as subsidiary law in the Dutch Republic. Van der Marck used a wide variety of arguments to make his point. He even responded to Luzac's brief critical comments in the *Nederlandsche Letter-Courant* with a separate lengthy pamphlet.[157] Briefly summarized, he took the following position. Roman law, he claimed, was unfit for use in the Dutch Republic because of the immense historical differences between this state and ancient Rome. Given that fact, the application of Roman law might even be said to constitute a threat to Dutch liberty. Roman law had, moreover, never been officially and properly adopted as law in the Dutch Republic, nor was it evident that it should be regarded as customary law. To make things worse, it was no more than a confusing accumulation of particular decisions without general importance, a state of affairs leading to a high degree of uncertainty in legal practice. Finally, it was unacceptable that people should be judged on the basis of laws written in a language they were unable to comprehend.[158]

Luzac saw no reason to deny the validity of many of the points made by Van der Marck. On the contrary, he recommended Van der Marck's publications and remarked that his observations concerning the neglect of natural law and the abuse of Roman law, by applying it to situations it was clearly unsuited for, contained more than a little truth.[159] Where he chiefly disagreed with Van der Marck was in the practical conclusions to be drawn from these general observations. Given his polemical temper, Luzac's response was exceptionally mild and undogmatic. The fact that Roman law had emerged in a different country and at a different time did not in itself prove anything against it, he observed. What did it matter where a law came from or when it had been written if it proved to be useful in the present? To maintain that the adoption of foreign laws constituted by definition an assault on Dutch liberty was an obvious absurdity.[160] It was furthermore, to say the least, highly intriguing to deny that Roman law had legal force in the Dutch Republic, since it had

---

157. Luzac discussed Van der Marck's work in the *Nederlandsche Letter-Courant*, vol.1 (1759), 171-176; vol.6 (1761), 50-53, 59-62, 324-328, 332-334; vol.7 (1762), 124-126; vol.8 (1762), 171-174. Van der Marck's pamphlet against Luzac was entitled *Nadere verklaring over de vryheid van den burgerstaat van Groningerland, etc.*

158. Jansen, *Romeins recht of natuurrecht*, 161-173. For other recent and markedly less sympathetic discussions of Van der Marck's views on Roman law see Zwalve, "Frederik Adolf van der Marck en Marcus Tullius Cicero", and, by the same author, "Het Recht en de Verlichting".

159. *Nederlandsche Letter-Courant*, vol.6 (1761), 62.

160. *Ibidem*, 333.

been used for centuries and had thereby clearly acquired the status of customary law.[161] As to the uncertainty of Roman law, it was indeed true that it lacked system and was frequently inconsistent. Matters would be made worse instead of better, however, by simply replacing it with natural law in legal practice. It was, in a way, a choice between two evils of which the existing one was to be preferred. For to introduce natural law as the direct basis of judicial decisions was to open the door to arbitrary justice.[162] That Roman law was inaccessible to the common man, finally, was an argument not to be taken lightly, but ultimately of little importance, since the common man would also be unable to understand the intricacies of natural law and would therefore, one way or the other, always have to rely on professional advice.[163] Having pointed out these problems, Luzac once more hastened to dissociate himself from the camp of uncritical admirers of Roman law. When in 1762 Van der Marck's Groningen colleague Dionysius van der Keessel (1738-1816), who later became a well-known Leiden professor, called for the intensification of the academic study of Roman law, he openly dissented. Rather than invest yet more energy in the detailed analysis of the more obscure parts of Roman law, he characteristically observed, it would instead be much more beneficial to study and improve it in the light of modern natural law and philosophy.[164]

161. *Ibidem*, vol.8 (1762), 173-174.

162. *Ibidem*, vol.6 (1761), 61-62 and 334.

163. *Ibidem*, 334. See also *Ibidem*, vol.9 (1763), 318.

164. *Ibidem*, vol.8 (1762), 373.

CHAPTER IV

WEALTH, LIBERTY, AND THE STADHOLDERATE

Luzac's most voluminous writings on Dutch politics and society date from the 1780s, when he was confronted with the rise of the Patriot movement and felt compelled to respond to it energetically. His vehement anti-Patriotism may partly be understood as the product of his general intellectual outlook, as discussed in the previous chapters. But it was also the direct result of the views he had developed on the nature of the Dutch Republic. Any satisfactory account of the history and politics of the Dutch Republic, Luzac maintained, should be structured around the two main themes of commerce and the Stadholderate. He discussed both subjects at great length and combined them in the massive four-volume *Holland's wealth*. Having completed that work in 1782, he found himself in the midst of a deep political crisis and turned exclusively to direct anti-Patriot political polemics for over a decade. These polemics will be the subject of chapter five. The purpose of the present chapter is to analyze Luzac's views on commerce and the Stadholderate. The first section will deal with the various contexts in which the genesis of these views may be understood. In the second section, Luzac's general approach to commerce and commercial society will be explored. This will be followed by a section discussing his analysis of the nature and history of Dutch commerce. Luzac's convictions about the crucial role of the Stadholderate in the Dutch Republic will be the subject of the fourth and final section of this chapter.

1. *Texts and Contexts*

Luzac's very strong interest in the Stadholderate hardly needs explaining, for this institution had played a central role in Dutch politics and Dutch political discourse ever since the Republic was formed. It was discussed by almost every serious political publicist of the Dutch *ancien régime*. Luzac first formulated his views on the role of the Stadholder in a series of pamphlets published in the 1750s.[1] They were written with the express purpose of legitimating the restoration of the Stadholderate during the

---

1. These pamphlets were: *Het gedrag der stadhoudersgezinden, etc.* (1754); *Verantwoording wegens den uitgaaf van...Het gedrag, etc.* (1754); *Het gedrag der stadhoudersgezinden, etc.* Second, enlarged edition (1755); *De zugt van...Johan de Witt, tot zyn vaderland, etc.* (1757); *Het oordeel over...Johan de Witt, etc.* (1757).

revolution of 1747-1748 and represented Luzac's effort to develop a modernized theory of Orangism, much needed after the rather poor intellectual performance of the Orangist camp during the second Stadholderless era (1702-1747).[2] Luzac's argument in these early pamphlets was specifically intended for a situation in which the only relevant political fact was the traditional opposition between the States party and the Orangist party. This context, as will be seen below, led him to adopt a line of argument that he was forced to drop at the end of the century, when a profoundly changed political debate revealed it to have an unforeseen radical potential. Whereas Luzac's views on the Stadholderate thus showed a measure of discontinuity and change, his approach to commerce remained remarkably consistent throughout his writings. The rise of Patriotism, in other words, did not cause Luzac to reassess his fundamental convictions about the nature of commercial society. On the contrary, they proved to be excellently suited for use in anti-Patriot political polemics. The problem presented by Luzac's writings on commerce is not one of intellectual discontinuity, but one of textual history and of a wide variety of national and international contexts.

Luzac was, as H.C. Cras observed, "passionately interested in matters of commerce".[3] This interest ranged, it might be added, from the practical realm to that of theoretical abstraction. Luzac evidently took great pride in running his publishing business on a profitable basis. From his correspondence with Rey and Formey he emerges as a shrewd businessman, someone who, in the words of Y.Z. Dubosq, "was a master in maintaining and expanding his own wealth".[4] It is as if he regarded successful entrepreneurship as a mark of Dutchness, as a measure of his full assimilation to the values of Dutch culture. When urged to abandon his commercial activities so as to be able to devote more time to his other talents he refused, explaining to Formey that he was "disinclined to give up a profession that is so admirably suited to our spirit of liberty".[5] As a lawyer, he was repeatedly involved in cases where the freedom of trade was at stake.[6] But it was in his writings that this fascination with the

---

2. On the poverty of Orangist political thought during the first half of the eighteenth century see the present author's "God, de deugd en de oude constitutie".

3. Cras, "Beredeneerd verslag", 83 ("De Heer Luzac was zeer gevat op zaken van koophandel...").

4. Dubosq, *Livre français*, 26.

5. *Corr. Formey*, Luzac to Formey, [1756] ("...mon humeur ne me porte pas à quitter une profession, qui convient le mieux à notre esprit de liberté.").

6. Cras, "Beredeneerd verslag", 88c; Schutte, *Patriotten en de koloniën*, 138.

world of commerce was most evident. In his general comments on the course of modern European history or on the nature of Dutch society commerce always figured prominently. It equally played an important role in his writings on natural law. His commentary on Wolff was intended, among other things, to demonstrate the utility of that author's principles "in legal cases concerning commerce and navigation".[7] One of the longest chapters of his final synthesis of natural law, *Du droit naturel, civil, et politique*, was devoted to the blessings of commerce.[8] His most extended treatment of the subject, however, was contained in the four volumes of *Holland's wealth*, published between 1780 and 1783 and reprinted early in the nineteenth century.

Recognized by contemporaries as of major importance, *Holland's wealth* was in the course of the nineteenth century elevated to the status of the most authoritative early modern work on Dutch commerce.[9] E. Laspeyres, the author of what has regrettably remained the only full survey of early Dutch economic writing, described it in 1863 without hesitation as "the internationally best-known work of the whole of Dutch economic literature".[10] Luzac's volumes are still being consulted by present day historians. Recently, his assessment of the Dutch eighteenth-century economic situation has even been called superior to that of many a modern study.[11] Given this continued attention, it is all the more remarkable that the complicated textual history of this work has never adequately been told. It is generally recognized that *Holland's wealth*, as indeed Luzac himself indicated, was derived from a work entitled *La richesse de la Hollande*, published in 1778 and written by one Jacques Accarias de Sérionne. For reasons that remain unclear, many subsequent historians have taken Sérionne to be non-existent. S. Schama, for instance, as late as 1977 confidently asserted that Luzac's *Holland's wealth* "had appeared in French in 1778 under the pseudonym Jacques Accarias de Sérionne".[12] Since Schama's error is no isolated instance, but repre-

---

7. The quotation is part of the full title as cited in the bibliography ("...pour juger les causes rélatives au commerce et à la navigation...").

8. *Droit naturel*, vol.3, 150-232 ("Sur le prix des choses et de l'argent et sur l'utilité du Commerce").

9. The work was used and praised by, among others, A. Kluit and G.K. van Hogendorp. See Van Rees, "Het collegie van Adriaan Kluit", 251 and Overmeer, *Economische denkbeelden van Van Hogendorp*, 98.

10. Laspeyres, *Volkswirtschaftlichen Anschauungen*, 37.

11. Israel, *Dutch Primacy in World Trade*, 379.

12. Schama, *Patriots and Liberators*, 660.

sentative of the widespread confusion surrounding this matter, it seems worthwhile to discuss the genesis and history of this important text in some detail.

It has already been observed that Luzac showed a thorough interest in the study of commerce by the time he came to write his commentary on Montesquieu's *Esprit des lois* in the late 1750s.[13] Over the next decade, political economy became an extremely fashionable topic in France.[14] Luzac, always carefully monitoring European intellectual trends, was quick to express his approval of this remarkable efflorescence of the "economic sciences". It was a branch of knowledge he judged to be eminently useful in furthering mankind's progress towards happiness and perfection.[15] His enthusiasm was strongly reinforced when in 1765 he was approached with the request to publish a manuscript entitled *Les intérêts des nations de l'Europe développés relativement au commerce*. This work, he wrote to Formey, was unique in its genre and clearly deserved to be read by "all those who have the good of mankind at heart".[16] By June 1766 Luzac was reading it for the third time. He now judged it to belong to the best books he had recently studied.[17] The author of these remarkable *Intérêts* was none other than Jacques Accarias de Sérionne (1706-1792), about whose adventurous life little is known.

Sérionne, born in the Dauphiné, had initially pursued a promising career in Paris as *avocat aux conseils* and *secrétaire du roi*. By the mid-1750s, however, financial difficulties forced him to leave his native country. He moved to the Austrian Netherlands, where he acted as an economic adviser to the government and where he played an important role in the publication of the *Journal de Commerce* (1759-1762). After a sojourn in the Dutch Republic during the 1760s, Sérionne departed in 1769 for Hungary to enter the service of the Count of Batthyany. Apart from the fact that he died in Vienna in 1792, almost nothing is known about the final decades of his life.[18] What is known, however, is that he was a prolific writer on economic matters, with a special interest in com-

---

13. See 55-56.

14. Hutchison, *Before Adam Smith*, 265.

15. *Nederlandsche Letter-Courant*, vol.1 (1759), 229 and vol.3 (1760), 3 ("...dat gedeelte der Weetenschappen, welken *Oeconomische* genoemd worden...").

16. *Corr. Formey*, Luzac to Formey, Leiden, August 20 and November 30, 1765 ("...tous ceux qui ont le bien de l'humanité à coeur.").

17. *Ibidem*, June 3, 1766.

18. Accarias, "Publiciste dauphinois"; Hasquin, "Jacques Accarias de Sérionne".

merce.[19] His economic thought, showing clear similarities to that of Luzac, has been described as "eclectic liberalism", a term chiefly intended to convey the fact that he rejected both mercantilism and physiocracy.[20] Sérionne was particularly fascinated by the Dutch as a trading nation. Early in 1760, while still living in the Austrian Netherlands, he was already thinking about a book on Dutch commerce. "Some day I want to write about Holland's commerce in particular", he wrote to Marc-Michel Rey on March 10 of that year.[21] His resolve was strengthened upon meeting Luzac, who published the *Intérêts* in 1766. The two men discussed Holland's commerce at length and Luzac provided Sérionne with all kinds of useful information on the subject.[22]

It is therefore no exaggeration to conclude that Luzac contributed to the genesis of *La richesse de la Hollande*, the work he would later transform into *Holland's wealth*. Sérionne, in fact, wrote two books about the Dutch economy. In 1768 his *Le commerce de la Hollande, ou tableau du commerce des Hollandois dans les quatre parties du monde* appeared in Amsterdam. A decade later, it was finally followed by *La richesse*. It was published by Luzac, who had been given the official privilege to print it on April 6, 1778.[23] Luzac initially planned to publish a Dutch translation of Sérionne's *Richesse*, but upon closely studying the book he decided that it contained too many flaws.[24] In 1779 he therefore announced his intention to publish a greatly expanded and improved version of *La richesse* under the title *Holland's wealth*.[25] A comparison of the two works shows that this is indeed exactly what he did. While following the general plan of Sérionne's book, Luzac treated the history of Dutch commerce in greater detail, added a large number of appendices containing sources of importance to the study of Dutch economic history, and particularly expanded the sections dealing with the relation between polity and economy and with the Stadholderate. The work, in other words, was transformed. The eighteenth-century story of the text does not completely end at this point, however, for Luzac's volumes in turn were enthusiastically taken up in Germany. An abbreviated German translation by the

19. For his bibliography see Cioranescu, *Bibliographie*, vol.1, 216.

20. Airiau, *Opposition aux Physiocrates, passim*.

21. Personal Archive Rey, J. Accarias de Sérionne to M.M. Rey, March 10, 1761 ("Je dois traiter un jour particulièrement le Commerce de la Hollande.").

22. Cras, "Beredeneerd verslag", 54-55.

23. *Ibidem*, 78; Van Eeghen, *Amsterdamse Boekhandel*, vol.5, 220.

24. *Hollands rijkdom*, vol.4, 359.

25. *Berigt, passim*.

historian A.F. Lüder, pupil of the famous Göttingen professor A.L. Schlözer and later an important figure in the German reception of Adam Smith, appeared in 1788.[26] In 1790, finally, the four-volume German translation of the whole work was completed under the title *Elias Luzacs Betrachtungen über den Ursprung des Handels und der Macht der Holländer.*[27]

The above reconstruction of the textual history of Luzac's best-known work does not, of course, provide sufficient insight into the intellectual context of his writings on commerce. In his discussions of the Stadholderate Luzac participated in and modified a clearly identifiable and ongoing national political debate. His writings on commerce and commercial society, on the other hand, formed part of a number of debates, both national and international, and freely crossed the still fluid or even non-existent borders between natural law, political economy, and politics proper. Before discussing them in detail, some preliminary remarks are therefore in order. Luzac, to point out the obvious, lived and wrote in early modern Europe's most thoroughly commercialized society. Whereas in many other European countries a relatively sudden leap into modernity gave rise to prolonged and agonized eighteenth-century discussions about the merits and demerits, or even the viability, of a truly commercial society, in the Dutch Republic its existence was, to a large extent, simply taken for granted. It has already been observed, however, that Luzac was always sharply aware of the international intellectual scene. In the case of his paeans to commerce, too, it is clear that he intended to intervene in a general European exchange of opinions. It was his firm conviction that the blessings of commerce were still insufficiently appreciated.

On this most general level he therefore strove, with all the intellectual means at his disposal to establish the superiority of modern commercial society over all previous and possible alternative arrangements. One way to do this was by means of natural law, whose importance to the development of eighteenth-century political economy has recently been emphasized.[28] Luzac indeed firmly anchored the main features of commer-

---

26. *Geschichte des holländischen Handels. Nach Luzacs Hollands Rykdom bearbeitet von August Ferdinand Lüder.* Leipzig, 1788. On Lüder see Roscher, *Geschichte der National-Oekonomik*, 619-624; Schutte, "'A Subject of Admiration and Encomium'", 122; Tribe, *Governing Economy*, 168-169.

27. *Allgemeine Literatur-Zeitung*, December 15, 1791, 526-527.

28. Hont and Ignatieff, ed. *Wealth and Virtue*; Hont, "The language of sociability and commerce: Samuel Pufendorf and the theoretical foundations of the 'Four-Stages Theory'" in: Pagden, ed. *Languages of Political Theory*, 253-276; Hutchison, *Before Adam Smith*, 5. A pioneering study exploring this topic for the Dutch Republic is Nijenhuis, "University of

cial society - sociability, the acquisition of property, monetarized exchange and the market - in natural law. Given this point of departure in
natural jurisprudence, it is less than surprising to find him consistently
rejecting all classical republican criticism of commercial society. He did
his utmost to combat the paradigm of virtue in whatever form it reared its
head.[29] It was, he contended, based on a misplaced idealization of life in
the ancient republics, on a regrettable misunderstanding of the nature of
commerce, and ultimately on a static and primitivist vision of man as
primarily a political animal. Luzac unfavorably contrasted ancient conquest with modern commerce and expansionist states with peaceful
trading republics. He argued at length that there was no intrinsic connection between the rise of commerce and the growth of corruption. He
finally dwelled upon the contrast between the rich life of modern polite
and sociable man and the brutish and impoverished existence of the
ancient citizen-soldier.

Moving from the international to the national dimension of Luzac's
writings on commercial society, the first relevant context is that of a
specifically Dutch tradition of discourse concerning the relation between
economy and polity. This was the so-called system of True Liberty,
which was mainly formulated during the first Stadholderless era (1651-
1672), but continued to exercise a powerful influence. Central to this
mode of thought was the conviction that successful commerce required
both a certain highly specific kind of political structure and a clearly
defined foreign policy. Its adherents argued that trade was the eminent
interest of the Dutch state. Therefore, they insisted, that state must be
both republican and bourgeois, for neither a monarchy nor a military aristocracy could offer the necessary rule of law and justice. It should
furthermore be non-expansionist and as neutral as possible, for both the
possession of an extensive territory and the participation in wars interfered with the interests of trade.[30] The most authoritative formulation of
this view stems from the 1660s and from the pen of Pieter de la Court
(1618-1685). In his *Interest van Holland*, the expanded 1669 version of
which was translated into English early in the eighteenth century as *The*

Leiden".

29. For the opposition between the early modern paradigms of natural jurisprudence and
civic humanism the reader may be referred to the works of J.G.A. Pocock as listed in the
bibliography.

30. On True Liberty see P. Geyl, "Het Stadhouderschap en de partijliteratuur onder De Witt"
in: Geyl, *Pennestrijd over Staat en Historie*, 3-71; Kossmann, *Politieke Theorie*, 30-58;
Smit, "The Netherlands in Europe"; Leeb, *Ideological Origins*, 29-40; Rowen, *John de Witt*,
380-401.

true interest and political maxims of the republic of Holland, De la Court
had left his readers in no doubt as to his combined political and economic
intentions.[31] "Since all men", he wrote in his preface, "know that the
preservation and prosperity of a country depends upon such a government
as is consistent with itself; and reason informs us, that the welfare of Holland is founded upon manufactures, fishery, trade and navigation, I think
myself obliged particularly to consider these means of subsistence and
pillars of the state, with some observations upon the late government of a
Stadholder and Captain General, which some ignorant and mistaken Hol-
landers still desire".[32] Luzac greatly appreciated De la Court's attempt to
present a comprehensive analysis of Dutch commerce and to investigate
the relationship between politics and prosperity. He used the *Interest*
throughout *Holland's wealth*.[33] What he vehemently rejected, however,
was its main thesis concerning the connection between successful commerce and republicanism, interpreted as a government without a head. To
Luzac the exact opposite was true: Holland's wealth depended for a
substantial part on the presence of a Stadholderly government. With that
contention, aimed against the system of True Liberty, he made himself
into a prime target for Patriot attacks.

Luzac's writings on commerce, *Holland's wealth* in particular, may
also be approached as contributions to the eighteenth-century debate on
the economic decline of the Dutch Republic. Modern economic historians
sharply disagree about the extent of that decline, with some even denying
it altogether.[34] To the intellectual historian, however, the only relevant
fact is the widespread contemporary perception of economic malaise. By
the mid-eighteenth century the vast majority of Dutch commentators were
convinced that something had badly gone wrong with the economy. From,
at the latest, William IV's *Proposition for a limited porto-franco* (1751)
until the very end of the century, this problem played a central role in

---

31. *Interest van Holland, ofte Gronden van Hollands-welvaren* was first published in 1662
and later expanded into *Aanwysing der heilsame politike gronden en maximen van de
republike van Holland en West-Vriesland*. On the three English editions (1702, 1743, 1746)
see Wildenberg, *Johan en Pieter de la Court*, 53; on Pieter de la Court's political and
economic thought see Van Tijn, "De la Court"; Haitsma Mulier, *Myth of Venice*, 120-169;
Blom and Wildenberg, ed. *Pieter de la Court in zijn tijd*.

32. [De la Court], *True interest*, viii-ix.

33. References to the *Aanwysing* in *Holland's wealth*: vol.1, XIX-XXI; vol.2, 272, 324, 326;
vol.3, 150, 176, 190; vol.4, 76 ff., 405, 409, 414, 421, 444 ff., 473 ff., 490 ff., 508, 523.

34. The standard work remains De Vries, *Economische achteruitgang*. Its conclusions have
recently been challenged by Israel, *Dutch Primacy in World Trade*, 377-404.

Dutch public discourse.[35] It was endlessly discussed in spectatorial periodicals such as *De Koopman* (1768-1776) and *De Borger* (1778-1779).[36] It was also made the subject of essay competitions, of which that held by the Hollandsche Maatschappij der Wetenschappen (Holland Society of Sciences) in 1771 proved to be the most influential and important. "What", the question had been, "is the basis of Dutch commerce, of its increase and flourishing? Which causes and accidents have led to changes in and decline of that commerce? What are the most suitable and the easiest means to protect it in its present state, to improve it, and to bring it to the highest perfection?" The answers of H.H. van den Heuvel (the winner), A. Rogge, and C. Zillesen were printed in 1775 and received widespread attention.[37] Luzac, too, closely studied these texts, but ultimately deemed them to be unsatisfactory. *Holland's wealth*, he announced to his readers, was partly written to cover the same ground once more and to discuss the matters neglected or inadequately treated by the authors of the prize essays.[38] The work was meant, he confidently remarked, "to show the path which, it seems to me, should be followed if one desires to investigate these subjects [i.e. "the decline of our navigation, commerce, and manufactures, and the means to resuscitate the same"]; a path which, as far as I know, has until now not been followed by any writer on matters of commerce".[39]

35. An exhaustive treatment of the *Proposition* is provided by Hovy, *Voorstel van 1751*. On the contemporary debate about economic decline see most recently Nijenhuis, *Een joodse philosophe*, 95-122.

36. On *De Koopman* (The Merchant) see Brugmans, "De Koopman"; on *De Borger* (The Citizen) see Nefkens, "Denkbeelden van De Borger". Unfortunately, there is no general modern study of Dutch eighteenth-century spectatorial literature. For some important observations on the subject see Buynsters, *Nederlandsche literatuur*, 36-46 and 58-85 and, by the same author, *Spectatoriale geschriften*.

37. "Welke is den grond van Hollandsch Koophandel, van zynen aanwas en bloei? Welke oorzaaken en toevallen hebben dien tot heden aan veranderingen en verval bloot gesteld? Welke middelen zijn best geschikt en gemakkelykst te vinden, om denzelven in zyne tegenwoordige gesteldheid te bewaaren, zyne verbetering te bevorderen, en den hoogsten trap van volkomenheid te doen bereiken?" On this essay competition see Bierens de Haan, *Oeconomische Tak*, 1-6 and Leeb, *Ideological Origins*, 108-109.

38. *Berigt*, 4-6; *Hollands rijkdom*, vol.3, 407-408.

39. *Hollands rijkdom*, vol.4, 534 ("...ter aanwijzinge van het spoor, het welk, zoo 't mij voorkomt, gehouden moet worden, wanneer men zich tot een onderzoek van die onderwerpen [i.e. "het verval van onze Vaart, Koophandel, Manufacturen en Trafieken, en de middelen om die te doen herleeven"] wil begeeven; en 't welk tot nog toe, zoo veel ik weet, door geen Schrijver over zaaken van Koophandel betreeden is geworden.").

2. *In Praise of Commercial Society*

There was still plenty to do, Luzac realized, for those wishing to establish the superiority of modern commercial society. Many writers, it was obvious, remained doubtful about its blessings. First of all, there were certain scholars who ascribed the rise of commerce to a corruption of manners and to vice. Then there were those, like Montesquieu and Rousseau, who claimed that commercial states were of necessity short-lived. The excessive admiration, moreover, for the world of classical Greece and Rome, a world more of conquest than of commerce, blinded many people to the superiority of the moderns, whose ease of life was incomparably greater than that of the ancients. Most existing historiography, finally, neglected the peaceful arts of trade and industry in favor of lengthy descriptions of war and politics. Luzac considered the refutation of these points of view to be an urgent task and he energetically took it up.

Very little, Luzac remarked, was known about the earliest history of mankind. On the basis of "the natural course of human effort", however, it was possible to arrive at a number of "conjectures" about the natural history of commerce.[40] It has already been observed that, in his writings on natural law, Luzac discarded a number of cherished concepts. Refusing to take constructs such as the primitive community of property seriously, he proclaimed property to be a most natural phenomenon. So, in a way, was commerce. Luzac's state of nature, indeed, already showed many of the characteristics of a highly developed society. The early inhabitants of the earth, diverse in talents and capacities, had tried to stay alive in different ways. All, however, had craved an easy, prosperous, and satisfactory life. It was soon discovered that the most convenient way to reach this goal was a mutually beneficial exchange of goods and services. "It is...very natural that the exchange of things against things, or against labor, and of labor against labor, has been the way in which since the beginning of the world its inhabitants have tried to communicate and to provide for their subsistence and livelihood". From the very start, there had thus been "that constant communication of reciprocal gifts that is called commerce". A society totally without such commerce seemed to be almost inconceivable. Evidently, this wonderful mutual exchange, soon greatly improved by the introduction of money, had nothing to do with a

---

40. *Hollands rijkdom*, vol.1, 219 ("...de natuurlijke loop der menschelijke poogingen..."); *Droit naturel*, vol.3, 152.

corruption of manners or with vice.[41]

Having made this basic point, Luzac turned to the analysis of the historical growth of commerce, a subject about which much more could and should be said than about its natural origin in man's desire to live as pleasantly as possible. Although commerce was a natural phenomenon, it was also true that historically it had not been the dominant mode of existence for the majority of states. It could exist in an endless variety of forms, from exchange *in natura* to the highly sophisticated *commerce d'oeconomie*. From its modest beginnings, it had grown "gradually and imperceptibly", with the increase of population constituting one of the more important causes of its expansion.[42] Contrary to his French and Scottish contemporaries, Luzac did not construct a four stages theory of human economic development. He did not clearly distinguish separate hunting, pastoral, agricultural, and commercial stages in the development of society. Instead of chronologically following upon each other, these productive modes could co-exist. History showed no societies altogether without commerce, but also relatively few totally dependent upon it.[43] It could not be doubted, however, that commerce was the highest and most noble form of human economic endeavor. So evident was this to Luzac, that he frequently and without further explanation referred to "polite and commercial nations".[44]

Of the many factors that, besides the growth of population, could stimulate the development of commerce, Luzac first mentioned nature. It was obvious that the inhabitants of a country with a rich soil would be less inclined to engage in trade than those living on poor grounds.[45] In his commentary on Montesquieu, however, Luzac had already expressed his belief that physical causes never played a decisive role in human history. They were also quite subordinate as factors contributing to the expansion of commerce. Of far greater and even decisive importance was the existence of a free and moderate political system. "Nobody is more

---

41. *Droit naturel*, vol.3, 151-154 ("Il est...très naturel, que la voye des échanges de choses contre choses, et contre des travaux, ainsi que de travaux contre des travaux a été celle par laquelle dès le commencement du monde les habitans de la terre ont cherché à se communiquer mutuellement leur aises et à subvenir à leur subsistance et entretien."; "...une communication continuelle de dons réciproques que l'on nomme commerce ou négoce.").

42. *Ibidem*, 156-157 ("...graduellement et d'une manière imperceptible.").

43. On the four-stages theory see Meek, *Social Science and the Ignoble Savage*.

44. E.g. *Hollands rijkdom*, vol.3, 16 ("...eenen beschaafden en handeldrijvenden burgerstaat...").

45. *Ibidem*, 7.

convinced than I am", he repeatedly remarked, "that commerce cannot
exist without Liberty". Liberty, indeed, was the very soul of commerce.[46] Since he realized that liberty belonged to the most overworked
and abused terms in the political vocabulary of his time, Luzac took the
utmost care to establish its meaning properly. With a wealth of references
to his beloved exponents of natural law, from Grotius to Wolff, he
defined liberty in a thoroughly negative way as *independentia ab alterius
voluntate*, a definition implying two things. As far as the internal situation
of a country was concerned, it meant protection against the arbitrary will
of other individuals, or the rule of law. In its second meaning, the
definition stood for safety, or the adequate defense of the state and its inhabitants against foreign intervention and violence.[47] In relation to commerce it was especially liberty in the first of these meanings that was
crucial. Without a regular and independent administration of justice,
security of property and the sanctity of contracts nobody would engage in
trade, a view also expounded in Adam Smith's *Wealth of Nations*.[48] It
was primarily in international trade that liberty in the second sense was
important. If maltreated, the merchants of a commercial state should be
able to rely on the military. Without a well-trained and well-equipped
army and navy to protect and support them, the trade and navigation of
no state would be respected.[49]

There was, however, still a third sense in which liberty should be
understood in its relation to commerce. Free competition, the undisturbed
interplay of the forces of supply and demand, was a fundamental prereq-
uisite for successful commerce. The price of any given commodity was
determined by "a confluence of the desires of all nations".[50] If a government prevented its merchants from acting according to that rule, that is to
say if it made it impossible for them to compete internationally, it
destroyed their existence. Governments, in other words, should abstain
from too much interference with commerce, either directly or indirectly.[51] High taxes, for instance, could be ruinous.[52] All coercion, as

---

46. *Ibidem*, Aan den Leezer ("Niemant is meer dan ik overtuigd, dat de koophandel zonder
Vrijheid niet bestaan kan...").

47. *Ibidem*, 197-216.

48. *Ibidem*, vol.4, 470-471. On Smith's conception of liberty see Forbes, "Sceptical
Whiggism, Commerce, and Liberty".

49. *Ibidem*, 294-295.

50. *Droit naturel*, vol.3, 229 ("...un concours de désirs de toutes les nations...").

51. *Hollands rijkdom*, vol.4, 400-401 and 520-521.

52. E.g. *Nederlandsche Letter-Courant*, vol.1 (1759), 96.

Luzac was fond of observing, was contrary to the nature of commerce.[53] Commerce would flourish, to sum up, if the state protected its citizens with a flawless and orderly system of justice at home, a strong military abroad, and for the rest gave them a maximum of independence and a minimum of rules.

Having treated the political preconditions for the growth of commerce, Luzac proceeded to discuss the advantages of a commercial way of life at great length. Basically, commerce was no more than "the art of meeting the needs of life, and of offering people the objects that can satisfy their wants".[54] It was simply the high road to prosperity and to a pleasant life. Commerce increased the riches of a country and gratified people's varied desires and tastes in all possible ways. Merchants could fittingly be described as "servants...of the Public".[55] Not, Luzac added, because they were motivated by noble sentiments, but because the system of commerce forced them into that role. That the wealth and luxury generated by commerce were the subject of the scorn of so many a moralist was altogether beyond comprehension. Those fulminating against so-called superfluous needs should realize that they were in fact fundamental to the functioning of commercial society and, indeed, to human progress. To oppose this was utterly unrealistic. "As long as people have senses and taste and do not, like savages, approach the state of animals, they will be inclined to splendor and luxury".[56] The condemnation of wealth and luxury was based on nothing but outdated and superfluous prejudice. "The desire for riches is not...a sin, nor is the accumulation of riches a blameworthy act; the same holds for luxury".[57]

Not only did commerce lead to an affluent and civilized national existence, it also greatly improved the relations between nations. The contrast between expansionist military states and peaceful commercial states recurred throughout Luzac's work. It partly coincided with the opposition between ancient and modern. Luzac failed to understand and

---

53. *Hollands rijkdom*, vol.4, 520.

54. *Ibidem*, 248 ("...de kunst, om de behoeften des leevens te vervullen, en den menschen voorwerpen aan te bieden, welken hunne begeerten kunnen voldoen...").

55. *Ibidem*, 433 ("...dienaars...van het Publiek...").

56. *Ibidem*, 52-55 and 243-248. The quotation is on 248 ("Zoo lange de menschen zintuigen en smaak zullen bezitten, en zij niet, gelijk de wilden, bijna tot den staat van redelooze dieren vervallen zullen weezen, zullen zij tot pracht en overdaad geneigd zijn...").

57. *Droit naturel*, vol.1, 225 ("Le désir des richesses n'est...pas un vice, ni le soin d'en acquérir, un acte blamable: le luxe ne l'est...pas d'avantage..."). For the eighteenth-century debate on luxury see Sekora, *Luxury*, 63-131.

emphatically rejected the widespread admiration for the bellicose states of antiquity. It has already been observed how, in his polemics with Rousseau, he drew attention to the fact that Rome's much praised greatness had largely been founded upon aggressive expansion at the expense of neighboring states. Luzac also frequently used the example of Sparta to make the same point. Those extolling the ancient military virtues, he remarked, certainly held curious opinions as to what constituted human happiness. "Is it then in the horrors of carnage and destruction that the happiness of social life and of its participants should be sought?"[58] What lent these observations great urgency was the fact that their relevance was not limited to the contrast between ancient conquest and modern commerce. Luzac was sharply aware of the fact that, although it did now not seem unlikely, the triumph of commerce was still far from certain. Expansionist and militarist absolutism, with Louis XIV's France as the prime recent example, continued to pose a threat to the peaceful existence of the moderate and commercial European states.[59] The superiority of the *voyes douces* of commerce, however, could not be doubted. Commerce kept up an uninterrupted communication between the nations and was incompatible with war, for violence ended all possibility of peaceful exchange.[60] It was therefore the enlightened self-interest of commercial states to abstain from war and to behave in a peaceful way, to the great benefit of mankind as a whole.[61] The matter could, in fact, be summed up in one simple rhetorical question: "Is the idea of forming a bellicose nation, always acting by force and driven by a taste for slaughter, more sublime than the idea of obtaining one's well-being and power by means of industry, frugality, and work?"[62] Or, as that great defender of modern commercial society Benjamin Constant would later put it: "war is impulse, commerce is calculation".[63]

There was yet another advantage to commerce. It transformed human behavior. "Commerce makes people more sociable, or, if you wish, less

---

58. *Lettres sur les dangers*, 108 ("Est-ce donc dans les horreurs du carnage et de la désolation, qu'il faut chercher le bonheur de la vie sociale, et celui des membres qui la composent?").

59. On Louis XIV e.g. *Hollands rijkdom*, vol.4, 332.

60. *Ibidem*, vol.1, 171.

61. *Ibidem*, vol.4, 522-523.

62. *Lettres sur les dangers*, 114-115 ("L'idée de former une nation guerrière, d'agir toujours par la force, d'inspirer du goût pour le carnage, est-elle plus sublime, que celle d'obtenir son bien-être, et sa puissance, par l'industrie, l'économie, et le travail?").

63. Constant, *De la liberté chez les modernes*, 498.

unpredictable, more industrious, more active", Luzac observed in his commentary on Montesquieu.[64] It has been seen that he regarded reason as man's most valuable asset. Yet he realized that strong passions constantly interfered with and even obstructed man's capacity to reason. "Human actions are usually not directed by judgment, but by the passions and affects, which may be depicted as being without ears or eyes, because they simply respond to external impulses".[65] For the great majority of people, reason alone was an insufficient counterbalance to the passions. This was no cause for despair, however, for fortunately the passions could also be tamed and directed towards innocent or even beneficial ends by the operation of the social system. One of the strongest passions, for instance, was the desire to equal and surpass other individuals.[66] It could express itself in many different ways, depending on the organization of society. In military and conquering societies the highest glory consisted of excelling in the *vertus militaires*, and ambition could only be satisfied by fire, steel, and the destruction of countries, that is to say by sacrificing the happiness of other human beings.[67] In commercial societies, on the other hand, competition could take an innocent and even productive form. "Merchants are engaged in a sort of war of industry. He who shows most foresight, acumen, activity, perseverance and skill in this battle will emerge victorious".[68] Commerce, in other words, channelled and transformed the passions into a blessing for humanity.[69]

To many eighteenth-century theorists, one of the central problems posed by the rise of commercial society was that of specialization and the division of labor. Critics of classical republican persuasion viewed these phenomena as incompatible with the existence of a citizenry composed of virtuous and independent political actors and therefore condemned them as disastrous. More revealing, perhaps, is the fact that even many com-

---

64. *Esprit des loix*, vol.2, 228 (book XX, chapter 1) ("Le commerce rend les hommes plus sociables, ou, si l'on veut, moins farouches, plus industrieux, plus actifs...").

65. *Droit naturel*, vol.3, 121-122 ("Ce n'est pas ordinairement le jugement qui dirige les actions humaines; mais les passions et les affections; qu'on pourroit dépeindre sans oreilles et sans yeux, parce qu'elles ne suivent que les impulsions qui leur viennent du déhors.").

66. *Ibidem*, vol.1, 211-213.

67. *Ibidem*, vol.3, 216.

68. *Ibidem*, 207 ("Les Négocians font une espèce de guerre d'industrie l'un contre l'autre: c'est à celui, qui aura mis le plus de prévoyance, de pénétration, d'activité, d'assiduité et d'adresse dans ce combat, que la palme réviendra.").

69. On this theme see Hirschman, *The Passions and the Interests* and Lerner, *Thinking Revolutionary*, 195-221.

mitted modernists were aware that the rise of commercial society was
attended by a certain narrowing of the human personality, as no reader of
Adam Smith can doubt.[70] Luzac identified the problem, discussed it at
length, and arrived at the conclusion that it was no cause for great concern. He was, as we have seen, convinced that commercial society
transformed human behavior and made people less savage and more industrious. It also made them less courageous, more insistent upon strict
justice, and less charitable.[71] All this, Luzac repeatedly observed, was
quite evident from the behavior of merchants, a subject he found highly
fascinating.

Merchants, in a way, were the heroes of the unheroic modern age. If
"utility and the good of society" were the criteria to judge a profession
by, it was hard to think of a more respectable one than that of merchant.[72] The successful merchant had to be a man of amazing skills.
Only by mastering an infinite variety of complicated data could he arrive
at the right decisions. "He needs genius. His mind must always follow
potential merchandise in an observant and active manner. He must be able
to take all relevant circumstances into account and to apply the principles
of his business to them".[73] Aided by these skills, merchants relieved
sellers of their superfluous products and took them to desirous buyers, if
necessary at the other end of the globe. They provided "ease of circulation" and thereby greatly contributed to the general welfare. Merchants, in short, were the essential cogs in the complicated machine of
commerce.[74] This, however, at the same time implied the existence of
clear limits to their behavior. Merchants were, of necessity, slaves to the
capricious tastes of the public and their lives were dominated by the
requirements of the market. Structurally, they were forced to strive after
profit. If they failed to do so, they would ruin themselves. This clearly
had consequences for the role merchants could be expected to play in
society. Their outlook was highly individualistic and essentially limited.
"The system of the merchant frequently comes down to this principle:
everyone works for himself, as I work for myself; I ask you nothing

70. E.g. Smith, *Wealth of Nations*, vol.2, 781-784. A good discussion of Smith's at times
somewhat ambivalent modernity is Winch, *Adam Smith's Politics*.

71. *Esprit des loix*, vol.2, 228 (book XX, chapter 1).

72. *Droit naturel*, vol.3, 212 ("...l'utilité et le bien que la société en rétire...").

73. *Ibidem*, 199 ("Il lui faut du génie, et un esprit toujours attentif et actif par rapport aux
objets; il faut qu'il en sache calculer les circonstances et y appliquer les principes sur
lesquels il doit régler ses opérations.").

74. *Ibidem*, 199-218. The quotation is on 211 ("...l'aisance dans la circulation...").

without offering its value; do the same".[75] The whole of a merchant's attention was engrossed by his trade. He could by definition not make the general interest the object of his attention or activity. "The aim of commerce is profit: whoever wants a merchant to act from love of country..., benevolence, or any other moral principle, expects him to act against the fundamental principles of his trade; one might as well ask an architect to erect his structures on quicksand".[76]

Merchant behavior, in short, demonstrated in the extreme the general truth that commercial society entailed specialization and a certain narrowing of the human personality. The same mechanism could be observed in many other areas, for instance in military affairs. In ancient times, Luzac pointed out, all citizens had been warriors in defense of their country. Modern commercial man, constantly engaged in his highly specialized occupation, was no longer able to perform the same role. This, however, was far from disastrous, since the flow of riches generated by trade enabled a commercial state to keep up a standing army and a strong navy. In the modern world, the richest state was also the strongest and most powerful one. Defense had simply become a specialism, best left to trained experts.[77] Commercial society was thus, in Luzac's view, composed of specialists, whether they be merchants, manufacturers,

---

75. *Esprit des loix*, vol.2, 228 (book XX, chapter 1) ("Le systême du commerçant se réduit souvent à ce principe: que chacun travaille pour soi, comme je travaille pour moi; je ne vous demande rien qu'en vous offrant la valeur; faites en autant."). It is worth noting that Dirk Hoola van Nooten, who translated both Montesquieu and Luzac's commentary into Dutch at the end of the century, was outraged by Luzac's disenchanted evaluation of merchant behavior. If it were correct, he remarked, "than a merchant would make a truly despicable citizen." ("... dan zou een koopman waarlijk een veragtelijk burger zijn.") *Geest der Wetten*, vol.2, 336.

76. *Hollands rijkdom*, vol.4, 432 ("Het doelwit des koophandels is winst: indien men wil, dat een koopman zich in de zaaken zijns koophandels gedraage uit liefde tot het vaderland..., weldaadigheid, of eenig ander zedelijk grondbeginsel, dan begeert men iet, dat tegen den grond, op welken den koophandel gebouwd is, en staan moet, aanloopt; het zoude even zoo veel zijn als of men begeerde, dat een bouwmeester, om deze of gene reden, een gebouw zoude aanleggen op grondslagen, welke hetzelve niet kunnen draagen.").

77. *Hollands rijkdom*, vol.1, 6 and vol.4, 325. Adam Smith, in his *Lectures on Jurisprudence* (541), was rather less sanguine on this issue: "Our ancestors were brave and warlike, their minds were not enervated by cultivating arts and commerce, and they were all ready with spirit and vigor to resist the most formidable foe". This, however, was now no longer the case, as was particularly evident in the Dutch Republic: "Holland, were its barriers removed, would be an easy prey. In the beginning of this century the standing army of the Dutch was beat in the field, and the rest of the inhabitants, instead of rising in arms to defend themselves, formed a design of deserting their country and settling in the East Indies... These are the disadvantages of a commercial spirit."

soldiers, or scholars. They all, in their own way and in their own social station, contributed to the common good, regardless of their personal motivation.[78] But they had neither the time, nor the inclination, nor - given their essentially limited outlook - the capacity to make the general interest of the state the sole object of their attention or effort.

The single-minded promotion of the general interest, then, was the task left for the political administrators of the commercial state. Although clearly of a limited nature, it was, Luzac maintained, of crucial importance. Nothing about all this, Luzac repeatedly emphasized, was inherently wrong, let alone dangerous. On the contrary, the existence of industrious and specialized modern man was, on the whole, greatly to be preferred to the primitive life of the ancient citizen-soldier. Luzac's works abounded in passages exalting the happiness to be found in apolitical pursuits such as the acquisition of goods, the cultivation of the mind and a pleasant social life. His was a world of hard-working and economically successful *burgers*, perfectly satisfied with their station in society, and enjoying a happy private life of familial bliss, quiet conversation, and material well-being. To the very end of his life he kept insisting that the negative liberty to be enjoyed in the non-participatory commercial state was in no way inferior to the classical ideal of active and politically virtuous citizenship. The very opposite, indeed, was true. "I do not desire that kind of liberty. I prefer a government that gives me the opportunity to enjoy the fruits of my industry in the bosom of my family. I leave it to those dissatisfied with such prosperity to call it slavery".[79]

Having enumerated the various advantages of a commercial way of life, Luzac proceeded to expound his views on historiography. The importance of historical knowledge, he was convinced, was hard to overrate. History could teach invaluable lessons and was indispensable to the education of the young.[80] Given this essential role, it was truly remarkable how inadequate much of existing historiography remained. All serious historical writing, Luzac insisted, should find its basis in an intimate knowledge of the sources.[81] The contempt displayed by many *philosophes* for the erudition and painstaking scholarship of the great

---

78. *Droit naturel*, vol.3, 211-212.

79. *Lettres sur les dangers*, 47 ("Pour moi...je ne veux point de cette liberté; je préfère un gouvernement, qui me donne la faculté de jouïr dans le sein de ma famille de mon industrie, et de mon labeur. Je laisse à ceux, qui ne peuvent s'accomoder de cette aisance, le plaisir de la nommer esclavage.").

80. E.g. *Nederlandsche Letter-Courant*, vol.1 (1759), 379-380; *Lettres sur les dangers*, 7-8.

81. *Nederlandsche Letter-Courant*, vol.3 (1760), 130.

seventeenth-century *savants* was not only unfounded, but also disastrous, for it resulted in admittedly elegant, but wholly inaccurate accounts of the past. "Voltaire is an elegant author, but one would be quite wrong to consult him for factual information", Luzac observed.[82] Yet he was the first to admit that a satisfactory historiography entailed more than the accumulation and subsequent narrative rendering of bare facts.[83] It had to penetrate below the surface of events. It had to trace and explain causes. It had, indeed, to be philosophical. This should, he emphasized, not be taken to mean that it was the historian's task to bore his readers with all kinds of gratuitous moral and political judgments.[84] What it meant was that the historian should devote his attention to the fundamentally important aspects of human history. It was exactly in this respect, Luzac contended, that much of eighteenth-century historiography, still classical in inspiration, was flawed. The overwhelming majority of historians remained obsessed with political events and wars, while neglecting the true sources of power, prosperity, and happiness.

An excellent example of such flawed historiography was Jan Wagenaar's *Vaderlandsche historie*.[85] Luzac criticized this enormously popular work on many grounds. He strongly disapproved of Wagenaar's political orientation and accused him, not altogether without foundation, of being a hack writer in the service of the regents.[86] He blamed him for being careless with his sources and unaware of many an anachronism in his interpretation of Dutch history.[87] Yet Wagenaar's gravest short-

---

82. *Lettres sur les dangers*, 207 ("Voltaire est un élégant Auteur, mais on auroit tort de s'en rapporter à lui pour la véracité des faits."). See also *Nederlandsche Letter-Courant*, vol.1 (1759), 253. On the *philosophes* and historical erudition see Gay, *Enlightenment*, vol.2, 372-379.

83. *Nederlandsche Letter-Courant*, vol.5 (1761), 5.

84. *Ibidem*, vol.6 (1761) 283.

85. (21 vols., 1749-1759). On Wagenaar see Castendijk, *Jan Wagenaar* and Wessels, "Jan Wagenaar (1709-1773)".

86. The two pamphlets (*Zugt* and *Oordeel*) Luzac wrote in 1757 as part of the so-called *Wittenoorlog* were specifically intended to refute Wagenaar's interpretation of the first Stadholderless era and, more in general, to expose the weaknesses in his glorification of True Liberty. On the *Wittenoorlog* see P. Geyl, "De Witten-oorlog, een pennestrijd in 1757" in: Geyl, *Pennestrijd over Staat en Historie*, 130-273 and Leeb, *Ideological Origins*, 86-96. Luzac also wrote a lengthy and devastating review of Wagenaar's history of Amsterdam: *Nederlandsche Letter-Courant*, vol.5 (1761), 235-240; vol.8 (1762), 70-72; vol.9 (1763), 228-231, 235-238, 244-246, 253-254, 261-262, 269-270, 276-278, 284-286, 292-294, 299-302. On Wagenaar as a hack writer see *Ibidem*, vol.5 (1761), 235-237.

87. On inaccuracy e.g. *Zugt*, 209-215 and *Hollands rijkdom*, vol.1, 84, note a; on anachronism e.g. *Oordeel*, 124, note h and Moreau, *Pligten der overheden*, 376-378.

coming in Luzac's eyes was his failure to pay attention to the central elements in the history of the Dutch Republic: commerce, navigation, and wealth.[88] *Holland's wealth* was, among other things, intended as a corrective to Wagenaar's imperfect but influential chronicle. Fortunately, Luzac pointed out, his was not an isolated plea for a transformation of historiography. Growing numbers of modern writers, David Hume and "the excellent historian" William Robertson among them, were now attempting to create a new kind of history, in which commerce and prosperity were considered to be as important as political events and military affairs.[89] "In recent years", Luzac observed with evident satisfaction, "people have begun to write a different kind of history. It is no longer considered beneath the dignity of the human mind to know how countries became populated, how civil societies arose and developed. This new history has established that civil society owes more to industry and diligence in the arts, commerce, and navigation, than to the devastating art of war; and that, where the latter is needed for the protection of country and people, it is only the former that can assure a happy and pleasant life".[90]

One of the most persistent myths this inspiring new historiography should be able to dispel, Luzac finally remarked, was that concerning the brief life span of commercial states. In his *Considérations sur les causes de la grandeur des Romains et de leur décadence*, Montesquieu had contended that the grandeur of commercial states could only be of brief duration.[91] Rousseau had voiced a very similar opinion in his *Contrat social*. He had, it is true, advised those living on suitable and extended shores to cover the sea with vessels and to expand their commerce and navigation, but he had added: "you will have a brilliant if short exis-

---

88. *Hollands rijkdom*, vol.1, 147 and vol.4, 538-540.

89. On Hume: *Nederlandsche Letter-Courant*, vol.1 (1759), 330 and *Hollands rijkdom*, vol.4, 539; on Robertson: *Ibidem*, 26 ("...de voortreffelijke Historieschrijver Robertson...").

90. *Hollands rijkdom*, vol.1, 146-147 ("Sedert eenige jaaren...heeft men begonnen de historiekunde op eenen anderen voet te behandelen, en te denken, dat het niet beneden de waardigheid van 't menschlijk vernuft was eenigermaate te weeten, hoe de landen zijn bevolkt geraakt, de burgerstaaten opgekomen, en tot eene zekere grootheid geklommen. In die beschouwing heeft men opgemerkt, dat men het welweezen van eenen Burgerstaat meer aan den ijver, de vlijt en de naarstigheid, in 't oeffenen van kunsten, koophandel en vaart, te danken heeft, dan aan de vernielende oorlogskunde; en dat, deeze noodig zijnde ter bescherminge van land en volk, het andere alleen in staat is om de landzaaten een gelukkig en genoeglijk leeven te doen genieten."). Cf. *Lettres sur les dangers*, 192-193.

91. Montesquieu, *Oeuvres complètes*, vol.2, 87.

tence".[92] Luzac energetically attacked these in his opinion completely unfounded views in *Holland's wealth*.[93] There was, he insisted, no intrinsic reason why in the long run commerce should lead to the decline of states. It was indeed impossible to think of one single state ruined by its commerce. As history both ancient and modern amply demonstrated, the decline and fall of states was invariably brought about by political and moral causes. Carthage's tragic end had not, as Montesquieu mistakenly held, been caused by the overextension of its commerce, but by bad government.[94] Similarly, the problems confronting the eighteenth-century Dutch Republic were not to be interpreted as signs of the inevitable fate of commercial states. This, obviously, was a point of great importance. It was, to put it more strongly, the basis of Luzac's firm conviction that the problems of the Dutch could be remedied.

3. *The Dutch Experience*

Luzac's favorite example of a commercial state was, unsurprisingly, the Dutch Republic at the seventeenth-century height of its powers. That state, with its liberty, industrious populace, peaceful international aspirations, and remarkable wealth, had offered "the most attractive tableau that can be presented to the view of a sage".[95] It had, indeed, been of enormous historical significance, in that its commercial power had driven many surrounding nations to emulate its success, "so that nowadays it is the volume of commerce which decides the power of a nation".[96] Clearly, the history of Dutch commerce was a subject that deserved to be treated in detail. Such a treatment was, in fact, of great urgency, since Dutch commercial prominence was evidently threatened. The only way to reverse this trend, Luzac was convinced, was to expose the true causes of the commercial rise and decline of the Dutch. These causes, he insisted, were primarily of a political nature and had long been obscured by the rhetoric of the adherents of True Liberty. Once they were identified, a return to prosperity would be a relatively simple matter.

Luzac started his story with the observation that the watery estuary the

---

92. Rousseau, *Oeuvres complètes*, vol.3, 392.

93. *Hollands rijkdom*, vol.4, 315-352.

94. *Ibidem*, 316-317.

95. *Lettres sur les dangers*, 114 ("...le tableau le plus attrayant, que l'on puisse exposer à la vuë du Sage.").

96. *Ibidem* ("...de façon que c'est aujourd'hui le plus ou moins de commerce, qui décide de la puissance d'une Nation.").

earliest inhabitants of the Low Countries had dwelled in had evidently been unsuited for agriculture. This natural poverty, he remarked, was an important key to much of subsequent Dutch history. It had been a blessing in disguise, for not only had it greatly contributed to the formation of Dutch character traits such as frugality and industriousness, it had also forced the Dutch to engage in commerce and navigation from the very beginning of their history.[97] In Dutch history commerce, although it had greatly expanded over the centuries, had always been of fundamental importance. So, Luzac added, had liberty. Commerce and liberty, indeed, were two of the most significant threads of continuity in the existence of the Dutch. This contention, simple as it sounded, was heavy with political implications and polemical intentions. It was, in fact, specifically intended to administer the death blow to the already ailing ideology of True Liberty. In the course of the eighteenth century one of the main props supporting that ideology had been swept away by historical research: the theory that the States-assemblies had been sovereign since time immemorial, later to become known as the Batavian myth. In his influential *Deduction*, written as early as 1587, François Vranck had contended that the sovereignty of Holland's States-assembly could be dated back eight hundred years.[98] Grotius, in his *De antiquitate reipublicae Bataviae* (1610), even saw it going back to the time of the Batavians.[99] These views had not been entirely uncontested in the seventeenth century, but it was only in the eighteenth century that historians and antiquarians systematically began to show from the documents how untenable a position this was.[100] Starting with the writings of Simon van Slingelandt (1664-1736) early in the century, this process culminated in the work of Adriaan Kluit (1735-1807).[101]

Luzac, who eagerly used this new research, clearly recognized that it left the *Loevesteiners* or *Staatsgezinden* a way of escape. For the adherents of True Liberty, while acknowledging the indisputable collapse of their ancient constitutionalism, could still reverse their argument and

---

97. *Hollands rijkdom*, vol.3, 7-10.

98. The *Deduction* can be found translated into English in Kossmann and Mellink, ed. *Texts concerning the Revolt of the Netherlands*, 274-281.

99. Kossmann, *Politieke Theorie*, 11-12.

100. On the seventeenth century see Kampinga, *Opvattingen over onze oudere vaderlandsche geschiedenis*, and Schöffer, "Batavian Myth".

101. On the first half of the eighteenth century see Haitsma Mulier, "'Hoofsche papegaaien'"; on Kluit see Boutelje, *Bijdrage tot de kennis van Kluit's opvattingen*; Hugenholtz, "Adriaan Kluit"; Schöffer, "Adriaan Kluit".

claim that freedom and prosperity had only emerged after the Dutch Revolt and mainly as a result of the particular brand of republicanism they favored. If, however, it could be shown that the Dutch, long before the Revolt and the establishment of a republican form of government, had been both free and prosperous, the adherents of True Liberty would have no case left. Their parochial republicanism would definitively be exploded. It was therefore no wonder that Luzac provided exhaustive descriptions of the growth of Dutch commerce before the second half of the sixteenth century, supporting his narrative with a wealth of source material.[102] It was also perfectly understandable that he dwelled on the clear marks of liberty to be found before the Revolt.[103] At no time in their early history, Luzac emphasized, had the Dutch been governed by an arbitrary ruler. The Frankish conquerors, it is true, had possessed extensive powers, yet the very nature of the feudal system had prevented them from dealing arbitrarily with their vassals and subjects. The Counts that filled the void created by the disintegration of Frankish power had from the very start been less than absolute in their sovereignty, since their power remained limited by the original nature of their office. They had furthermore voluntarily bridled themselves by granting a great variety of irrevocable privileges. The medieval Dutch had therefore enjoyed a very substantial measure of civil liberty. Their property was safe, they could not be taxed without their consent, a regular system of justice based on the *ius de non evocando* guaranteed their personal security, and they were protected from foreign attacks.[104]

These circumstances in themselves had greatly contributed to the growth of commerce, but the medieval Counts had also diligently promoted it by means of an active policy of toll-freedoms, tax-exemptions, and foreign treaties.[105] By the late fifteenth century the Low Countries had become a territory both wealthy and free, the staple market for much of Europe. Briefly but rudely interrupted by the despotism of Philip II, this liberty and prosperity had returned after the Revolt, to the satisfaction of all. Indeed, it had not been until the middle of the seventeenth century, Luzac at this point added, that a number of misguided Dutchmen began to imagine that liberty consisted of being ruled by a government without a head and, even worse, began to act upon that conviction.[106] It was, to

102. *Hollands rijkdom*, vol.1, 1-231.

103. *Ibidem*, vol.3, 216-260.

104. *Ibidem*, 253-255.

105. *Ibidem*, 33-61.

106. *Ibidem*, 260.

say the least, remarkable that Dutch commercial decline seemed to have started at roughly the same time.

That the commerce and navigation of the Dutch had considerably declined since the seventeenth century was a conviction that Luzac shared with most of his contemporaries. Where he disagreed with many of them was in the analysis of what had caused this decline. The debate on the subject, Luzac insisted, was to a large extent dominated by prejudice. We have already noted how he contemptuously dismissed the view that the downfall of successful commercial states was inevitable. Not only, he claimed, was there no particular valid reason to suppose that commercial states were short-lived, there were also no grounds for the widespread belief that all states had a limited life span. Such cyclical pessimism, he held, was based on a flawed analogy between the state and the human body. That all human beings had to die sooner or later was a simple biological law, but there was nothing in the nature of a state or civil society "that *necessarily* or *inevitably* has to bring it down; it is therefore my opinion that a civil society, however far advanced its decline may be, can always be revived and restored to its former prosperity, or be given a new life".[107]

Then there was the theory that the decline of Dutch commerce was the inevitable result of the growing strength of foreign competition. Luzac did not altogether deny the importance of this factor. The emulation of Dutch commercial success had meant an increase in the total number of European merchants and a threat to the Dutch staple market.[108] England and France, moreover, had in the second half of the seventeenth century started to pursue aggressive protectionist policies, to the detriment of Dutch commerce and navigation.[109] Yet in the final analysis this growing competition was but a weak excuse for Dutch commercial decline. To blame the outside world, Luzac observed, was always the easiest solution At no point in time had there been a lack of competitors. The real question therefore was why, contrary to former times, the Dutch were now apparently no longer able to beat them.[110] That, as many a contem-

---

107. *Ibidem*, vol.4, 4 ("...daar niets in den aart van eenen burgerstaat te vinden is, dat dien *noodzaakelijk* of *onvermijdelijk* ten verderve of tot een ondergang moet brengen: waarom het mij dan voorkomt, dat, tot welk verval een burgerstaat geraakt moge zijn, 'er altoos mogelijkheid en kans is, om dien op te beuren, en tot eenen voorigen welstand te brengen, of, wil men liefst, om dien een ander, en als 't ware een nieuw leven, te geeven.").

108. *Ibidem*, 108-111.

109. *Ibidem*, 235-242.

110. *Ibidem*, 11-52.

porary commentator claimed, the debilitating effects of luxury constituted a sufficient answer was strongly gainsaid by Luzac. While he did not deny that under certain specific circumstances luxury might be harmful, on the whole it was to be regarded as a great boon to commerce. It could even be said, as we have seen, to belong to the very essence of commercial society.[111]

It was neither inevitable decline, nor increased competition, nor the growth of luxury, but the unfortunate development of the relationship between polity and economy that, according to Luzac, was at the heart of the problems of the Dutch. All of history demonstrated "that commerce has flourished in countries to the extent that governments have followed the basic rules and principles favoring commerce and navigation".[112] The most fundamental of those rules, Luzac had already observed, was that commerce had to be free. This, indeed, was particularly true for the Dutch Republic. "A wise statecraft adapts itself to the character of the nation. The character of Holland is dominated not only by a desire for commerce, but by a desire for *free* commerce".[113] Unfortunately, however, ever since the Dutch Revolt governments had increased in- and export duties, excises, and other taxes, a development resulting in a constant raising of the cost of commerce, and therefore, given the laws of competition, ultimately in its decline.[114] This process, Luzac maintained while carrying his polemic with the system of True Liberty yet another step further, had been particularly evident during the two Stadholderless periods.

A Stadholderless era inevitably meant a loss of both internal unity and stability and of international prestige, with war as a consequence. War in itself, as we have seen, was directly harmful to commerce and navigation, but it also had a long-term crippling effect on these activities by necessitating further financial impositions. It was especially the first Stadholderless period, with its three economically disastrous wars with England and its inglorious demise amidst an invasion by the troops of Louis XIV, that had been ruinous to Dutch commerce. Luzac discussed

---

111. *Ibidem*, 52-55.

112. *Ibidem*, vol.1, xviii ("...dat de koophandel in onderscheiden landen heeft gebloeid, naar maate dat de regeering de grondregels en grondbeginsels, die den handel en de scheepvaart begunstigen, heeft aangenomen en gevolgd.").

113. *Staatsbeschouwers*, vol.3, 668 ("Een wyze Staatkunde schikt zich naar het caracter van de Natie. Handelzucht niet alleen, maar zucht tot *vryen* handel maakt in dit opzicht het caracter van de Hollandsche Natie uit.").

114. *Hollands rijkdom*, vol.4, 55-133.

its horrors at length in his two 1757 pamphlets dealing with the merits, or rather the lack thereof, of that hero in the pantheon of True Liberty, John de Witt. It was deeply regrettable that no lesson had apparently been learned from that disastrous episode, for after William III had restored security, stability, and prosperity at great cost, the same cycle had started again. The second Stadholderless period had shown nothing but corrupt, unchecked family government by the regent oligarchy, with a loss of unity and military strength, high taxation, and a further decline of commerce and navigation as a result. Unsurprisingly, this era had once more ended in war and French invasion.[115] From all this, Luzac remarked, it was abundantly clear that "the more one attentively studies the history of our state, the more one is forced to the conclusion that its power and prosperity are inextricably linked with the Stadholderly government".[116]

It could not reasonably be doubted, Luzac was convinced, that a crucial precondition for the renewed flourishing of Dutch commerce had been met with by the restoration of the Stadholderate in 1747. There had, he pointed out, indeed been substantial improvement since that time. The utterly corrupt system of tax farming had, for instance, been replaced by a more efficient mode of tax collection.[117] William IV and his advisers, moreover, had pointed the way to the full recovery of Dutch commerce in their admirable 1751 *Proposition for a limited porto-franco*.[118] Yet despite these hopeful signs, Luzac was forced to admit, it was evident that even after several decades of Stadholderly government the Dutch had not yet succeeded in fully regaining their former economic position. There were several factors, he pointed out, that contributed to this continued economic stagnation. First of all, it was very hard to win back commerce once it had been lost. "Commerce may well be compared to a river giving itself a new bed. A river's first deviations from its regular course are almost unnoticeable, but once the new bed has been formed, it is very difficult to bring the stream back to its old course".[119]

115. *Vryaart*, vol.4, part 12, 1-92.

116. *Hollands rijkdom*, vol.3, 173 ("Hoe meer men de geschiedenis van onzen Staat met opmerkzaamheid doorleest, hoe meer men overtuigd moet zijn, dat deszelfs magt en welvaaren aan de stadhouderlijke regeering verknocht zijn...").

117. *Ibidem*, vol.4, 388.

118. Luzac frequently used the *Proposition* throughout *Holland's wealth*.

119. *Hollands rijkdom*, vol.4, 121-122 ("Men kan den koophandel beschouwen als eene rivier, die zich een nieuw bed maakt. Haare eerste afwijkingen zijn bijna niet bemerkelijk; doch als zij eens een nieuw bed heeft gemaakt, is het zeer moeielijk haar op haaren ouden loop te brengen.").

Secondly, there was the alarming emergence of what might be termed a post-commercial mentality. When writing his commentary on Montesquieu's *Esprit des lois*, Luzac had already been deeply impressed by the President's shrewd observations on the potential dangers threatening the "spirit of commerce". A commercial republic, Montesquieu had remarked, would never, even with individuals amassing great private fortunes, be seriously endangered as long as the spirit of commerce, ingraining the habits of frugality, moderation, and industry, continued to reign. For that spirit to survive, he had added, it was necessary that, among other things, the most important citizens themselves remained engaged in active commerce, that all laws favored commerce, and that no other spirit was allowed to challenge the spirit of commerce.[120] Luzac could not have agreed more and was consequently greatly alarmed by the changes he observed in contemporary Dutch values. Commercial society could only function, he believed, if commerce was generally perceived as the most important battle ground for competing ambitions. "Competition in business" was, it has been noted, at the very heart of commercial society and merchants should preferably think of nothing else.[121] "The merchant should have no other aim than to increase his funds for another and greater transaction".[122] When, for whatever reason, ambition became primarily focused on other activities than commerce a trading nation was in deep trouble.

This, Luzac observed, was precisely what threatened to happen in the Dutch Republic. Increasingly, the desire to excel in commercial affairs was being replaced by "a competition in status".[123] Social status, nowadays expressing itself in contempt for hard and honest work, in conspicuous consumption, and in frivolous Frenchified cultural tastes, was coming to be looked upon as more important than anything else. Commerce was beginning to be seen as no more than a quick way to get rich, as an activity to be abandoned for something more elevated at the first possible moment.[124] It was a development very ably satirized, Luzac pointed out, in Pieter Langendijk's excellent play *Mirror of fatherlands*

---

120. Montesquieu, *Oeuvres complètes*, vol.2, 280 (book V, chapter 6).

121. *Esprit des loix*, vol.1, 84 (book V, chapter 6) ("...l'émulation de se surpasser en affaires.").

122. *Ibidem*, vol.2, 249 (book XX, chapter 22) ("Le négociant ne doit avoir d'autre émulation que celle d'augmenter ses fonds pour faire une plus grande négoce.").

123. *Ibidem*, vol.1, 84 (book V, chapter 6) ("...une émulation de se surpasser en condition.").

124. E.g. *Vryaart*, vol.1, part 3, 18-34.

merchants.[125] It was imperative that this potentially ruinous change in mentality be reversed before it infected several generations. Such a reversal, Luzac was confident, would in the long run be brought about by completely freeing commerce from the unnecessary impositions accumulated and thereby allowing it to regain its status as the most essential component in the Dutch way of life.

Unfortunately, however, there was a third obstacle to commercial regeneration. Impatience with prolonged economic stagnation was beginning to lead a growing number of people to question the long-standing consensus that commerce was and ought to be the main pillar of Dutch prosperity. This trend was particularly evident in the Economic Branch, a new section of the Holland Society of Sciences, founded in 1777 as a result of the debates generated by the 1771 essay competition on the Dutch economy. A significant group of members of the Economic Branch was convinced that the Dutch staple market definitively belonged to the past. The course to follow, these so-called Economic Patriots argued, was one of economic reorientation and diversification. They pleaded for an increased emphasis on domestic agricultural and industrial production, preferably behind protectionist barriers. The Economic Patriots also urged Dutch citizens to consume domestic products, demanded sumptuary laws, and in general adopted a highly moralistic tone.[126]

To Luzac, unsurprisingly, these suggestions, however well intended, seemed utterly unrealistic and completely contrary to the nature of Dutch history and society. The Dutch would never, he emphasized, regain their preeminence by artificially closing themselves off from the international market. It was in international commerce that they had always excelled and the only possible route to the restoration of their former glory was through the removal, not the imposition of limitations on free trade.[127] "Keep too tight a rein on liberty in a commercial country and you will destroy the source of the wealth and power of a people".[128] The choice, indeed, was relatively simple. It was a choice between facing open

---

125. Luzac reviewed Langendijk's *Spiegel der vaderlandsche kooplieden* in the *Nederlandsche Letter-Courant*, vol.2 (1759), 366-374.

126. Bierens de Haan, *Oeconomische Tak*, 1-76; De Vries, "Oeconomisch-Patriottische Beweging"; Hovy, *Voorstel van 1751*, 638-640; Leeb, *Ideological Origins*, 109-110; Mijnhardt, *Tot Heil van 't Menschdom*, 109-110.

127. *Hollands rijkdom*, vol.4, 520-521.

128. Wolff, *Institutions*, vol.2, §1021, note o ("Mettez un frein trop sensible à la liberté dans un pays de commerce, vous détruisez la source des richesses et de la puissance d'un peuple.").

competition on the world market and declining into economic insignificance on a tiny and infertile territory. There was, Luzac kept repeating, no reason for despair about the commercial future of the Dutch Republic. It was, after all, still true that no European country was as advantageously located for international trade or possessed as much money. No other country, moreover, knew such freedom or such security under the law. No country, finally and most importantly, had such an excellent form of government.[129] That so many people still failed to recognize this last point was, Luzac held, the fourth and final remaining obstacle blocking the restoration of Dutch greatness. The ruinous precepts of True Liberty, it seemed, still exercised their baleful influence over the mind and behavior of many a Dutchman. In an attempt to dispel their power forever, Luzac wrote longer and more eloquent treatises legitimating the Stadholderate than any of his contemporaries.

4. The Soul of Government

In 1747, after almost half a century of True Liberty in the Dutch Republic's most important provinces, the Stadholderate had once again been restored. In the first waves of enthusiasm and optimism, the institution was even declared hereditary in both the male and female line. During the late Spring and early Summer of 1747, William IV triumphantly toured the country. On June 29, he visited Leiden, where elaborate preparations had been made for his arrival. Triumphal arches had been erected and the whole inner city had been illuminated. On the day of the visit, church bells rang, cannons were fired, and the streets were packed with crowds shouting "Vivat Orange". After a meeting with the city government, William was taken to the university, the seat of learning his ancestors had helped to found. There, professor Tiberius Hemsterhuis, Luzac's preceptor in history, publicly and lengthily lauded him as the savior of the Fatherland. Late that evening the Prince and his wife, Anna of Hannover, attended a magnificent display of fireworks prepared in their honor by the students of the university.[130] It was in short a happy and festive occasion and one of which the young Luzac, then about to launch his career as a publicist, heartily approved. He was, and would always remain, a warm supporter of the Orange Stadholderate.

It is indeed no exaggeration to say that Luzac was the most eminent, innovative and prolific Orangist political theorist of the final decades of

---

129. *Hollands rijkdom*, vol.4, 525.

130. *Nederlands wonder-toneel*, vol.1, 133-140.

the Dutch *ancien régime*. The actual position of the Stadholder in the Dutch Republic was based on an ill-defined assembly of special rights, privileges, usurpations, and informal influence.[131] The Stadholderate in fact was, it has recently been remarked, an improvisation that lasted more than two centuries.[132] It is therefore perhaps understandable that until well into the eighteenth century, as E.H. Kossmann has observed, no comprehensive and adequate Orangist political theory had been developed.[133] There had, of course, never been a shortage of defenders of the Orange Stadholderate. This institution had, for instance, always found and in the eighteenth century continued to find large numbers of adherents among Dutch reformed ministers, who regarded the Stadholders as instruments of God's providence and as the protectors of true religion.[134] Given his intellectual outlook, it is unsurprising that Luzac distanced himself from this primarily religious mode of Orangism. He was, however, clearly also less than satisfied with the existing secular defenses of the Stadholderate. Whereas in his attacks on True Liberty he regularly referred to important seventeenth- and eighteenth-century authors of that persuasion such as the brothers De la Court and Lieven de Beaufort (1675-1730), he seldomly invoked the older Orangist literature.[135] A modern defense of the Stadholderate, Luzac was convinced, was urgently needed. It should, first of all, establish beyond doubt that the restoration of the Stadholderate during the revolution of 1747 had been perfectly legitimate. Secondly, and even more importantly, it should exhaustively explain how indispensable an institution the Stadholderate was in Dutch politics.

It was the former issue that Luzac first addressed. In 1754, he began his career as a commentator on Dutch political matters with what would always remain his most radical political pamphlet: *The conduct of the*

131. For an exhaustive account of the post-1747 Stadholderate see A.J.C.M. Gabriëls's recent *Heren als Dienaren*. This extremely Namierite work is remarkable for its detailed scholarship, but even more for its almost total neglect of contemporary discussions of the Stadholderate, thereby implicitly grossly underestimating their significance.

132. Rowen, *Princes of Orange*, IX.

133. Kossmann, *Low Countries*, 40.

134. For the eighteenth century see Huisman, *Neerlands Israel*.

135. De Beaufort was the author of the posthumously published classical republican *Verhandeling van de vryheit in den burgerstaet* (1737). See Haitsma Mulier, "Controversial republican", 258-259 and Velema, "God, de deugd en de oude constitutie", 478-485.

Stadholder's party defended.[136] The pamphlet was occasioned by the campaign against the former *Doelisten* leader Daniel Raap and was intended to justify the restoration of the Stadholderate in 1747.[137] The main theoretical argument Luzac used to support his case was the existence of a popular right of resistance to unjust authority. As his motto he took a quotation from the last paragraph of John Locke's *Second Treatise of Government*, in which it is stated that when the supreme power is forfeited by miscarriages of those in authority, it then "*reverts to the society, and the people have a right to act as supreme, and continue the legislative in themselves, or erect a new form, or under the old form place it in new hands, as they think good*".[138] Luzac adopted the following line of argument. The fundamental and God-given law, the foundation of all human duties, is the rule that man should promote his own and his fellow man's well-being as much as he can. From this a second rule follows, namely that every man should contribute as much as he can to the well-being of the civil society he belongs to. The promotion of the general well-being has been entrusted to governments, but it is inconceivable that this absolves the people from their duty to adhere to God's first law. If governments therefore violate that law, resistance by the people as "original and rightful rulers of themselves" is entirely justified.[139] As Locke had done, Luzac assured his readers that such a situation would seldom occur.[140] He then proceeded to show that Stadholderless governments ruined the country or, as he would put it in 1757, "destroy civil society", and that in 1747 the very survival of the Republic had been at stake.[141] The people had therefore been entirely justified in restoring the Stadholder to power.

Throughout the theoretical part of his argument Luzac leaned heavily on Locke. His use of the *Second Treatise* was highly selective and almost

---

136. The pamphlet was banned by the Amsterdam government on the grounds that it was contrary to that city's laws, seditious and libellous. It was publicly burned in Amsterdam on May 15, 1754. In his own defense Luzac wrote the *Verantwoording*. In 1755 he published a second and revised edition of *The conduct*, more than twice as long as the first one. See Wessels, "Jan Wagenaar's 'Remarques' (1754)", 19-21.

137. On *The conduct* in general see Geyl, *Pennestrijd*, 189-195; Leeb, *Ideological Origins*, 68-73; Wessels, "Jan Wagenaar's 'Remarques' (1754)".

138. Locke, *Two Treatises*, 446.

139. *Gedrag*, 11-30; *Gedrag* (1755), 1-63. The quotation is on 29 and 61-62 ("...als oorspronkelyke en rechtmaatige Heerschers over zich zelven...").

140. Locke, *Two Treatises*, 432-434; *Gedrag*, 26-29; *Gedrag* (1755), 43-50.

141. *Gedrag*, 30-42; *Gedrag* (1755), 76-106; *Oordeel*, 116 ("...den Burgerstaat vernietigt...").

all quotations came from chapter nineteen, "Of the dissolution of government". Luzac did not speak of compacts or natural rights. He emphasized the fact that the people were normally, and rightly, excluded from the process of government.[142] He stressed, particularly in the second and enlarged edition of *The conduct*, the duty to obey established governments under normal circumstances.[143] Yet he did state that the people had restored the Stadholder and had removed a number of regents. He also seemed to imply the existence of a residual popular sovereignty.[144] And in his 1757 pamphlets, written against Wagenaar, he emphasized that all legitimate governments were based on consent.[145] Apparently, at the time of writing, Luzac gave little thought to the possibility that his line of argument might conceivably be turned against the Orangists, as indeed it later would.

It is obvious why Luzac remained unaware of this potential danger. In the first place, the historical association between brief and limited popular movements in times of crisis and the Orangist cause was firm. In the 1750s it was hard to imagine that the people would ever independently formulate anti-Orangist political demands or desire large-scale permanent participation in politics.[146] Secondly, Luzac's right of resistance and theory of consent were completely aimed at what he perceived to be the absolutist tendencies of the regent aristocracy and were totally unconnected with "democratic tendencies".[147] It was only in highly exceptional and desperate circumstances that the people were allowed to act as a safeguard against repressive regent despotism. As the century progressed, however, it gradually transpired that the coalition between Orange and the people could no longer be taken for granted. It also became clear that elements from Luzac's line of argument could be used to attack all constituted authority. As a result, it will be seen below, Luzac dropped the position he had taken in *The conduct* and adopted an altogether different and far less explosive approach to the events of 1747. The

142. *Gedrag*, 14-16; *Gedrag* (1755), 9-12.

143. *Gedrag* (1755), 16-17 and 21-22.

144. *Gedrag*, 20-21, 29-30, 36-37; *Gedrag* (1755), 34-35, 61-62, 100-101.

145. *Zugt*, 1-18; *Oordeel*, 91-126. On these pamphlets see Geyl, *Pennestrijd*, 195-202 and 217-226; Leeb, *Ideological Origins*, 92-96.

146. On the weakness and lack of independence of eighteenth-century popular movements before the Patriot era see J. Hovy, "Institutioneel onvermogen in de achttiende eeuw" in *Algemene Geschiedenis der Nederlanden*, vol.9, 136-138.

147. *Gedrag*, 55-58; *Gedrag* (1755), 119-121. The phrase "democratic tendencies" is, of course, Geyl's.

profoundly changed political scene had caused *The conduct* to become somewhat of an embarrassment, an unfortunate youthful statement now better passed over in silence. The business of modernizing Orangism, Luzac had painfully found out, could be full of unintended consequences.

Fortunately for Luzac, his arguments intended to demonstrate that the Stadholderate was necessary and indispensable in the Dutch Republic proved to be more resistant to subsequent abuse. Although they might well be contradicted, as indeed they were, it was next to impossible to reverse their meaning. Not only were these arguments free from any trace of ambiguity, they were also remarkably comprehensive, ranging from constitutional history to the very structure of the universe. When, during the 1780s, Luzac came to realize that Patriotism had replaced True Liberty as the main political threat, he saw no reason whatsoever to adapt his views on the functions of the Stadholder. To repeat and expand them, he judged, was sufficient a response. The most fundamental misunderstanding that prevented the Stadholderate from being properly appreciated, Luzac insisted, was a misconceived notion of liberty, ultimately of classical origin. Since the middle of the seventeenth century the opponents of the Stadholderate had, without exception, claimed that it was incompatible with liberty. Liberty, they were convinced, primarily meant the total absence of a monarchical element in government. "This notion, or rather misconception", Luzac observed, "was spread among the population by the Romans after they had chased away Tarquin, and has ever since found a wide following".[148] To this in his opinion curiously parochial and flawed notion of liberty Luzac opposed, as we have seen, his own definition of liberty as *independentia ab alterius voluntate*.

With that clear and simple definition as the point of departure, it was easy to show that the Stadholders had never violated liberty. This was even true for the two cases always brought up to prove the tyrannical, or at least the monarchical ambitions of Stadholders, Maurice's conflict with Oldenbarnevelt during the twelve year truce, and William II's war with Amsterdam in 1650. According to Luzac Oldenbarnevelt and the city of Amsterdam had been guilty of trying to violate the constitution. In the ensuing crises, the Stadholders had only acted to restore the *status quo ante*.[149] It was, in fact, only in Stadholderless periods that liberty was threatened by unchecked oligarchical government. Such government,

---

148. *Staatsbeschouwers*, vol.1, 125 ("Dit denkbeeld, of wanbegrip, is door de Romeinen, wanneer zy *Tarquinius* verjaagd hadden, het gemeen ten sterkste ingeprent, en voorts door hun by andere Volkeren voortgeplant.").

149. Zugt, 19-50 and 70-88; *Hollands rijkdom*, vol.3, 180-186 and 263-278.

Luzac observed in his commentary on Montesquieu, was no more than "the despotism of a certain group of people, intent upon keeping their families rich by means of easy jobs and a position beyond the reach of justice".[150] The only freedom, indeed, that the Stadholderate could fairly be said to threaten was the freedom of urban magistrates to do exactly as they pleased.[151]

History not only demonstrated that the Stadholderate was compatible with liberty, it was also essential in understanding the Stadholder's constitutional position. It has already been noted that Luzac was well acquainted with the new scholarship that had definitively exploded the Batavian myth, or the belief that the assemblies of the States had been sovereign since time immemorial. In the 1780s, he came to use this scholarship in support of his contention that democratic Patriotism was deeply foreign to the history and nature of Dutch society. In his writings on the constitutional position of the Stadholder he found it of great help in establishing that the Stadholder was much more than a mere servant of the States, to be dismissed at will. Before the Revolt, Luzac explained, William of Orange had been Holland's first noble, seated in the assembly of the States in that capacity, and connected to Philip II by a feudal tie. He had also been Philip's Stadholder, representing the whole of sovereignty.[152] After the Revolt, therefore, the position of the Stadholder was that of member of the new sovereign assembly of the States, vassal of that same assembly, and representative of its whole sovereignty.[153]

It was thus clearly wrong, even ludicrous, to deny that the Stadholderate was an essential and integral part of the constitution, as the *Staatsgezinden* regularly did. Luzac's historical account not only allowed him to clarify the constitutional position of the Stadholder, it also enabled him to draw attention to the continuity in Dutch constitutional development. The Revolt, he pointed out, had not interrupted the slow process of institutional growth that had started in the early middle ages. Ever since that time, the consistency of the Dutch governmental structure had depended on the presence of a head. The whole state had grown up

---

150. *Esprit des loix*, vol.1, 195 (book VIII, chapter 6) ("...un despotisme d'un certain ordre de personnes, qui n'auront d'autres vues que de conserver l'opulence dans leurs familles, par des emplois aisés, et à l'abri de toute perquisition.").

151. *Gedrag*, 43-44.

152. *Vryaart*, vol.3, part 9, 76-77.

153. *Ibidem*, vol.4, part 12, 316-319. Although it was about Holland that Luzac was writing, he explicitly stated that *mutatis mutandis* the same was true for the other provinces. *Ibidem*, 263.

around this principle and all inhabitants had adapted their behavior to it. To claim that a sudden deviation from this age-old structure, by the institution of a government without a head, would not have ruinous effects was obviously absurd. The very opposite had, unfortunately, been demonstrated twice in the recent past.[154]

Having firmly anchored the Stadholderate in the Dutch constitution, Luzac turned to a discussion of its many functions in the Dutch political system. The Revolt, he repeatedly observed, had by accident created a form of government widely regarded as the very best: the mixed form.[155] The Dutch mixed government consisted of the familiar one (the Stadholder), few (the nobility), and many (the representatives of the towns), both on the national and on the provincial levels.[156] Luzac duly pointed out the many shortcomings of the various simple forms of government and proclaimed the superiority of the mixed form. Yet he did not treat Dutch mixed government in any detail. The reason for this is clear. It has already been noted that he regarded mixed government as a somewhat empty formula and that, under the influence of Montesquieu, he was much more taken with the relatively novel notion of the separation of powers.

Luzac, in fact, was the first author to apply the theory of the separation of powers to the Dutch Republic. He found it of great utility in constructing a modern defense of the Stadholderate. In the Republic, Luzac contended, the legislative power resided in the assemblies of the States, of which the Stadholder was also a member. The executive power was in the hands of the Stadholder. This was a perfect combination, for legislation required the mature deliberations of an assembly, whereas execution demanded the speed and efficiency of a single person.[157] A similar combination, Luzac added, worked well in matters of defense: the final decisions on war and peace were taken by the Estates General, but the actual warfare was directed by the Stadholder in his capacity of Captain and Admiral General.[158] The judiciary was largely independent of both other powers, but in extraordinary cases people could appeal to the Stadholder. His presence insured the possibility of a *regressus ad*

---

154. *Hollands rijkdom*, vol.3, 171-173; *Lettres sur les dangers*, 67-68.

155. *Hollands rijkdom*, vol.3, 325.

156. *Ibidem*, 126.

157. *Ibidem*, 331-332.

158. *Ibidem*, 333-334.

principem and he saw to it that the rule of law was maintained.[159] The Stadholderate, it is clear, formed the all-important link between the otherwise separated powers of government and balanced them. By doing so, it guaranteed the survival of the kind of moderate government that best protected the people from oppression.

All of the above, Luzac continued, did not yet constitute a full demonstration of the necessity of the Stadholderate. Both the commercial nature of Dutch society and the weakness of the ties binding the seven provinces together also needed to be taken into account. Commerce, it has already been noted, entailed specialization and made the largest part of the population unfit to participate in politics. The direct pursuit of the common good should, as a result, be left to trained administrators. The Dutch Republic, however, was not only a commercial, but also a fragmented and particularist state. The 1579 Union of Utrecht, the basis of this fragile structure, had provided for no more than a bare minimum of central authority.[160] The representatives of the various provinces in the Estates General, Luzac repeatedly emphasized, were all primarily inclined to promote the good of their own region and thus all had their special interests.[161] It was only the Stadholder, Luzac was convinced, who could fully transcend special interests, promote the common good, and establish unity. "The union of the seven provinces", he remarked, "is the basis and support of the state. It rests on the influence of the Stadholder. That influence, therefore, is the most essential part of the form of government of the state".[162] This unity was both a political and an economic necessity. "Of all defects that can exist in a civil society, division among the rulers is the worst; it is also the defect most harmful to our navigation and commerce".[163]

The question that, of course, remained to be answered was why the Stadholder necessarily promoted the common good. It was because, Luzac contended, the interests of the Orange Stadholders and those of the Dutch

---

159. *Ibidem*, 335 and *Lettres sur les dangers*, 84-85.

160. On the Union of Utrecht see Groenveld and Leeuwenberg, ed. *Unie van Utrecht* and Boogman, "Union of Utrecht".

161. *Hollands rijkdom*, vol.3, 157-159.

162. *Ibidem*, 159 ("De vereeniging der zeven gewesten is de grondslag en steun van den Staat: deze vereeniging rust op den invloed des Stadhouders. Die invloed is derhalven het weezenlijkste en voornaamste gedeelte van deszelfs regeeringsvorm...").

163. *Ibidem*, 156 ("Dewijl nu van alle de gebreken, die in een burgerstaat plaats kunnen hebben, de verdeeldheid onder de gezaghebbers het grootste is; zoo is ook die verdeeldheid het schadelijkst gebrek voor onze scheepvaart en koophandel.").

state were identical.[164] The Oranges were one of the oldest and most venerable noble houses in the Netherlands.[165] The foundations of the free Republic had been laid by William of Orange and the work of state building had been completed by Maurice and Frederick Henry.[166] Since an independent state was the most beautiful thing man could create, the psychological consequence was that these Oranges, and their descendants, identified themselves with the welfare of the state in its entirety. Their power and prestige, furthermore, actually depended on the power and prestige of the whole Republic.[167] Unless the order of nature were to reverse itself, a Stadholder could have no other will, no other intention, and no other desire than to promote the interests of the Republic.[168]

It was for his final and most abstract argument in defense of the Stadholderate that Luzac returned to his beloved theme of harmony. The necessity of a monarchical element in every state, and of a Stadholder in the Dutch Republic in particular, could, he was convinced, be demonstrated from the orderly and harmonious structure of the universe, ultimately maintained by a single directing force. The whole cosmos proclaimed the naturalness of a head. "Nothing lives, nothing exists, nothing moves that does not make it clear to us that a civil society needs a head, just as there is a first principle to everything", it was clear to Luzac.[169] "In the physical world, we observe the reign of a harmony, which departs from a fixed point and rests on a common center...It is the same with civil societies. They need unity and the confluence of the different actions of the members towards one goal...They need a soul, a spirit".[170] Luzac's work abounded in analogies and metaphors further illustrating these abstractions. He saw their truth confirmed in the spacious firmament but also in various social microcosms: passengers in a carriage

---

164. *Zugt*, 30-31.

165. *Lettres sur les dangers*, 93-94.

166. *Hollands rijkdom*, vol.3, 159.

167. *Lettres sur les dangers*, 89-90 and 98.

168. *Hollands rijkdom*, vol.3, 161. On the theme of the harmony of interests between ruler and country in contemporary French thought see Hirschman, *The Passions and the Interests*, 97-100.

169. *Staatsbeschouwers*, vol.1, 185 ("Niets leeft'er, niets is'er, niets roert'er, dat ons niet toeroept dat'er in een Burgerstaat een Hoofd moet zyn, gelyk'er een grondbeginsel tot alles is.").

170. *Lettres sur les dangers*, 274-275 ("Nous voyons régner dans le monde physique une harmonie, qui part d'un point fixe et repose sur un centre commun...Il en est de même des Sociétés civiles. Il leur faut une unité et un concours des différentes opérations de tous les membres à une même fin...Il leur faut une âme, un esprit...").

needed a driver, an orchestra could not play without a conductor, and a ship needed a captain.[171] So it was with the state. Without the Stadholder, the soul of government, the political universe of the Seven United Provinces would fall apart.[172]

171. *Vryaart*, vol.1, part 2, 168-169 and vol.4, part 12, 187-191.

172. *Hollands rijkdom*, vol.4, 135.

CHAPTER V

THE ASSAULT ON CIVILIZATION

Late in August of 1783 Luzac, having returned from a business trip to Germany, joined his wife Geertruy in Utrecht in order to spend a few pleasant and relaxing days in that city. On his first stroll through town, however, he was suddenly recognized as the author of *Vryaart's letters* by members of the Utrecht citizen militia. They abused him verbally, beat him up, followed him back to his tavern, and forced him to spend the night in hiding. Separated from his wife, the bruised Luzac succeeded in secretly leaving town on the following day. Although he deeply deplored it, the whole incident had not greatly surprised him. It had, in fact, done no more than confirm his view that previously unknown forms of sociability were rapidly emerging in the Dutch Republic. They were collectively known under the ridiculously inappropriate name of Patriotism.[1]

What the incident, in a very basic way, illustrates for the modern historian is the depth of the divisions in the Dutch Republic during the 1780s. Yet in the historiography dealing with this period, the so-called *Patriottentijd*, it is not uncommon to find the differences, particularly those of an ideological nature, between the various existing or emerging political groups minimized. The Dutch Patriots, so a frequently heard argument goes, cannot be called radical in any sense of the word before their forced exile in France between 1787 and 1795. They shared much common ground with their opponents, the anti-Patriots, conservatives, or Orangists. The two groups were, to quote an eminent representative of this approach, separated by no more than "a minor quarrel about the practical form of the executive".[2] This consensual interpretation of Dutch political thought in the 1780s, however, makes it virtually impossible to understand why the country came to be torn apart by revolution and civil war for years. It is indeed wholly inadequate and misleading. Even the most superficial perusal of the political literature of the period makes it abundantly clear that Patriots and anti-Patriots disagreed on almost

---

1. On the Utrecht incident see *Nieuwe Nederlandsche Jaerboeken*, 1783, part 3, 1612-1615; *Brief van een heer te Utrecht*; De Bie, *Petrus Hofstede*, 409-416.

2. Leeb, *Ideological Origins*, 176 and *passim*. For a more recent interpretation along similar lines see L.H.M. Wessels, "Over heden en verleden in het tweede tijdvak. Historie, Verlichting en Revolutie: enkele impressies bij een beoordeling van de ideologische positie van de Nederlandse Patriotten" in: Van der Zee, et al., ed. *1787*, 218-245 and, by the same author, "Tradition et lumières".

everything, so much so that there was a total breakdown of communication. It is the purpose of the present chapter to demonstrate the fundamental nature of the ideological conflict in the Dutch Republic in the years after 1780 by analyzing the anti-Patriot arguments put forward by Luzac. After a first section outlining the general contours of the ideological struggle of the 1780s, sections two and three will discuss Luzac's negative assessment of the practice and principles of Patriotism. Section four, finally, will provide a brief sketch of Luzac's attempt to formulate an alternative to Patriotism.

1. *Patriotism and Anti-Patriotism in the Dutch Republic*

The Patriot movement emerged during the Fourth Anglo-Dutch War (1780-1784), when the weaknesses of the Dutch state became painfully obvious.[3] The earliest criticisms directed against the established regime concentrated on issues of foreign policy and on the position and behavior of Stadholder William V. Soon, however, the Patriots proceeded to formulate a comprehensive program for the regeneration of the Dutch nation. In doing so, they frequently used arguments drawn from Dutch history. Contrary to what has often been suggested, however, this was not the most important weapon in their ideological arsenal. The Patriot program, in fact, found its theoretical basis and its explosive force in an eclectic mixture of elements drawn from several political languages. Most importantly, it combined notions derived from the classical republican tradition with an ultra-Lockean interpretation of the natural, permanent and inalienable rights of the sovereign people.[4]

As true late eighteenth-century classical republicans, the Dutch Patriots viewed human history as a perennial battle between power and

---

3. Important accounts of the political history of the Patriot era include Colenbrander, *Patriottentijd*; Geyl, *Patriottenbeweging*; De Wit, *Strijd tussen aristocratie en democratie* and *Nederlandse revolutie van de achttiende eeuw*; Schama, *Patriots and Liberators*. The recent commemorations of this period have demonstrated a remarkable resurgence of interest. It has, however, not yet resulted in a new synthesis. For discussions of the most recent literature see Reitsma, "'Altoos gedenkwaardig'"; Huussen jr., "1787. De Nederlandse revolutie?"; Te Brake, "Staking a new claim".

4. Patriot political thought has unfortunately not been studied in depth. Leeb, *Ideological Origins*, still is the most comprehensive work available. The possible presence of classical republican elements in Dutch late eighteenth-century political thought has briefly been explored by Pocock, "Problem of political thought" and Kossmann, *Politieke theorie en geschiedenis*, 224-233. It is clearly a subject that deserves further study. See most recently Fritschy, *Patriotten en de financiën*, 79-86.

liberty.[5] All of history, according to the lengthy Patriot program *Constitutional restoration* (1784-1786), showed an "incessant struggle between sovereigns, desirous of arbitrary power, and peoples, trying to defend and maintain their liberty".[6] In the Dutch Republic the usurpation of power could not, of course, be attributed to a monarch, but the Stadholder could equally well be held responsible for what the Patriots saw as the almost total extinction of republican liberty. Every single act of William V, Joan Derk van der Capellen observed in his famous *To the people of the Netherlands* (1781), demonstrated his ambition to become a despot. He was trying to build a strong standing army composed of servile mercenaries. He had greatly increased his powers of appointment at all levels, thereby establishing a system of influence and corruption. His personal behavior, moreover, was utterly debauched.[7] The Stadholder, the important *Leiden draft* (1785) insisted, was creating a state dominated by "the most incompetent, base, and shameless court-flatterers and oppressors of the people".[8] In the exact, slightly paranoid language of their Anglo-American contemporaries, the Patriots diagnosed their own time as the period in which liberty had to seize its last chance.[9] The only two alternatives left, they were convinced, were liberty and slavery.[10]

The liberty the Patriots were referring to was the positive liberty of the civic humanist tradition. Citizen participation in government, they held, was absolutely essential in and a defining characteristic of a free state. "In a republican state", according to the authors of *Constitutional restoration*, "one may distinguish between civil and political liberty. The first consists of being allowed to do as one pleases, provided it does not harm others. Political liberty is the right...to influence the government...It could easily be shown that the growth or decline of civil liberty parallels

---

5. On this theme see Bailyn, *Ideological Origins*, 55-93 and Wood, *Creation of the American Republic*, 3-45.

6. *Grondwettige herstelling*, vol.1, 61 ("...gestaadigen Twist tusschen Souvereinen, naar eene willekeurige magt haakende, en Volken, hun best doende om hunne Vryheid daartegen te verdedigen..."). On *Constitutional restoration* see Leeb, *Ideological Origins*, 185-195; De Wit, *Ontstaan van het moderne Nederland*, 15-49; Van Himbergen, "Grondwettige Herstelling".

7. [Van der Capellen], *Aan het volk*, 60-88. On Van der Capellen see most recently Van Dijk, et al., ed. *Wekker van de Nederlandse natie*.

8. *Ontwerp*, 14 ("...de ongeschiktste, de laaghartigste, de onbeschaamdste Vleiërs en Gunstelingen van het Hof, en verdrukkers van het Volk...").

9. Wood, "Conspiracy and the paranoid style".

10. *Grondwettige herstelling*, vol.1, 18-19.

the maintenance or suppression of political liberty.[11] To make a system of political liberty function, the Patriots claimed, the citizenry had to be armed, independent, and virtuous. Citizen armament was, ever since the publication of Van der Capellen's *To the people*, a veritable Patriot obsession. During the 1780s citizen militias, claiming a variety of roles, sprang up all over the country.[12] These armed, independent, and virtuous citizens constituted, the Patriots maintained, the sovereign people.

Popular sovereignty, in fact, was inalienable. Its exercise could temporarily and provisionally be entrusted to others, but the sovereign people could resume its full role whenever it wanted and change the government at will.[13] Active republican citizenship on the basis of permanent popular sovereignty would, the Patriots were convinced, have extremely beneficial results and would regenerate the nation. "The larger the number of people influencing the process of government is..., the larger the number of people identifying with the public good will be and, as a consequence, the stronger patriotism, the soul of all republican governments, will be".[14] With the rebirth of political virtue, the state would be transformed. It was high time indeed, as the author of the radical pamphlet *The aristocracy* insisted, to replace the old and rotting structures of the established regime with something altogether new and better. "We tear down old buildings, and better ones are erected on the same grounds. Why then, if we see old deficiencies, should we hesitate to replace them with something better? The older they are, the sooner they should be eradicated...".[15] It was in disseminating these revolutionary

11. *Ibidem*, 189 ("In eenen Republicainschen staat onderscheidt men de burgerlyke en de staatkundige vryheid. De eerste bestaat daarin, dat men doen mag 't geen men wil, mits men anderen niet benadeele. De staatkundige vryheid bevat het recht, om...invloed in het Staatsbestier te hebben...Men zou gemaklyk kunnen aantoonen, dat, naar maate de staatkundige vryheid gehandhaafd of onderdrukt wordt, ook de burgerlyke vryheid meer of minder wordt beveiligt.").

12. Schulte Nordholt, *Dutch Republic and American Independence*, 271-273; H.L. Zwitzer, "De militaire dimensie van de patriottenbeweging" in: Grijzenhout, et al., ed. *Voor Vaderland en Vrijheid*, 27-50.

13. [Van der Capellen], *Aan het volk*, 38; *Grondwettige herstelling*, vol.1, 63-64.

14. *Grondwettige herstelling*, vol.1, 443 ("Hoe grooter het getal is dergeenen, die invloed hebben op het Staatsbestuur, ...hoe meer elk inwooner in het geval is, om het algemeen welzyn als zyn eigen aan te merken en hoe grooter gevolglyk het Patriotismus, de ziel van alle Republikeinsche Regeeringen, zyn moet.").

15. Anonymus Belga, *De adel*, 107 ("Wy werpen oude gebouwen om ver, en nieuwe verschynen met meerder luister op derzelver gronden. Wy zien oude gebreken, en we zouden ze met geene nieuwe goede inrigtingen durven vervangen? In teegendeel, hoe ouder ze zyn, hoe eerder men ze dient uitteroeien..."). This pamphlet has been attributed to P. de

views that the Patriots showed their greatest skills. They were veritable masters in the art of political propaganda. The Republic was flooded with the products of their new political journalism. They energetically experimented with novel forms of political organization and direct action. Their central messages were presented in an appealing and accessible language of symbols, signs, and public rituals. Because of all this, it has recently been suggested, the Patriots greatly contributed to the birth of modern Dutch political culture.[16]

Whether or not the Patriots succeeded in bringing about an enduring transformation of Dutch political culture, it is certain that those wishing to preserve the established regime were up against a formidable enemy. For a number of reasons, the position of these anti-Patriots was extremely difficult. First of all, they were stuck with Stadholder William V who, to put it mildly, was not the most inspiring political leader. Whatever qualities he may have had, in politics he was an extremely unimaginative conservative, who clung to the letter of law and was incapable of firm and creative behavior in a situation of political crisis.[17] The disastrous course of the Anglo-Dutch War, moreover, made it easy to point to the Stadholder, who after all was also Captain and Admiral General, as the scapegoat for all national disasters. The anti-Patriots' second major problem was the success of their opponents in winning over a substantial part of the population to their side. Traditionally used to wide public support, the Orangists were now suddenly forced to develop their own versions of the successful strategies adopted by the Patriots.

The third and for our purposes most important problem confronting Dutch conservatives was the need to formulate an adequate theoretical response to the Patriot challenge. It was impossible, though some tried to do so, simply to fall back on the old arguments used by the Orangists in their struggles with the *Staatsgezinden* or *Loevesteiners*. Since Patriotism was essentially a new phenomenon, the anti-Patriots had to come up with a new set of answers. Their performance in this field was important and impressive. It is therefore both remarkable and regrettable that anti-Patriot

Wakker van Zon.

16. N.C.F. van Sas, "Opiniepers en politieke cultuur" in: Grijzenhout, et al., ed. *Voor Vaderland en Vrijheid*, 97-130 and, by the same author, "The Patriot Revolution: New Perspectives" in: Jacob and Mijnhardt, ed. *The Dutch Republic in the Eighteenth Century*, 91-119. On the Patriot language of symbols see Grijzenhout, *Feesten voor het Vaderland*.

17. On William V see Schutte, "Willem IV and Willem V", 202-224; Rowen, *Princes of Orange*, 186-229; Gabriëls, *Heren als dienaren*, 108-115.

political discourse has been largely ignored by subsequent historiography.[18] In order to combat their opponents the anti-Patriots first of
all tried to demonstrate that the Dutch Republic was one of the most free,
tolerant, prosperous, and humane societies in Europe. Once this was
established, they proceeded to show that the political thought of the
Patriots was archaic and primitivist. Finally, they discussed the disastrous
consequences the introduction of a popular government, which they took
to be the Patriots' main aim, would have.

The government of the Dutch Republic was defined as mixed and
therefore moderate by almost all defenders of the old order of things. A
balance between monarchical, aristocratic and democratic elements
precluded the arbitrary use of power.[19] The role of the Stadholder,
obviously, was of crucial importance for the continued existence of this
balance.[20] The moderation and mildness of the existing government was
not only assured by a balance, but also by the presence of a multiplicity
of representative institutions on all levels and by a stable constitution.
These excellent arrangements enabled the inhabitants of the Republic to
enjoy the highest possible degree of liberty, so the anti-Patriots claimed.
The Dutch Republic as a free state was their most beloved theme. The
liberty they sang the praises of was, of course, not the classical republican
liberty exalted by the Patriots, but the negative liberty of the rule of
law.[21]

Everyone in the Dutch Republic, without exception, was subject to the
same laws and therefore equal. A unique system of independent and
incorruptible civil and criminal justice not only protected the person and
goods of each individual inhabitant, but also saw to it that the government
would not abuse its power. The inhabitants of the Dutch Republic were,
in fact, almost completely free to behave as they wished.[22] Yet liberty
was not limited to the rule of law. The Dutch Republic was also an

---

18. The only thorough book-length studies of late eighteenth-century Dutch conservatism
available are devoted to Gijsbert Karel van Hogendorp (1762-1834). The interest in Van
Hogendorp, however, seems to owe more to his role in the early nineteenth-century
founding of the Kingdom of the Netherlands and his subsequent place in the development of
Dutch liberalism than to his contribution to the political thought of the late eighteenth
century. The best book on the subject is Van der Hoeven, *Gijsbert Karel van Hogendorp*.

19. The theme was extensively discussed by, among others, Canter de Munck, *Tegenswoordige regeeringsvorm*.

20. For a lengthy and exhaustive defense of the Stadholderate see De Vogel, *Katechismus*.

21. E.g. Meerman, *Burgerlyke vryheid*, 5-8.

22. *Missive van een oud regent*, 35; Decker, *Proeve*, 25-29; Meerman, *Burgerlyke vryheid*,
9-16.

extremely tolerant and open society. This was true in the field of religion, where the combination of an established church with a large measure of religious toleration represented, so the anti-Patriots claimed, the maximum of religious liberty that could exist in a well-ordered society. But it was also evident from the free exchange of opinions and knowledge, a phenomenon that corresponded with the free exchange of goods and services characteristic of commercial society. A free press, the presence of dissident political voices, a large measure of openness in government - all this, according to the anti-Patriots, proved the fact that the Dutch Republic was a uniquely free state.[23]

Having established how excellent a state the Dutch Republic was, the conservatives proceeded to demonstrate that the political thought of their opponents was extremely dangerous because it was archaic and primitivist. The regressive nature of Patriot political thought, they claimed, was clear from the way it handled natural rights, from its inability to guarantee any measure of political continuity, and from its misplaced invocation of the distant past. The Patriots were positively intoxicated with notions of natural liberty and equality. Yet the state of nature they based their contentions on, their opponents pointed out, was no more than a hypothesis. It was a figment of their imagination and did not correspond to anything known about the earliest history of mankind. If hypotheses concerning the state of nature were to be of any use at all, they should at least be constructed along more realistic lines. The Patriot conjectures about man's natural liberty and equality were, in short, wholly unfounded. What made them truly objectionable and dangerous, however, was the Patriot insistence that they could directly be used in judging the legitimacy of the political arrangements of an established and well-ordered state.[24]

Not only did the Patriot use their largely imagined natural rights as yardsticks for the established order, they also claimed them to be inalienable. This, the conservatives were convinced, prevented them from having any conception of a continuous process of political development. A political system based on inalienable rights was no system at all, the anti-Patriots contended. The living would never be bound by the wise decisions of the dead and even within one and the same generation all

23. [Van Goens], *Ouderwetse Nederlandsche Patriot*, nr. 22, 473-486; [Kluit], *Rechten van den mensch*, 153-175.

24. De Vogel, *Katechismus*, vol.2, 116-142; Vreede, ed., *Van de Spiegel*, vol.4, 571-581. On Van de Spiegel see Boogman, *Raadpensionaris L.P. van de Spiegel*.

decisions would be instantly reversible, with chaos as a result.[25] The regressive nature of Patriot thought, finally, was also clear from the fact that it failed to take the complex development of states and societies into account in yet another way. The Patriots' constant normative invocation of the distant past, be it Roman republicanism or Batavian virtue, was misplaced and even slightly ridiculous. It simply ignored such factors as the transition from a primitive agrarian to a highly developed commercial economy, the historical increase in institutional complexity, and the emergence of professional and technically sophisticated forms of warfare.[26] The Patriots, their opponents were convinced, were blind to modernity.

That this was indeed the case, they insisted, was also abundantly clear from their most essential political demand, the introduction of a popular government or democracy. The conservatives used a wide range of arguments to prove that the introduction of such a popular government in the Dutch Republic would be a disaster. They tried to show that it was incompatible with modern commercial society, that it had no basis whatsoever in Dutch history, and that the desirability of its introduction could only be argued on the basis of a flagrant abuse of the generally accepted meaning of key political concepts. A popular government was the very opposite of, and would most certainly destroy, the liberty now enjoyed by the inhabitants of the Dutch Republic. It testified to their complete lack of understanding of the development of societies, Cornelis Willem Decker thought, that the Patriots refused to admit "that it does not belong to the *essence* of every citizen, however free, personally to participate in appointing the government".[27] A democracy might be viable in a very small state with a limited population and a primitive economy, but it was unthinkable in the Dutch Republic.[28] Civil liberty was the only liberty appropriate to the commercial system.

The anti-Patriot consensus on this issue was perfectly summed up by Gijsbert Karel van Hogendorp. "I wish", he wrote in 1785, "the present fanatical parties had a better understanding of the commerce that makes

---

25. E.g. Kluit, *Souvereiniteit der Staten van Holland*, 71-74 and [Kluit], *Rechten van den mensch*, 377-393. On Kluit's political thought see Veen, "Legitimatie".

26. E.g. Canter de Munck, *Tegenswoordige regeeringsvorm*, 50-53.

27. Decker, *Proeve*, 35 ("...dat uit de *essentie* van ieder burger, hoe vry hy ook zyn mag, geenzints afvloeit of spruiten kan, dat hy de Regeerders of Bestuurders voor zich moet helpen aanstellen...").

28. Canter de Munck, *Tegenswoordige regeeringsvorm*, 50-53; Meerman, *Burgerlyke vryheid*, 27.

the state what it is, and of the reasonable liberty that is the foundation of commerce and that is reinforced by it...; as much liberty, that is, as is compatible with the advanced state of our society. Whoever wants more will only bring about confusion and, with a misconceived love of liberty, will plunge us into anarchy or despotism".[29] Popular participation in politics was simply impossible in a highly developed commercial society, characterized by an advanced division of labor. Nothing could be more absurd than the thought that everybody was competent or had the time to arrive at sound political judgments. "The political merchant or laborer", in the words of a 1783 pamphlet, "is a miserable being, and such a political fool is a great fool indeed".[30] Nothing, too, could be more absurd than the suggestion that industrious citizens should prove their virtue by bearing arms and by engaging in military exercises.[31] This half-baked Patriot notion would, according to Decker, only result in the replacement of the salutary spirit of commerce by an archaic and detrimental "military spirit".[32] Politics should be left largely to politicians, just as fighting should be left largely to soldiers. The citizen should strive after personal fulfillment in his family life and in his occupation.[33] For the rest, to quote the Utrecht conservative Rijklof Michael van Goens (1748-1810), it was his simple duty to uphold "a sincere and intense, but calm love of the Fatherland, of which the most important elements are subjection to the legitimate government and devotion to the established laws and constitution".[34]

Not only was the introduction of a popular government made impossible by the nature of Dutch society, the anti-Patriots claimed, it also

---

29. Van Hogendorp, *Brieven en Gedenkschriften*, vol.2, 280 ("Zoodanige partijen, welke in hunnen blinden ijver de zaak van het vaderland vergeten, ware het te wenschen, dat een beter besef hadden èn van den koophandel, die den Staat doet zijn al hetgeen hij is, èn van de redelijke vrijheid, op welke de koophandel steunt, ja welke door denzelven bevorderd wordt...; zooveel vrijheid, meen ik, als met den gevorderden staat der maatschappij onder ons bestaanbaar is. Wie naar meer haakt, zal niets dan verwarring verwekken, en ons door zijn gewaande vrijheidsliefde of anarchie of despotie op den hals halen.").

30. *Verhandeling over den alouden en tegenswoordigen staat*, 36 ("De Staatkundige Koop of Arbeidsman is een ellendig wezen, en zodanig een Staatkundige nar een groote nar.").

31. *Spiegel der vryheid, passim*; *Samenspraak*, 6.

32. Decker, *Proeve*, 12 ("...l'Esprit Militair...").

33. *Samenspraak*, 7.

34. [Van Goens], *Ouderwetse Nederlandsche Patriot*, nr.5, 100 ("...eene oprechte en vurige, doch geregelde Vaderlands-liefde, waarvan de eerste plicht is onderwerping aan de wettige Overheid en gehechtheid aan de vastgestelde Wetten en Constitutie."). On Van Goens see most recently Bos, *Van Goens*.

lacked a basis in Dutch history. Patriot attempts, for instance in *Constitutional restoration*, to prove the opposite were skillfully refuted by Adriaan Kluit en Johannes Canter de Munck. It was not possible, they argued, to find any sign of permanent popular sovereignty in Dutch history. The popular influence that could admittedly be found in the established regime had nothing to do with the Patriot conception of democracy.[35] Only the flagrant abuse of the concepts of sovereignty and representation could explain these Patriot misconceptions about the history of Dutch institutions. In general, the anti-Patriots insisted, the abuse of these concepts was the basis of most Patriot theories about popular government. The Patriots, whether they wanted a Rousseauist democracy or a democracy by representation, completely ignored the meaning of the word sovereignty. Their contention that the people always remained sovereign was a gross distortion of the writings of authorities such as Grotius and Locke. For Grotius, as Kluit explained at length in his reply to the authors of *Constitutional restoration*, had argued the precise opposite.[36] And Locke too, Jan Willem Kumpel claimed, had stressed the transfer of sovereignty.[37] The Patriot refusal to admit that sovereignty could be transferred led, the anti-Patriots argued, to a total misunderstanding of the concept of representation. For if the people always remained sovereign, representatives could be no more than servants of the people, always answerable to their principals and removable at will. To claim this, however, was to destroy the basis of government by making it impossible to distinguish between governors and governed. The essence of representation, the anti-Patriots emphasized, was the very real replacement of those represented. Anything else would result in chaos.[38]

The conservatives had shown, to sum up, that the Dutch Republic had basically been a free and happy country before 1780, that the Patriot attack on the established order was based on dangerous and primitivist arguments, and that the introduction of a popular government - the Patriots' main aim - was highly undesirable. One of the leading and most prolific representatives of this sophisticated anti-Patriotism was Elie Luzac. It is against this wider background that his contributions to the

---

35. Canter de Munck, *Tegenswoordige regeeringsvorm, passim*; Kluit, *Souvereiniteit der Staten van Holland, passim*.

36. Kluit, *Souvereiniteit der Staten van Holland*, 76-82.

37. [Kumpel], *Philarche*, nr. 3 and 4, 27-35.

38. Kluit, *Misbruik van 't algemeen staatsrecht*, 51-64; Canter de Munck, *Tegenswoordige regeeringsvorm*, 173-174; *Onpartydige beschouwing*, 26-29.

political thought of the last decades of the Dutch *ancien régime* must be discussed and may be understood.[39]

2. *Luzac and the Rise of Patriotism*

It took a while before Luzac fully realized what was happening to the Dutch Republic in the 1780s. When confronted with the first manifestations of domestic commotion, he took them to be just another episode in the familiar struggle between Orangists and *Staatsgezinden*, as many other contemporary observers did. The Stadholderate, once again, seemed to be the main issue. The most important critical reaction to *Holland's wealth*, for instance, completely concentrated on Luzac's treatment of that institution. It showed him to be, F. Bernard claimed in his *Free thoughts of a citizen on the decline of the Republic*, a "hotheaded lover of the Stadholders" and a pseudo-monarchist. The least that should be done, this author insisted, was to ban the whole work.[40] Luzac drew his conclusions and, under the pseudonym Reinier Vryaart, started to write and publish a series of letters chiefly intended to free the Stadholder from blame for recent events and to protect him against unjustified attacks.[41]

It was nonsense to hold William V responsible for the Republic's military humiliation, Luzac remarked, since even the slightest familiarity with the constitution was sufficient to know that "His Serene Highness cannot execute anything unless he is enabled to do so by the necessary means".[42] The regents, who were now desperately trying to remove the Stadholder, were the real culprits, for they had consistently blocked increases in military expenditure over the past decades.[43] Luzac would never entirely give up his analysis of the Patriot movement as a Catilinarian conspiracy of aristocratic regents, who used the people to further

---

39. For a more detailed discussion of anti-Patriot political discourse between 1780 and 1795 see W.R.E. Velema, "Contemporaine reacties op het patriotse politieke vocabulaire" in: Bots and Mijnhardt, ed. *Droom van de Revolutie*, 32-48 and "Revolutie, contrarevolutie en het stadhouderschap".

40. [Bernard], *Vrye gedachten*, 135 ("...een heethoofdig...liefhebber der Stadhouders..."), 140, 144.

41. *Vryaart*, vol.4, part 11, 1.

42. *Ibidem*, vol.3, part 8, 35 ("...dat Z.D. Hoogheid niets kan uitvoeren, ten zy Hoogst-dezelve'er toe door de noodige middelen in staat gesteld worde.").

43. The military is an important theme throughout *Vryaart's letters*. On the late eighteenth-century Dutch debate about the army and the navy see Bartstra, *Vlootherstel en legeraugmentatie*.

their own despotic ends.[44] He would also keep denying that the Patriots spoke for a majority of the Dutch population. Yet as the movement expanded, he was forced to the conclusion that Patriotism was something without precedent in Dutch history. Patriotism had developed into a movement profoundly different from the intentions of its regent originators. It would not stop at the removal of the Stadholder, but threatened every aspect of civilized life.

It was imperative that this assault on civilization be halted. Luzac attempted to do so by means of a constant stream of polemical writings, totalling well over six thousand pages in a ten year period. *Vryaart's letters* were followed by the equally lengthy *Vaderlandsche staatsbeschouwers*.[45] Having completed those, Luzac needed another three volumes to discuss *The advantages and disadvantages of popular influence on government*.[46] He wrote the final work in this series of anti-Patriot polemics after the outbreak of the French Revolution. It was the deeply conservative *Lettres sur les dangers de changer la constitution primitive d'un gouvernement public*, published in 1792, when he was in his early seventies. Luzac, indeed, became a symbol of the established regime. Patriot political caricatures of the period invariably depicted him as a thin, repulsive looking member of a shady court-*clique*.[47] He was, it is true, known at the court and held in high regard there.[48] Yet he always scrupulously kept his distance and guarded his independence.

Nothing illustrates this better than his refusal to involve himself with subsidized political journalism. The Orangists, it has been noted, were desperately trying to imitate the effective political strategies of their opponents. This was particularly true in the field of political journalism, where the unprecedented success of the new Patriot newspapers simply had to be countered. In order to do so, the court subsidized the talented Rijklof Michael van Goens to write his conservative *Oldfashioned Dutch*

---

44. *Voor- en nadeelen*, vol.2, 60-90.

45. A title that is rather hard to translate, but means something close to National Observers of the State.

46. *De voor- en nadeelen van de invloed des volks op de regeering, etc.* 3 vols. Leyden, 1788-1789.

47. Van Rijn, *Atlas van Stolk*, vol.5, nr. 4420 and 4425; vol.6, nr. 4497, 4529 and 4572.

48. Luzac was first introduced at court in 1757. See *Corr. Formey*, Luzac to Formey, Leiden, January 24, 1758. The Duke of Brunswick, William V's most important advisor and a man much hated by the Patriots, repeatedly praised his qualities in public. Hardenbroek, *Gedenkschriften*, vol.4, 559.

Patriot (1781-1783).[49] Wanting all the help he could get, William V also sent Luzac a sum of money, accompanied by the request to write for this journal. Luzac, however, immediately returned it, remarking that he had never done anything in politics "with a view to monetary gain".[50] To him, as his pupil and close friend H.C. Cras recorded, "an independent state, and above all independence in sentiment and judgment, was...the most desirable thing in life".[51] It was disinterested political conviction that led Luzac to his completely negative assessment of Patriot behavior.

During the 1780s, it has already been noted, the Dutch Republic, for the first time in its history, was flooded with vernacular political weeklies, replacing the political pamphlet as the primary means of communication. With their newspapers such as the *Post van den Neder-Rhijn* and the *Politieke Kruyer* the Patriots brought about a veritable, albeit short-lived, press revolution.[52] Luzac, it has been seen above, had always belonged to the most principled defenders of the freedom of the press in the Dutch Republic. He had, indeed, paid a high price of public persecution and forced secrecy for these strong convictions. Yet radical as his position was, it had primarily been intended to defend the freedom of an elitist Republic of Letters against clerical interference and governmental repression. Luzac had never denied the desirability of punishing those who, blinded by their passions, abused their freedom for purposes of indecency or slander.[53] He never abandoned these views. To the end of his life, he remained a "lover...of free thought and free speech" and he kept insisting that everybody possessed the right to publish "such truths as belong to abstract learning".[54] But by the 1780s the problem, as he saw it, no longer was the defense of scholarly inquiry and intellectual freedom. The issue now had become the defense of reputation or good name against the scandalous, libellous, and seditious filth that streamed from the Patriot presses. Liberty of the press had turned into licence. "Newspaper writers", he bitterly observed, "who turn their liberty to relate the

---

49. On the *Oldfashioned Dutch Patriot* see Peterse, "Publicist voor Oranje".

50. De Beaufort, ed. *Van Goens*, vol.3, 40 and 65-66 ("...dans des vues pécuniaires...").

51. Cras, "Beredeneerd verslag", 23 ("...eene onafhankelijke staat, en vooral ook een vrije onafhankelijkheid van gevoelen en oordeel, de wenschelijkste zaak...in dit leven was...").

52. On the *Post van den Neder-Rhijn* see Theeuwen, "Pieter 't Hoen". See also the articles by Van Sas mentioned in note 16.

53. See 6-22 and 75-80.

54. *Vryaart*, vol.1, part 1, 113 ("...Liefhebber...van het vry denken en vry spreeken..."); *Staatsbeschouwers*, vol.2, 203 ("...zulke waarheeden, die tot de weetenschappen in 't afgetrokken behooren.").

news into the impertinence of publishing everything that surfaces in their raging and sick brains are a disgrace to nature and the pests of society. They may with justice be regarded as the scum of the earth".[55]

Luzac formulated two main objections to Patriot political writing. First of all, there were clear limits to what should be written about politics. Affairs of state should only be discussed in the abstract by writers of sufficient ability and knowledge, who should carefully abstain from publicly damaging the Fatherland.[56] Discussion of specific policies and persons was highly undesirable, because it disturbed peace and unity, ruined the essential trust of the subjects in their rulers, inflamed the passions, and undermined the foundations of quiet sociability by sowing discord.[57] Once, however, the business of government was "drawn from the circle in which it should remain enclosed", it became everyone's duty to participate in the public debate and to combat dangerous opinions.[58] This was precisely what the Patriot newspapers had brought about with their Athenian demagoguery.[59] It was Luzac's first justification for his own voluminous political writings.

Secondly, the accusations brought against the Stadholder and the Orangists in the Patriot press were completely unfounded.[60] They were slanderous and libellous and as such contrary to Scripture, natural law, Dutch law, and common decency.[61] Luzac insisted that reputation was as important as life and property. Defamation therefore belonged in the same category as murder and theft and should be punished accordingly.[62] It was the government's duty to do so. But the government, dominated by anti-Orangist regents, refused to take its responsibility. The result was,

---

55. *Vryaart* vol.2, part 4, 144 ("Courantiers die de vryheid van nieuws te verhaalen, met welke zy begunstigd zyn, veranderen in eene vrypostigheid van alles op 't papier en in 't licht te brengen, wat hunne bandelooze en ongestelde harsenen opleveren, zyn schandvlekken van de natuur, pesten van de samenleeving, en konnen met recht voor 't schuim van 't menschelyk geslacht, en voor het schadelykste ongedierte des Burgerstaats gehouden worden.").

56. *Ibidem*, vol.3, part 7, 3-6.

57. *Staatsbeschouwers*, vol.1, 191 and vol.2, 200-202.

58. *Ibidem*, vol.1, 193 ("... het bedryf der Regeeringe...getrokken word uit den kring daar het in besloten moet blyven...").

59. The comparison between Patriot newspaper writers and Athenian demagogues in *Voor- en nadeelen*, vol.1, 102 and *Lettres sur les dangers*, 220-222.

60. This is a continuous theme in both *Vryaart's letters* and the *Vaderlandsche Staatsbeschouwers*.

61. *Vryaart*, vol.2, part 5, 41; *Staatsbeschouwers*, vol.2, 194-202.

62. *Staatsbeschouwers*, vol.1, 46-47.

Luzac claimed, that every individual gained the duty and right to engage in *"self-defense in writing"*.[63] This was his second and most important justification for his own political publications.[64] When by the mid-eighties the anti-Orangist regents in turn became the target of radical Patriot attacks, Luzac could only conclude that they had themselves to blame for this unfortunate fate, for they had started and encouraged something which they could now no longer control.[65]

Luzac followed a similar line of argument in condemning the Patriot campaigns of petition and assembly. The right to petition, he stressed, was extremely useful and valuable. The inhabitants of a country should always be allowed to present their government with specific grievances and even to form societies and appoint delegates for that purpose. Governments would never be in a position to promote the common good if they completely closed their ears to the voice of the population.[66] But the Patriots were now perverting these simple truths by presenting their petitions as demands instead of as requests. "They have disguised their compulsory and criminal way of making demands as a right to petition. They are trying to obscure the punishable nature of their behavior by calling it a natural right to make requests".[67] Equally, the Patriot societies and their delegates had no intention of voicing specific and limited grievances. Instead, the delegates were used for the purpose of over-throwing the established government and of seizing power.[68] The Patriots were enabled to bring things to this point by what Luzac considered to be the most abominable feature of their behavior, the formation of citizen militias. "Arm yourselves, compatriots!", Van der Capellen had exclaimed in his 1781 *To the people of the Netherlands* and his suggestion was widely followed in the years thereafter.[69] To Luzac it was clear

---

63. *Vryaart*, vol.3, part 7, 30-52. The quotation is on 52 ("...*noodweer in geschrifte*...").

64. *Ibidem*, 95-96.

65. *Staatsbeschouwers*, vol.2, 247-248 and 555-561.

66. *Voor- en nadeelen*, vol.3, 140-145.

67. *Ibidem*, 145-146 ("Zy hebben de stoutheid, om op die wys afvorderingen te doen, en hunne dwingende stem te laaten hooren, looslyk doen voorkomen, als een recht tot het inleveren van Requesten, ten einde de strafwaardigheid hunner stappen, onder het natuurlyk recht van verzoeken te mogen doen, onbespeurd mogte blyven..."). On the difference between legitimate and illegitimate petitioning see also *Vryaart*, vol.4, part 12, 230-240 and 349-350; *Staatsbeschouwers*, vol.2, 423-431.

68. *Voor- en nadeelen*, vol.3, 148-149.

69. [Van der Capellen], *Aan het volk*, 37 ("O Landgenooten!...wapend u allen..."). See also *Ontwerp*, 50-56.

that these new free corps of armed citizens, products of the "restless and seditious brain of Van der Capellen and other regents", served no purpose in either external defense or the maintenance of internal order.[70] Not only were they superfluous, they were both illegal and anachronistic. Indeed, a close scrutiny of their behavior suggested that the members of these free corps aimed for nothing less than "the violent introduction of a North American form of government".[71]

External defense should be left in the hands of a professional army and the maintenance of peace and quiet in the towns was the task of the *schutters*. It was undeniably true, Luzac admitted, that the institution of the urban guard had decayed over the centuries. This was unfortunate, for even in modern times it still had the useful function of promoting sociability and manliness.[72] But the decay of the urban guard certainly did not warrant the formation of completely new militias. The history of Dutch medieval towns clearly showed that the *schutters* had originally been established by the sovereign, or at least with his permission. The citizen militias, by contrast, had been organized independent of all established authority and were therefore illegal.[73] Dreams of a return to pre-medieval Batavian manners were preposterous. The Batavians, after all, could hardly be said to have lived in a civil society.[74] Was it the Patriots' desire to turn the well-ordered Dutch Republic into a "monstrous assembly of people, with more resemblance to a band of savages than to a civilized nation?"[75]

The appeal to the distant past, indeed, clearly revealed the anachronistic nature of the citizen militia ideal, for it completely ignored modern military and economic developments. Luzac not only ridiculed the Batavian example, he also held the Patriot belief that imitation of the classical republics was still feasible to be pathetic: "...these smartheads have heard about a Roman burgomaster who stepped from behind a plough to command an army, and hence conclude that they are capable of

70. *Staatsbeschouwers*, vol.1, 107 ("...den onrustigen en woelenden geest van Van der Capellen, en andere regenten...").

71. *Ibidem*, 326 ("...eene Noord-Americaansche Regeringsvorm met geweld in te voeren...").

72. *Voor- en Nadeelen*, vol.3, 174.

73. *Staatsbeschouwers*, vol.1, 89-103.

74. *Vryaart*, vol.4, part 12, 149 and 254-260.

75. *Staatsbeschouwers*, vol.3, 191 ("...een wanschaapen zaamenvoeging van menschen..., die eerder naar een bende van raazende wilden, dan naar een beschaaft volk zoude gelyken...").

similar things".[76] On the one hand, the introduction of standing armies had made modern warfare so sophisticated and demanding an activity that only full-time professionals were fit for the task. Nothing could be more ridiculous than the thought that a band of armed citizens could equal or surpass the strength of a huge and well-disciplined modern army. On the other hand, the modern system of commerce, with its advanced and time-consuming specialization, had made the notion that all male citizens should engage in intensive military exercise utterly unrealistic.[77] The actual behavior of the free corps, their intimidation of Orangist citizens and regents, their increasing impatience with regents altogether, and the growing shrillness and radicalism of their demands convinced Luzac that he was dealing with "a conspiracy to destroy the legitimate and established government...and to exercise a violent tyranny over those who disagree with these aims".[78]

Licentious newspaper writing, seditious petitioning, and violent armed action were, to sum up, the three most salient characteristics of the practice of Patriotism according to Luzac. He closely followed the movement from day to day and wrote detailed and well-informed case studies of Patriot activity in towns such as Utrecht, Amsterdam, and his hometown Leiden. He persisted in thinking that Patriotism had been initiated by anti-Orangist regents. But he came to realize that their aristocratic desire to rule without a Stadholder had rapidly been supplanted by a strong demand for "popular influence on government".[79] Luzac found it impossible to associate democratic Patriotism with one particular group in the Republic. Patriots could be found among the intelligent and the stupid, among the literate and the illiterate, among rich and poor, among theologians and unbelievers.[80] What finally united these people, other than pure wickedness and unfocused dissatisfaction, was their perverse political thought. It was therefore of the utmost urgency to expose the fallacies of Patriot doctrine.

---

76. *Vryaart*, vol.3, part 9, 25 ("...die schrandere koppen hebben van een Romeinschen Burgemeester hooren spreeken, die van agter den ploeg is gehaald om een leger te gebieden; en maaken daar uit op, dat...zy zelve, bekwaam zyn om aan 't hoofd van een leger gesteld te worden.").

77. *Voor- en nadeelen*, vol.3, 150-153.

78. *Staatsbeschouwers*, vol.1, 104 ("...een vloekgespan der Ingezeetenen, om aan de wettige, en vastgestelde Regering den bodem in te slaan...en een geweldige tierannye over allen die 't met hun niet eens zyn te oeffenen.").

79. On the split between aristocratic regents and a democratic wing in the Patriot movement e.g. *Staatsbeschouwers*, vol.2, 278 and 317.

80. *Ibidem*, 271.

3. *Democratic Patriotism Refuted*

Luzac at times wondered whether there was such a thing as a coherent body of Patriot political thought at all. Patriotism, indeed, seemed to show a close resemblance to the religious enthusiasm he so abhorred. "There are", he disparagingly remarked about Van der Capellen, "both political and religious forms of enthusiasm".[81] Like religious enthusiasts, the Patriots had come to regard certain notions derived from their "seething imagination" as incontrovertible truths.[82] This had made them incapable of listening to reasonable arguments. They had become totally divorced from the normal process of communication. Factual truths, rational proof, and elementary logic had lost their meaning for these modern zealots. Their fanaticism was so strong that, like their religious predecessors, they felt an urgent need to persecute anybody who dared to disagree with their mad ravings.[83] It certainly was no coincidence, Luzac repeatedly remarked, that Dissenters and especially Baptists were so powerfully attracted by Patriotism.[84]

Patriot political language, moreover, seemed to be an incomprehensible "mixture of gibberish and humbug".[85] Luzac, it has been seen above, was both a trained jurist and an admirer of the Wolffian mathematical or demonstrative method. One of the reasons why he thought modern moral and political reasoning vastly superior to the ancient understanding of these topics was the modern sensitivity to the importance of unambiguous definitions and a rigorous logic. But the whole achievement of enlightened modern moralists since Grotius was now threatened by a return to ancient rhetoric. Luzac had first discerned this tendency in the work of the French *philosophes* in general and particularly in the writings of Jean-Jacques Rousseau. In his anti-Patriot polemic, he repeated many of the points he had previously made against Rousseau. The Patriots were incapable of logical and systematic reasoning, they abstained from defining their concepts, and they used terms with generally accepted meanings in highly idiosyncratic ways.[86] "If there is anything to be admired in the behavior of these state-deformers", he ironical-

81. *Vryaart*, vol.3, part 9, 26 ("...daar is ten opzichte van 't geloof in staatszaken even zoo wel als in den Godsdienst een dweepery.").

82. *Staatsbeschouwers*, vol.2, 315 ("...ziedende verbeelding...").

83. *Ibidem*, 332.

84. *Vryaart*, vol.4, part 11, 67-69, 86; part 12, 31, 104, 185.

85. *Staatsbeschouwers*, vol.3, 183 ("...een mengsel van wartaal en beuzelpraat...").

86. E.g. *Ibidem*, vol.1, 417, 421, 451-452.

ly remarked. "it certainly is their art of inventing words and sayings that seem to imply much, but in fact mean nothing".[87] Patriot political discourse, Luzac was convinced, consisted largely of empty sounds.

The conceptual structure erected by the Patriots, Luzac pointed out, was a strange composite of meaningless battle cries such as "constitutional restoration", "ancient rights and privileges", "inalienable rights" and "popular influence on government". He summarily dismissed the demand for constitutional restoration and a return to ancient rights and privileges.[88] First of all, it was completely ridiculous to pick some arbitrary point of time in the country's past and then desire that things return to that point, ignoring subsequent developments, the progress of society and institutions, and all acquired rights.[89] Secondly, and even worse, the historical foundation on which the Patriots based their demands was non-existent. They might proclaim the need for constitutional restoration, but what they in fact were bringing about was the total destruction of the established constitution under the pretense of restoring it to some imagined earlier state.[90]

But fortunately for them, Luzac sarcastically observed, the Patriots found it remarkably easy to switch from historical arguments to those derived from the state of nature when this happened to be convenient.[91] He judged their talk about inalienable natural rights to be dangerous because it ignored the essential differences between a supposed state of nature and civil society.[92] Nothing could be more subversive than to confront a well-ordered state with all kinds of random natural rights. "To dig up natural rights, to peddle them as truths, and to desire their enforcement regardless of the civil laws and regardless of a country's constitution and the patterns of its social life is, in our eyes, a sign of enormous foolishness".[93] Only rights that directly flowed from natural

---

87. *Ibidem*, vol.4, 48 ("Zoo'er in het gedrag der Staats-Vervormers iet te admireeren is, dan is het zekerlyk de kunst die zy bezitten, om woorden en zeggens uit te vinden, die veel schynen te beduiden, en met dat al niets betekenen..."). Ancient and Patriot rhetoric compared: *Ibidem*, 272-273.

88. On the Patriot publication entitled *Constitutional restoration* see note 6.

89. E.g. *Vryaart*, vol.3, part 9, 22-24.

90. *Staatsbeschouwers*, vol.3, 178; *Voor- en Nadeelen*, vol.3, 169-170.

91. *Vryaart*, vol.4, part 12, 340-341.

92. *Staatsbeschouwers*, vol.2, 191.

93. *Ibidem*, 205 ("Uit het natuurlyk recht begrippen op te delven, voor waarheeden uit te venten, en die, in weerwil van de burgerlyke wetten, te willen opdringen, en 's Lands Staatsgesteldheid, zoo wel als den gemeenschappelyken ommegang en verkeering onder de

moral duties could truly be called inalienable. Such rights, however, could not directly be related to specific forms of government, which largely depended on specific circumstances.[94]

Having thus pointed out what he thought to be the most obvious absurdities in Patriot rhetoric, Luzac concluded that the essence of Patriot doctrine was the demand for "popular influence on government".[95] The core of the Patriot case according to Luzac was the contention that the people originally were sovereign and always remained so. They might elect representatives, but these were no more than servants or mandatories of the people, always answerable to their principals. The crucial and related concepts to be discussed, therefore, were popular sovereignty, popular government or democracy, and representation. These themes dominated Luzac's analysis of Patriot political thought. He tried to show that original popular sovereignty was an impossible concept. He addressed the dangers of democracy by discussing democratic theory and by appealing to the experience of the ages. Finally, he tried to prove that both popular government and real representation were foreign to the historical nature of the Dutch state.

Original popular sovereignty, Luzac remarked, was no more than a hypothesis. Nowhere was there to be found any factual proof of its existence. But even if one agreed to make a purely juridical and hypothetical argument about the origins of sovereignty, it would soon transpire that this was a most curious notion. The most simple definition of sovereignty could be found in Grotius's formula *ius gubernandi civitatem*. Now it was evident that the people, in the sense of all the inhabitants of a country, were incapable of ruling, since they lacked the means to produce the necessary unitary will. What they resembled most was a swarm of flies. But if this was true then it was also true that sovereignty could not originally reside in the people, because a right can never be vested in those who by their nature and essence are incapable of exercising it. The most that could be said then was that the people, once united in civil society, had the right to *create* a sovereign authority, without originally *being* sovereign themselves. The consequence of this line of argument,

---

Ingezeetenen vervormen, is, in ons oog, een blyk van overgroote dwaasheid.").

94. *Ibidem*, vol.3, 260-261.

95. On January 30, 1787, the town of Haarlem in the Holland States-assembly proposed the formation of a commission to investigate the proper influence of the people on government. The proposal was defeated at first, but finally adopted on March 23. Colenbrander, *Patriottentijd*, vol.3, 149 and 168. Luzac's *Voor- en Nadeelen* were occasioned by this proposal.

Luzac emphasized, was to make nonsense of the claim that the people, after instituting a sovereign authority, could still make subsequent changes at their will because they supposedly had never completely transferred their original sovereignty.[96] Judging by the amount of space he devoted to it, however, Luzac found the analysis of the theoretical and practical merits of popular government more to his taste than speculation about original popular sovereignty.

Democratic theory was by no means something new, Luzac observed, not even in the Dutch Republic. Indeed, he maintained that the principled democratic republicanism of some authors of the first Stadholderless period, although highly objectionable, was considerably more intelligent and consistent than the ambivalent ideas of the Patriots. It was, moreover, one of the more important sources of Patriot thought. *To the people of the Netherlands*, for instance, was "no more than a poor imitation...of certain far more learned and sensible books published over a century ago, but incomparably more impertinent, and adapted to our times by an admixture of those fanatical ideas of liberty...which inevitably lead to public turmoil".[97] To refute democratic theory in its most fundamental form, Luzac therefore concentrated on the arguments in favor of popular government to be found in the *Political balance* by Johan (1622-1660) and Pieter de la Court.[98]

Popular government was natural, reasonable, and in itself just, the De la Courts had claimed. They had explained this pronouncement by way of rhetorical questions. "What", they asked, "can be more natural than to live *by one's own judgment, order, and laws?* What can be more reasonable than to *obey those one has chosen oneself?* What can be more just *than to suffer mistakes and tolerate people that one can correct and punish?*[99] To the first question Luzac answered that it was a regrettable error to

96. *Vryaart*, vol.4, part 12, 106-123, 146-167, 186-204.

97. *Ibidem*, vol.2, part 4, 197-198 ("...enkelyk een kreupele nabootsing...van werkjes voor ruim een eeuw, met oneindig meer kundigheid en verstand, in 't licht gegeeven, doch deeze in onbeschaamdheid verre overtreffende, en tot op onze tyden verlengd met byvoeging van die dweepzieke gevoelens van vryheid, welken...regt geschaapen staan om alle Burgerstaaten in rep en roer te brengen...").

98. *Consideratien van staat, ofte polityke weegschaal, etc.* The first edition of this work was published in 1660. On Johan de la Court see Haitsma Mulier, *Myth of Venice*, 120-169 and Wildenberg, *Johan en Pieter de la Court*. On Pieter de la Court see Chapter IV, note 31.

99. *Consideratien van staat, ofte polityke weegschaal*, 530 ("Wat kan natureliker zijn, als te leven *naar zijn eigen oordeel, ordre, en wetten?* Wat kan reedeliker zijn als *te gehoorsamen die men zelfs gekooren heeft?* Wat kan billijker zijn, *als te dulden misslagen, en menschen die men zelfs beeteren, en straffen kan?*").

think that living in a democracy meant obeying one's own judgment. Rousseau had made the same mistake.[100] Nobody in civil society completely obeyed his own judgment and a democracy implied obedience to the judgment of the majority of the people. Given individual differences and the fact that the best were always the minority, it was perverse to call this natural. To the second question Luzac replied that the reasonableness of obedience did not depend on choosing one's own rulers, but on their superior capacity. Since the people had very limited ability to judge capacity, it was unreasonable to demand that they choose their own rulers. This same argument also served to disprove the contention of the brothers De la Court that merit was only sought after in popular governments. Luzac treated their last question as a poor joke. Is a disaster made less bad by causing it oneself? "Board a ramshackle ship, depart with an incompetent captain of your own choosing and, while sinking, comfort yourself with the thought that you are to blame".[101]

Luzac finally summarized his whole anti-democratic line of argument by vigorously contradicting the De la Courts's contention that the general good is promoted in popular governments only.[102] They were mistaken in thinking that the general good coincided with the sum of individual goods.[103] They had moreover neglected the fact that no people, however enlightened, can ever judge what constitutes the general good "because everybody is distracted too much by his *particular* affairs to worry about what is necessary for the *common good*".[104] Apart from that, there were several more factors which made the people unfit to judge. To begin with, in most states it was impossible to bring the people together in an orderly fashion.[105] Secondly, the people were fickle and generally more guided by their feelings and passions than by reason. Because of this, they were an easy prey for ambitious demagogues.[106] In the third place, the people could easily be bought, "which is why Plato called a popular government

---

100. See 69.

101. *Voor- en nadeelen*, vol.1, 45-49. The quotation is on 47 ("Men begeeve zich dan in 't een of ander wrak schip, men steeke in zee met een onbekwaamen Schipper, dien men zelf heeft aangesteld, en men trooste zich in 't vergaan, met het streelend nadenken, dat men'er zelf de oorzaak van is.").

102. *Consideratien van staat, ofte polityke weegschaal*, 530-531.

103. *Voor- en nadeelen*, vol.1, 17.

104. *Ibidem*, 15 ("...daar elk door zyne *byzondere* zaaken te veel afgeleid word van de beschouwing van 't geen 't *algemeen nut* vereischt.").

105. *Ibidem*, 20.

106. *Ibidem*.

a market, meaning that everything is for sale there".[107] All these things, Luzac insisted, had been known for a long time. They could find confirmation in the study of the practice of ancient democracy.

To study the history of ancient Greece for anti-democratic purposes was a well-known conservative strategy in the late eighteenth century. In England, this tendency culminated in William Mitford's *History of Greece*, published between 1784 and 1810.[108] The German reviewer of Luzac's *Lettres sur les dangers* remarked that it was a pity the author had not read at all the latest German publications on the subject, since he would have found his anti-democratic conclusions confirmed and reinforced there.[109] According to Luzac, most Greek states had been happy and prosperous monarchies at first, but for a variety of reasons had subsequently degenerated into democracy and despotism. We shall not follow him in his detailed discussions of the evolution of Greek government, nor shall we repeat all his harsh judgments on the people's capacity to act in politics. Instead, we shall concentrate on the single most important lesson that Luzac derived from his study of Greek history. This was the lesson that a real democracy, in the sense of political participation by all or most inhabitants of a state, had never existed and could never exist.

In the first place, all so-called democracies had in fact been aristocracies, because criteria of sex, age, occupation, or property had always been used to limit the definition of what constituted the people.[110] More important, however, was the fact that the body of citizens defined as the people was incapable of acting by itself and therefore dependent on a few of its members.[111] This meant that democracy could not be and had never been more than a struggle for power between various groups of ambitious and unscrupulous demagogues. The people were no more than "the plaything of a few power-hungry citizens" or "puppets in the hands of flattering orators".[112] This power struggle invariably ended in lawless despotism by one or a few. Since the victors in this struggle were not bound by any established order or limited by fundamental laws and since they claimed to embody the ever-changing will of the people, they could

---

107. *Ibidem*, 21 ("...waarom Plato aan een Volks-Regeering den naam van markt heeft gegeeven, betekenende daar meede, dat'er alles te koop was.").

108. Turner, *Greek Heritage*, 189-204.

109. *Göttingische Anzeigen von gelehrten Sachen*, April 15, 1793, 607-608.

110. E.g. *Vryaart*, vol.4, part 12, 201; *Voor- en nadeelen*, vol.1, 22.

111. *Lettres sur les dangers*, 149.

112. *Ibidem*, 126 ("...le jouet malheureux de quelques Citoyens avides de tenir les rênes du gouvernement.") and 220 ("...*jouet de la flatterie des harangueurs*...").

perpetrate the bleakest crimes without punishment. Indeed, the justice of a Turkish sultan was a wonder of mildness compared to the total arbitrariness to be found in so-called democracies, Luzac remarked.[113] Unfortunately, the Patriots failed to recognize that the same consequences would result from their attempts to introduce popular government in the Dutch Republic. Luzac held up to ridicule their claim that an increasing enlightenment would make the people capable of orderly political participation.[114] Were not the Athenians among the more enlightened people known in history, he asked them. Yet look at the results of their introduction of democracy.[115] He equally dismissed as irrelevant the Patriot argument that what they wanted was no more than popular government by representation. Popular government and representation were opposites, Luzac remarked, unless one made the representatives subservient instruments of the popular will. But if that were the case, then representation would entail all the disadvantages of pure democracy.[116]

The last element in Luzac's battle against democratic Patriotism was his attempt to show that popular sovereignty and real representation had no basis whatsoever in the history of the Dutch state. Their introduction would mean the sudden and complete destruction of a regime that had gradually developed over the centuries. Such a step could only be compared to "firing the directors of a well-ordered glass or porcelain trade and replacing them with monkeys".[117] It was in this context that Luzac, once again, gratefully used the new historical scholarship on pre-Revolt Dutch history.[118] Very little, he remarked, could be said with certainty about pre-Frankish times.[119] The fundamental and most relevant fact about medieval Dutch history, however, was that the Counts had been sovereign.[120] In their rule, they had always been assisted by a feudal nobility.[121] Gradually, as the population expanded and economic life became more complex, they had supplemented this nobility with deputies

113. *Ibidem*, 149, 151, 158.

114. *Staatsbeschouwers*, vol.2, 496; *Voor- en nadeelen*, vol.2, 18-25.

115. *Staatsbeschouwers*, vol.4, 101; *Voor- en nadeelen*, vol.2, 21.

116. *Voor- en nadeelen*, vol.1, 12; vol.2, 29-31.

117. *Ibidem*, vol.2, 37 ("...dat men in een florissante en welgeregelde glas of porcelein-negotie, de bestierders van dezelve ging afdanken, en'er eenige aapen in plaatsen, om dezelven waar te neemen.").

118. See 136 and 148.

119. *Vryaart*, vol.4, part 12, 254-260.

120. *Ibidem*, 265.

121. *Ibidem*, vol.3, part 9, 136-138.

from the rising towns.[122] Nobles and deputies from the towns together formed the assemblies of the States, representing the estates of the country. The burgomasters and city councils (*vroedschappen*), sending their deputies to the States-assemblies, represented the whole urban population. They did so, however, not because they had been elected by the urban inhabitants, but because the sovereign Count had so decided. The relation between the urban population and its representatives could best be compared to that between a pupil and his guardian, appointed by a third party.[123]

The crucial significance of the pre-Revolt situation for later times was "that the representative nature of our constitution does not result from *a popular election*, as if the people had originally appointed their representatives, like individuals appointing mandatories or like the delegates which have been appointed in our riotous days, but *from ordinances formerly made by the Counts and introduced to improve the stability of administration on all levels*".[124] For what had happened during the Revolt? The assemblies of the States had taken over the Count's sovereignty, without protest from the people and with their later consent as expressed in various oaths of allegiance to the constitution.[125] The assemblies of the States had acquired sovereignty in its sixteenth-century form, that is to say considerably limited by earlier laws, ordinances, and privileges.[126] Their sovereignty, moreover, was not exercised *jure proprio*, but *vi administrationis*, because they had been representatives before they became sovereigns.[127] The important point, however, was that nothing else had changed and that the one identifiable change had nothing to do with either the exercise of popular sovereignty or a modification of the nature of representation. Since the sixteenth century, the situation brought about by the Revolt had not been fundamentally altered. Accor-

122. *Ibidem*, 138-139; part 12, 261.

123. *Staatsbeschouwers*, vol.1, 69; vol.2, 348-349.

124. *Ibidem*, vol.4, 337-338 ("...dat het Representatief caracter, 't welk in onze Constitutie plaats heeft, niet voortvloeit *uit eene verkiesing van het volk*, als of door hetzelve hunne plaatsbekleeders of Repraesentanten oorsprongkelyk waren aangesteld, even als Particulieren Gemachtigden aanstellen, en gelyk in onze dagen van Landverderffelyke beroerten, Gecommitteerden en Geconstitueerden aangesteld zyn; maar dat die voortvloeit *uit verordeningen, door de Graaven in der tyd bepaald, en tot vastigheid van het algemeen en byzonder bewind ingevoerd*.").

125. *Vryaart*, vol.4, part 12, 309-310.

126. *Voor- en nadeelen*, vol.3, 211.

127. *Staatsbeschouwers*, vol.1, 429; vol.2, 349-351; *Voor- en nadeelen*, vol.3, 193-196.

ding to Luzac, the Patriot desire for government by the active and continuous consent of the governed was therefore misplaced. Both popular sovereignty and real representation were deeply foreign to the historical development and present structure of the Dutch state.[128]

4. *Final Thoughts on the Established Order*

During the 1780s, it is clear, Luzac came to reject everything that smacked of popular participation in politics. His new political opponents did not, of course, fail to call attention to his earliest political pamphlets, which had contained quite a different message. The authors of *Constitutional restoration* quoted Luzac's 1754 *The conduct* at length, opposed it to the deeply anti-democratic conservatism of *Vryaart's letters*, and accused him of unscrupulously changing his principles. Luzac's retreat from theories of popular sovereignty and consent, they maintained, could only be attributed to the basest of motives.[129] Their diagnosis of a change in argument was certainly correct: Luzac had completely dropped the Lockean line of reasoning adopted in *The conduct* to legitimate the revolution of 1747. Their explanation, however, was mistaken. Luzac had, in fact, abandoned his earlier position because his own political thought had evolved, but even more because both the political constellation and the conceptual universe had been transformed since mid-century. The Orangist uses to which Locke had been put were no longer feasible from the 1770s onward.

Very little, unfortunately, is known about the fate of Locke's politics in the eighteenth-century Dutch Republic. Locke's work was widely available in French translation.[130] M.C. Jacob has shown that the *Second Treatise* was used by both establishment and radical Orangists in the 1740s and 1750s.[131] Luzac seems to fit that pattern. But it is also known that later in the century Locke's writings came to serve as a source of inspiration to various Patriots such as Van der Capellen and Pieter Paulus.[132] In Patriot political writing, Locke's political thought was developed into a Lockean radicalism similar to and derived from the

---

128. For the position of the Stadholder before and after the Revolt see 148.

129. *Grondwettige herstelling*, vol.1, 69-72.

130. Locke, *Two Treatises*, 126.

131. Jacob, "In the Aftermath of Revolution".

132. De Jong Hzn., *Van der Capellen*, 212; Goslinga, *Rechten van den Mensch*, 70. A thorough investigation of Locke's role in eighteenth-century Dutch political thought is urgently needed.

variety that surfaced in England from the 1760s on, a doctrine insisting on a continuous active political role of the sovereign people.[133] The authors expounding this doctrine in England, such as Richard Price, Joseph Priestley, and Thomas Paine, were enormously popular in the Dutch Republic.[134] Luzac had clearly identified this development when, in 1784, he mentioned Locke and Price in the same breath as pernicious influences on Dutch political thought.[135]

While Locke was thus being appropriated by the Patriots, Luzac's thought had in the meantime, as we have seen, progressed in an altogether different direction. During the 1760s he bitterly came to oppose Rousseau, whom he judged to be a dangerous primitivist, whose doctrines of inalienable popular sovereignty and the general will moreover strongly smacked of arbitrary rule and popular despotism. Luzac's commentary on Christian Wolff, published in 1772, contained sharp criticisms of concepts like the state of nature, the original community of property, natural equality, and the original contract. In these notes on Wolff, he developed a conservative version of natural law, stressing man's natural inequality and dependence and the existence of a hierarchical cosmic and social harmony. Most of these themes clearly were foreign to the conceptual world of Locke and certainly to that of his late eighteenth-century heirs. In the 1770s, finally, Luzac turned to political economy and adopted the argument that only non-participatory forms of political organization were appropriate to highly developed commercial states.

Against this background Luzac, returning to a profoundly altered political scene, started to write his anti-Patriot political polemics in the 1780s. It was in these writings that he expressed his changed and more guarded views on the revolution of 1747. For the sake of peace and quiet it would be much better, he now first of all emphasized, not to keep returning to the events of 1747 and to let bygones be bygones.[136] If discussion was deemed necessary, however, then at least the important questions should be asked. "Did the people have a right to revolt? Were they entitled to do the things they did during that revolt? Did disturbances occur that should not have happened and that went too far? These are

---

133. Dickinson, *Liberty and Property*, 197-199; Kramnick, "Republican Revisionism"; Pocock, *Virtue, Commerce, and History*, 256-264.

134. De Jong, *Van der Capellen*, 211-225 and 523-525; Goslinga, *Rechten van den Mensch*, 17-21; Kossmann, *Low Countries*, 44.

135. *Vryaart*, vol.4, part 12, 341.

136. *Ibidem*, 58-59.

questions I shall not decide".[137] The only relevant questions were
"Whether the restoration of the Stadholderly government, by whatever
means it was brought about, has not been salutary? And whether our
present form of government, whatever its deficiencies may be, is not by
far the best for our state?"[138] Whether the events of 1747 had been
completely legitimate or not, in short, they had brought about a most
satisfactory situation and matters should be left at that. If the role of the
people had to be brought in, however, this should only be done on the
basis of a right to self-defense in an emergency situation, a right which
derived from the duty to self-preservation and certainly did not imply the
existence of original or residual popular sovereignty.[139] Finally, it was
undeniable that, although there had been popular commotion in 1747 and
1748, the Stadholder had not been restored by the people, but by the then
established regime.[140]

By limiting the discussion as much as possible to the happy factual
consequences of the revolution, by emphatically divorcing the right of
resistance from popular sovereignty of whatever variety, and by substituting the established government for the people as the main actor in
1747, Luzac in the 1780s eliminated all potentially dangerous and subversive elements from his analysis of the revolution of 1747. About doctrines
of consent, which he had still espoused in 1757, he now remarked that it
might well be asked "whether such systems which are not derived from
the nature of mankind as it exists, but from our arbitrary notions about
the nature of mankind as it never has existed, are not more harmful than
advantageous to learning".[141] Nobody, it is clear, was to be left in any
doubt about Luzac's political position.

Luzac's mature political thought has always been described as conser-

137. *Ibidem*, 37 ("Of het volk recht gehad heeft om tot dien opstand te komen? of het zelve
bevoegd is geweest tot die bedryven, die'er by dien opstand gepleegd zyn? en of 'er geen
ongeregeldheeden zyn voorgevallen, welken niet moesten gebeuren en te verre gegaan zyn?
zyn vraagen die ik niet beslissen zal...").

138. *Ibidem*, 40 ("...of de herstelling van de Stadhouderlyke Regering, zy mag dan geschied
zyn door welk middel men wille, niet is geweest allerheilzaamst? en of de tegenswoordige
Staatsvorm, met alle de gebreeken die zy onderheevig is, voor onzen Staat niet nog boven
allen de beste is?").

139. *Ibidem*, 195-197.

140. *Staatsbeschouwers*, vol.3, 198-199.

141. *Vryaart*, vol.3, part 9, 114 ("...of men met zulke leerstelselen, welke waarlyk niet
afgeleid zyn uit den aart van 't menschdom, zoo als het daadlyk bestaat, maar uit begrippen,
welken wy ons van den aart van 't menschdom, zoo als het nooit is geweest, willekeurig
maaken, aan de Weetenschappen niet meer nadeels dan voordeels doet.").

vative and there is every reason to continue doing so. But is should be stressed that he regarded the intellectual, socio-economic and political order of things he defended against Patriot attacks as essentially modern and enlightened. Intellectually, reasonable Christianity and an enlightened *science des moeurs* were recent triumphs over religious enthusiasm and ancient rhetorical moralism. On the socio-economic plane, modern commercial society and its attendant prosperity were vastly preferable to earlier systems of conquest. Politically, the moderate Stadholderly government, more firmly established since 1747 than ever before, was infinitely superior to both ancient forms of democracy and seventeenth-century forms of absolutism. Luzac could only regard Patriotism, whether it took the form of a relapse into classical rhetoric, a quasi-religious enthusiasm, Batavian primitivism, or the glorification of popular sovereignty and democracy, as a regressive movement that threatened the essentials of modernity. We have closely followed him in his complete rejection of Patriotism, a rejection he extended to what he thought were similar movements in surrounding countries and to the French Revolution in particular. Luzac's response to democratic Patriotism, however, was more than purely negative, for he went to great lengths to point to the existence of an alternative.

At the most fundamental level, this alternative consisted of substituting, with renewed emphasis, the primacy of the social life for the primacy of the political life. This tendency was evident both in his long-standing preference for a certain type of state and in the doctrine of historical utilitarianism he embraced in the final years of his life. Throughout his work, Luzac had insisted that an agreeable and happy existence was the supreme human goal. He explicitly defined this agreeable life in apolitical terms. He constantly referred to the happiness provided by "an orderly, pleasant, sociable life" and to the "the pleasures of social life" and he opposed this to the turmoil and discord generated by widespread political participation and to the stifling social effects of lawless despotism.[142] The fact that happiness was primarily a social achievement meant that the state, although clearly defined, had an essentially limited function in Luzac's thought. It never appeared as the creator of happiness, as it frequently did in German political discourse.[143] Instead, it was there to provide the structure within which happiness could be achieved through a life of calm, uninterrupted and ever-increasing

---

142. *Lettres sur les dangers*, 206 ("...une vie réglée, douce, sociable...") and 46 ("...les agréments de la vie sociale.").

143. See 109-110.

commerce, in both the social and economic senses of the word.[144] Between the two - sometimes overlapping - poles of democracy and despotism, a wide variety of political forms was acceptable. To fulfill its modest role, Luzac claimed, the state only had to be efficient and moderate.

Luzac was far from being blindly opposed to all reform. He repeatedly observed that states should constantly adapt themselves to changing circumstances.[145] He felt no need to deny that the democratic Patriots were right in some of the criticisms they leveled at the established regime in the Republic, although the remedies they proposed were utterly wrong.[146] The first problem with the Dutch state according to Luzac was the enormous complexity of the decision-making process, a complexity frequently resulting in the inability to reach any decisions at all. The most authoritative commentary on this state of affairs had been written in the early eighteenth century by Simon van Slingelandt, an author whose work Luzac greatly admired.[147] It was clear, Luzac remarked, "that the destruction of the Count's authority has broken the unity of our state too much. As a result, the administration now runs over too many wheels: it has become too complicated".[148] The only person who potentially could cut through the tangle and increase efficiency was, of course, the Stadholder. Any attempt to weaken his position was therefore disastrous.[149]

The second problem with the Dutch state was the incompetence, corruption, and sheer number of its regents. The Patriots had been absolutely right in pointing this out, Luzac thought. This situation could even be regarded as one of the main causes of the rise of the Patriot movement.[150] But Luzac rejected, as we have seen, the Patriot suggestion that matters would improve by making the regents into dependent instruments of the popular will. "Does it matter to a people", he asked, "by whom it

---

144. On the many meanings of commerce see Bruneau, "Commerce honnête".

145. E.g. *Vryaart*, vol.3, part 8, 116.

146. *Voor- en nadeelen*, vol.3, 39, 155.

147. *Vryaart*, vol.4, part 10, 84-99; *Staatsbeschouwers*, vol.1, 284-289. On Van Slingelandt see Leeb, *Ideological Origins*, 40-57.

148. *Voor- en nadeelen*, vol.3, 125 ("...dat door het vernietigen van het graaflyk gezach, de eenheid in onzen Burgerstaat te veel gebroken is geworden, en dat daardoor de werking van 't Staatsbewind aan te veel raderen is onderworpen geraakt: *l'administration est devenue trop compliquée*.").

149. *Vryaart*, vol.4, part 10, 99; *Staatsbeschouwers*, vol.1, 289-290.

150. *Voor- en nadeelen*, vol.2, 12-15; vol.3, 26-27, 37-60.

is governed or how the regents are appointed, as long as it is governed well?"[151] Democracy, in fact, was the direct opposite of efficient administration and contrary to the interests of the people.[152] The aim should be an enlightened, professional, efficient, and minimal administration. The professional administrators should be selected on the basis of merit and training, a training desperately in need of improvement by reforms of the academic curriculum.[153] They should, moreover, be supervised and kept in their proper place by the Stadholder.[154] The conclusion, once again, was that the Stadholder was indispensable if the state was to be efficient. The most urgent political reform, therefore, was a strengthening of the position of the Stadholder within the limits of the existing constitution.

But Luzac's plea for more efficiency was intended only to make the Dutch state better at performing its essentially limited task of providing the inhabitants with external security and the possibility to lead "a prosperous, pleasant, peaceful, and quiet life".[155] The crucial domestic precondition for the attainment of such a life was a reasonable civil liberty, which in turn depended on the limitation of the state's power. According to Luzac, as we have seen, the fundamental distinction to be made in judging political constitutions was that between arbitrary or absolute and limited or moderate government. This distinction firmly placed him in the mainstream of eighteenth-century constitutionalism and in the company of Montesquieu.[156] In the Dutch context, it allowed him to criticize the more specific demands of both *Staatsgezinden* and Patriots as not only dangerous, but also extremely parochial. Fundamental laws, the separation of powers, and mixed government were the central components of Luzac's constitutionalism, in this order of importance. These three devices to contain arbitrary power were, by historical accident, all

151. *Ibidem*, vol.3, 169 ("Is het niet voor een Volk om 't even door wien het zelve geregeerd worde? of de Regenten op deeze of gene wyze aangesteld worden, als het maar wel geregeerd worde?").

152. *Ibidem*, 60-64.

153. On merit: *Ibidem*, 55, 59; on the deficiencies of the future regents' academic training e.g. *Vryaart*, vol.3, part 9, 1-18 and 41-55.

154. This was a recurring theme in Luzac's writings from *Gedrag*, 43-49 to *Voor- en nadeelen*, vol.3, 229-254.

155. *Lettres sur les dangers*, 209 ("...une vie aisée, douce, paisible et tranquille...").

156. See 50-54.

present in the Dutch Republic, he claimed.[157]

Although he repeatedly described the Republic as a mixed government, he had growing doubts about the usefulness of this concept and
about the whole classical typology of governmental forms on which it
was based. Mixed government he came to consider as a rather vague and
unspecific term that could be applied to almost every existing government
and therefore clarified very little. "A public administration may be
organized in a thousand different ways. Everything depends on the
combination and connection of the constituent parts and on their particular
structure".[158] The continued reiteration of the simple formula of mixed
government, in short, contributed very little to a better understanding of
practical politics. Much more helpful, Luzac thought, was the way in
which Montesquieu had made the functional division of governmental
powers central to the definition of moderate government. The President's
seminal contribution to political thought, he insisted, had been to point
out that the combination of the full legislative, executive, and judicial
power in the hands of one person or group of persons destroyed liberty.
Having thus explained Montesquieu, Luzac proceeded to show that these
three powers were indeed exercised by different bodies and persons in the
Dutch Republic.[159]

The final, most simple, and perhaps most important mark of the
moderate state was the limitation of sovereignty by fundamental laws.
"Every government is either arbitrary or limited. It is arbitrary when there
are no fundamental laws determining the way in which the process of
governing is conducted; it is more or less limited when such laws restrain
public authority to a greater or lesser degree".[160] The way sovereignty
in the Dutch Republic had been acquired by the States-assemblies in the
sixteenth century meant, as we have seen, that it was limited by earlier
laws and privileges. Luzac firmly rejected any suggestion that sovereignty
simply consisted of the *ius de republica et ejus civibus pro lubitu dis-
ponendi*. He accused first the *Staatsgezinden* and later the Patriots of

---

157. On the importance of chance in the emergence of the Republic's moderate government
see *Hollands rijkdom*, vol.3, 126 and 325; *Voor- en nadeelen*, vol.2, 2.

158. *Lettres sur les dangers*, 312 ("L'organisation d'une administration publique est...suscep-
tible de mille modifications; tout dépend de l'ensemble et de l'enchaînement des différentes
parties, et de leur structure particulière.").

159. E.g. *Staatsbeschouwers*, vol.1, 335-337.

160. *Esprit des loix*, vol.1, 16 (book II, chapter 1) ("Tout gouvernement est arbitraire ou
limité. Il est arbitraire dès qu'il n'y a point de loix fondamentales qui fixent la façon dont il
faut se conduire dans la régie des affaires; il est plus ou moins limité, suivant que ces loix
restreignent l'autorité publique.").

adopting such unacceptable and despotic doctrine.[161]

Luzac's political norms, although clearly anti-absolutist and anti-democratic, were highly flexible. They could accommodate a wide variety of governmental forms and political arrangements. In the late 1780s and early 1790s, under the impact of the international expansion of political radicalism, this flexibility became even more pronounced. Clearly inspired by Montesquieu's relativism and in some ways parallelling Edmund Burke, that most famous conservative defender of a modern ruling order, Luzac was groping for a new discourse on politics.[162] Its outer limits remained defined by the laws of nature, but its language was non-jurid-ical. It may be described as a form of historical utilitarianism, in which practical success, historical experience, and political prudence appeared as the central elements.[163] The fundamental error of radical political re-formers all over Europe, Luzac claimed, was to think that established political structures could be changed on the basis of simplistic maxims or an abstract "plan of political construction".[164] A best form of govern-ment simply did not exist. Different circumstances demanded different political solutions. In the end, the only standard by which these solutions could be judged was their practical success. "It is fruitless to search for one single best form of government. It seems beyond doubt to me that the best form of government simply is the one that makes a state flourish and that gives its inhabitants a pleasant and prosperous life".[165] Not their juridical origin or their conformity to some abstract standard should deter-mine our judgment of political constitutions; the only relevant test was historical experience. The only acceptable standard was whether or not the life of the inhabitants had been prosperous, peaceful, and happy over a long period of time.

States, of course, were not unchanging and inert structures. They in

---

161. *Staatsbeschouwers*, vol.2, 546-547; *Voor- en nadeelen*, vol.3, 196-197.

162. On Burke as a "modernist" see J.G.A. Pocock, "The political economy of Burke's analysis of the French Revolution" in: Pocock, *Virtue, Commerce, and History*, 193-212.

163. The term historical utilitarianism has been used to characterize Burke's political thought. See Christie, *Stress and Stability*, 165. For a recent discussion of the conservative uses of utilitarian argument in late eighteenth-century Britain see Schofield, "Conservative Political Thought".

164. *Lettres sur les dangers*, 102 ("...un plan de construction politique..."); *Voor- en nadeelen*, vol.2, 32-33.

165. *Lettres sur les dangers*, 32 ("Qu'on dispute tant qu'on voudra sur les formes d'un Gouvernement, pour fixer quelle est la meilleure: à mon avis la meilleure en tout sens est incontestablement celle, qui fait fleurir un Etat, qui donne aux habitants une vie aisée et douce.").

fact kept changing and adapting themselves to the needs of the population. But these changes, Luzac emphasized, should always take place within the limits set by their original form, for a complex relationship existed between the form of the state and the life of the nation. This relationship grew more complex and consistent with historical development and should never be rudely disturbed.[166] This was true for the Stadholderly government in the Dutch Republic: "Our state has its form: the foundations have gradually been laid, and have become stable and firm. Domestically, everything has become adapted to these historical arrangements; the inhabitants have grown accustomed to them. Our relations with foreign powers, our whole commerce and navigation, ...everything has come to rest on the present form of our state".[167] But the same was true, for instance, for France.[168] What could be more foolish than to confront these structures, raised over the centuries and reasonably successful in practice, with demands for sudden and complete change? It was a fatal mistake not to consider "whether the measures that are thought to be useful, and that indeed are useful on an abstract level, will work in practice and whether they are compatible with the character, genius and inclinations of a particular people".[169] The conclusion was clear. Prudence dictated not risking the certain practical benefits of a reasonably successful established order, whatever its form, for the highly uncertain and probably disastrous results of radical political innovation.

---

166. *Ibidem*, 67-69. The language Luzac used was strongly reminiscent of certain passages in Montesquieu, for instance his *Pensée* 632: "Je ne pense nullement qu'un gouvernement doive dégoûter des autres. Le meilleur de tous est ordinairement celui dans lequel on vit, et un homme sensé doit l'aimer; car, comme il est impossible d'en changer sans changer de manières et de moeurs, je ne conçois pas, vu l'extrême brièveté de la vie, de quelle utilité il seroit pour les hommes de quitter à tous les égards le pli qu'ils ont pris". Montesquieu, *Oeuvres complètes*, vol.1, 1153.

167. *Voor- en nadeelen*, vol.2, 38 ("Ons Staatsweezen heeft zyne vorm: de gronden zyn langzamerhand gelegd, en hebben hunne vastigheid gekreegen. Voor 't inwendige heeft zich alles geplooid naar de beschikkingen van tyd tot tyd gemaakt; de Ingezeetenen hebben 'er zich aan gewend: de betrekkingen tot vreemde Mogendheeden, de gantsche Koophandel en Zeevaart, ...alles rust op de Staatsvorm zoo als die thans gevestigd is.").

168. *Lettres sur les dangers*, 91.

169. *Ibidem*, 107-108 ("...si les mesures, qu'on croit utiles, et qui le sont effectivement dans la spéculation, peuvent convenir à une nation, et si le caractère, le génie et les inclinations particulières d'un peuple, considéré soit en corps, soit individuellement, peuvent s'y prêter et s'y plier.").

EPILOGUE

In Luzac's intellectual universe reason, tolerance, moderation, and harmony were the central concepts. Member of an international community of enlightened Huguenots and heavily influenced by Christian Wolff and Montesquieu, Luzac inhabited the world of the Moderate Enlightenment. As a young man, he had every reason to be optimistic about the future prospects of that world. Intellectual freedom was, of course, still occasionally threatened by clerical intolerance and governmental repression, but it seemed to be increasing. The harmonious and orderly structure of God's universe had been laid bare and man's knowledge of the natural world was growing day by day. Man's moral life, too, was now, for the first time in history, being studied in a truly scientific way. The potential benefits of modern moral science, a branch of knowledge brought close to perfection by Christian Wolff's demonstrative method, seemed almost limitless. Improvement, however, was not limited to the intellectual sphere. There was also clear progress in manners. With the continued expansion of commerce, Europe was on the way to becoming a peaceful continent. The last remnants of the ancient system of conquest, it seemed, would soon be gone. On the whole the Dutch Republic, where Luzac lived and worked, exemplified the blessings of a commercial way of life. There were, it is true, some signs of decline, but the restoration of a moderate and balanced government with the return of the Stadholderate in 1747 augured well for the future.

Things, however, did not go the way Luzac had hoped and expected. On the contrary, the values he had so enthusiastically adopted as enlightened and modern early in his life increasingly came under attack as the century progressed. Luzac, indeed, was forced to devote most of his writing career to a defense of the worldview of the Moderate Enlightenment against growing threats. After mid-century, Luzac's systematic and still strongly rationalist approach to knowledge came under fire in France. To the *philosophes*, the approach Luzac favored represented a perverse *esprit de système*. To Luzac, *philosophie* stood for the denial of the importance of reason and a destruction of moral knowledge. At first, he thought he was dealing with a sensationalist misinterpretation of Newtonian science, with experimental philosophy run wild. By the time Rousseau's writings began to appear, however, Luzac increasingly began to interpret the attacks on the values of his Moderate Enlightenment in political terms. He linked them to the rise of a new and revolutionary political fanaticism. Motivated by political self-interest, the *philosophes* were destroying all solid moral knowledge, inventing a dangerous and incoherent political vocabulary, and poisoning the masses with their intoxicating but empty rhetoric. Their triumph in France and Europe, he feared and predicted, would have utterly disastrous results.

The rise of the late eighteenth-century revolutionary political movements, the Dutch Patriot movement in particular, confirmed Luzac's worst suspicions. What had begun as the destruction of knowledge now ended in a wholesale assault on civilization. Like their colleagues in other European countries and in America the Dutch Patriots, Luzac repeated over and over again, were primitivist political fanatics of the worst kind. They understood neither natural law, nor commercial society, nor even the most basic principles of political thought. There was no excuse whatsoever for their insane and violent attacks on the free, humane, and modern established order of the Dutch Republic. The final decades of the eighteenth century made the essentially moderate and tolerant Luzac into a conservative hardliner. Modern civilization, he was convinced, was threatened by a new barbarism. After 1787, when some of his fellow conservatives in the Dutch Republic urged a reconciliation with the defeated and partly exiled Patriots, Luzac dissented. With these people, he insisted, no compromise was possible or desirable. Who is to say that, from his perspective, he was wrong? In 1795 the Patriots he so loathed marched into the Dutch Republic and, with the help of the French army, brought the Dutch *ancien régime* to an end. Luzac had finally been completely defeated. He died the next year.

BIBLIOGRAPHY

I. MANUSCRIPT SOURCES

Algemeen Rijksarchief, The Hague.
Tweede Afdeling. Archive Kemper-Cras, Inventory number 2.21.98, nr. 50. H.C. Cras, "Beredeneerd verslag omtrent de geschriften van den Heer Mr. Elias Luzac, in zijn leven Advocaat te Leyden". 96 p.

Bibliotheek van de Vereniging ter Bevordering van de Belangen des Boekhandels, Amsterdam.
Correspondence Marc-Michel Rey. 60 letters from Elie Luzac to Rey.
Personal Archive Marc-Michel Rey. Letter from J. Accarias de Sérionne to Rey.

Deutsche Staatsbibliothek, Berlin.
Correspondence Jean Henri Samuel Formey. 182 letters from Elie Luzac to Formey, 2 letters from Elie Luzac and Jean Luzac to Formey, 5 letters from Jean Luzac to Formey.

Gemeentearchief Leiden.
Archives de l'Eglise Wallonne de Leyde, nr. 46, Records of the Consistory.
Family archive Van Heukelom.

Provinciale Bibliotheek Leeuwarden.
Four letters from Luzac to Herman Cannegieter, Hs 1152.

Universiteitsbibliotheek Leiden.
Two letters from J.D. van der Capellen to M. Tydeman, BLP 845 and Ltk. 997.

II. PRINTED SOURCES

A. Works by and attributed to Elie Luzac in chronological order

Luzac, E. "Avertissement de l'imprimeur" in: [J.O. de La Mettrie], *L'homme machine*. Leyde, 1748.
[Luzac, E.] *L'homme plus que machine*. A Londres, 1748.

Luzac, E. *L'homme plus que machine. Ouvrage, qui sert à refuter les principaux argumens, sur lesquels on fonde le materialisme.* Seconde edition. Gottingue, 1755.

[Luzac, E.] *Man more than a machine...In answer to a wicked and atheistical treatise, written by M. de La Mettrie, and entitled Man a machine.* London, 1752.

[Luzac, E.] *Essai sur la liberté de produire ses sentimens.* Au pays libre, 1749.

[Luzac, E.] *Onderzoek over de vryheid, van zyne gevoelens mede te deelen.* Amsterdam, 1782.

Luzac, E. *Disquisitio politico-moralis num civis innocens irae hostis, longe potentioris, juste permitti possit, ut exidium totius civitatis evitetur.* Lugduni Batavorum, 1749.

Luzac, E. "Reponse de l'imprimeur à mr...sur son examen de l'avertissement qui se trouve à la tête du livre intitulé l'Homme machine". *Nouvelle Bibliothèque Germanique*, 6 (1750), second part, 431-441.

[Luzac, E.] *Le bonheur, ou nouveau système de jurisprudence naturelle.* Berlin, 1753. Reprinted Amsterdam, 1820.

[Luzac, E.] *Het gedrag der stadhoudersgezinden, verdedigt door Mr. A.v.K. rechtsgeleerden.* S.l., 1754.

[Luzac, E.] *Verantwoording wegens den uitgaaf van het boekje; tot tytel voerende: Het gedrag der stadhoudersgezinden verdedigt, door Mr. A.v.K. rechtsgeleerden.* S.l., 1754.

[Luzac, E.] *Het gedrag der stadhoudersgezinden, verdedigt door Mr. A.v.K. rechtsgeleerden.* Tweede druk, vermeerdert. S.l., 1755.

[Luzac, E.] "Discours sur l'origine et les fondemens de l'inégalité parmi les hommes, par Jean-Jacques Rousseau, etc.". *Bibliothèque Impartiale*, 12 (1755) 213-230.

[Luzac, E.] "Examen et critique desinteressée du Discours de Mr. J. Rousseau, sur l'origine et les fondemens de l'inégalité parmi les hommes, soumise au jugement d'une société littéraire, par un des membres de cette société". *Bibliothèque Impartiale*, 14 (1756) 101-124 and 434-451.

[Luzac, E.] "Solution de la question, proposée par l'Académie Royale de Prusse, et qui fait le sujet du prix de 1751" in: [E. Luzac and A.J. Brugmans] *Recherches sur quelques principes des connoissances humaines.* Göttingue et Leide, 1756. Reprinted Amsterdam, 1820.

[Luzac, E. and Brugmans, A.] *Recherches sur quelques principes des connoissances humaines. Publiées à l'occasion d'un Mémoire sur les monades, inseré dans le Journal des Savans, Avril 1753.* Göttingue et Leide, 1756.

Luzac, E. "Lettre de Mr. Luzac aux auteurs de la Bibliothèque des

Sciences et des Beaux Arts". *Bibliothèque des Sciences et des Beaux Arts,* 8 (1757) 464-468.

[Luzac, E.] *De zugt van den heere raadpensionaris Johan de Witt, tot zyn vaderland en deszelfs vryheid: ter gelegenheid van twee boekjes over 's mans karakter in 't licht gezonden, uit zyne daaden naagespoort.* Leyden, 1757.

[Luzac, E.] *Het oordeel over den heere raadpensionaris Johan de Witt, zo als het in het werkje, genaamt De zugt van den heere raadpensionaris J. de Witt tot zyn vaderland en deszelfs vryheid, uit zyne daaden nagespoort, vervat is, tegen het onderzoek van dit werkje, als een aanhang gevoegt agter de Vrymoedige aanmerkingen over de zedige beproeving, enz. bekragtigd, bevestigd, beweezen, en den schryver van 't Onderzoek voorgelegt.* Leyden, 1757.

Luzac, E. *Specimen iuris inaugurale de modo extra ordinem procedendi in causis criminalibus.* Lugduni Batavorum, 1759.

De l'esprit des loix. Nouvelle édition. Revue, corrigée, et considerablement augmentée par l'auteur. Avec des remarques philosophiques et politiques d'un anonyme [E. Luzac]*, qui n'ont point encore été publiées.* 4 vols. Amsterdam and Leipzig, 1759. Reprinted 1763.

De geest der wetten, door den Heere Baron de Montesquieu. Uit het Fransch vertaald door Mr. Dirk Hoola van Nooten. Met wijsgeerige en staatkundige aanmerkingen, zo van eenen onbekenden [E. Luzac], als van den vertaaler. 4 vols. and an index. Amsterdam, 1783-1787.

[Luzac, E.] *Nederlandsche Letter-Courant, doende kortelyk verslach van de nieuwe boeken en geschriften, welken van tyd tot tyd, zo in de Vereenigde als andere Gewesten, uitkomen; als ook 't voornaamste nieuws, dat 'er in de geleerde werreld voorvalt.* 10 vols. Leyden, 1759-1763.

Luzac, E. "Betoog hoe veel de zedekunde, zoo ten aanzien haarer gronden, als beweegredenen, en eindoogmerken, door de Godlyke Openbaaring, volmaakter is geworden. 1762" in: *Verhandelingen over eenige voornaame stukken van de Kristelyke Zedenkunde in het Nederduits en in het Latyn geschreeven om te dingen naa den prys van het Stolpiaansch Legaat.* Volume I. Leyden, 1766.

[Luzac, E.] *Lettre d'un anonime à Monsieur J.J. Rousseau.* Paris, 1766.

[Luzac, E.] *Seconde letter d'un anonime à Monsieur J.J. Rousseau. Contenant un examen suivi du plan d'éducation, que cet auteur a proposé dans son ouvrage intitulé Emile ou de l'éducation.* Paris, 1767.

Luzac, E. and Luzac, I.E. "Memorie, gedaen maken, en overgegeeven aen de Edele Groot Achtbaere Heeren, die van den gerechte der Stad Leyden, door ofte van wegens Cornelis van Hoogeveen junior, en Pieter van der

Eyk en Daniel Vygh, tot apui van 't verzoek, door hun by Requeste aen hunne Edele Groot Achtbaerheden gedaen, omme te obtineeren, dat hun Edele Groot Achtbaerheeden gelieven te coöpereeren, ten einde het nader geredresseerd Concept-Placaet tegens Godslasterlyke Boeken en Geschriften by de Edele Groot Mogende Heeren Staeten van Holland en Westfriesland werde gedeclineerd". *Nieuwe Nederlandsche Jaerboeken*, 5, second part (July 1770) 809-896.

[Luzac, E. and Vaster, F.] *Briefwisseling van Philagathos en Philalethes over de leer van het zedelyk gevoel, uitgegeven, en met een voorbericht en uitvoerige aanmerkingen vermeerdert door Johannes Petsch.* Utrecht, 1771.

Institutions du droit de la nature et des gens, dans lesquelles, par une chaine continue, on déduit de la nature même de l'homme, toutes ses obligations et tous ses droits. Traduits du Latin de Mr. Christian L.B. de Wolff par Mr. M***. Avec des notes, dans lesquelles on fait voir la solidité des principes de l'auteur; l'application de ces mêmes principes au droit public, civil et Romain; et l'utilité qu'on peut surtout en retirer, pour juger les causes rélatives au commerce et à la navigation: par Mre. Elie Luzac. 2 vols. Leyde, 1772.

De pligten der overheden, of vertoog over de rechtvaardigheid: als den grond van alle de pligten van eenen vorst, den tegenwoordigen koning van Frankryk, voor deszelfs komst tot den troon, voorgesteld en aangeprezen: door den Hr. Moreau. Uit het Fransch vertaald. Zynde bij deze Vertaaling gevoegd eene voor-reden, en eenige aantekeningen van Mr. Elias Luzac, Adv. Leyden, 1779.

[Luzac, E.] *Berigt wegens een Hollandschen druk van het werk, onlangs in 't fransch uitgekomen, onder den tytel van Hollands rykdom, etc.* Leiden, 1779.

Luzac, E. *Hollands rijkdom, behelzende den oorsprong van den koophandel, en van de magt van dezen staat, de toeneemende vermeerdering van deszelfs koophandel en scheepvaart, de oorzaaken, welke tot derzelver aanwas medegewerkt hebben; die, welke tegenwoordig tot derzelver verval strekken; mitsgaders de middelen, welke dezelven wederom zouden kunnen opbeuren, en tot hunnen vorigen bloei brengen. Het Fransch ontwerp gevolgd. Het werk zelf geheel veranderd, merkelijk vermeerderd, en van verscheiden misslagen gezuiverd.* 4 vols. Leyden, 1780-1783. Reprinted 1801.

[Luzac, E.] *Reinier Vryaarts openhartige brieven, om te dienen tot opheldering en regte kennis van de vaderlandsche historie; en teffens ter aanwyzinge van de waare en wezendlyke oorzaaken van 's lands vervallen en kwynenden staat, mitsgaders van de middelen om tot beteren toestand te komen.* 4 vols., 12 parts. S.l., [1781-1784].

[Luzac, E.] *De vaderlandsche staatsbeschouwers, overweegende alles wat 'er binnen en buiten het Vaderland omgaat en tot deszelfs belang betrekking heeft.* 4 vols. S.l., [1784-1788].

[Luzac, E.] *De voor- en nadeelen van den invloed des volks op de regeering, overwoogen en voorgedraagen by brieven geschreeven aan een lid van de hooge regeering.* 3 vols. Leyden, 1788-1789.

[Luzac, E.] *Lettres sur les dangers de changer la constitution primitive d'un gouvernement public. Ecrites à un patriote hollandois.* London [Leiden], 1792.

Luzac, E. *Du droit naturel, civil, et politique en forme d'entretiens. Programme.* Leyde, 1796.

Luzac, E. *Du droit naturel, civil, et politique, en forme d'entretiens.* 3 vols. Amsterdam, 1802.

B. Other Primary Printed Sources

[A.B.] *De leer van het zedelyk gevoel, opgeheldert en verdeedigt in eenen brief aan een geleerd man.* Groningen, 1770.

Accarias de Sérionne, J. *Le commerce de la Hollande, ou tableau du commerce des Hollandois dans les quatre parties du monde; contenant des observations sur le progrès et les décroissemens de leur commerce, sur les moyens de l'améliorer, sur les compagnies des Indes Orientales et Occidentales, sur les loix et usages mercantils, sur le luxe, l'agriculture, l'impôt, etc.* 3 vols. Amsterdam, 1768.

Accarias de Sérionne, J. *La richesse de la Hollande, ouvrage dans lequel on expose, l'origine du commerce et de la puissance des Hollandois; l'accroissement successif de leur commerce et de leur navigation; les causes qui ont contribué à leur progrès, celles qui tendent à les détruire; et les moyens qui peuvent servir à les relever.* 5 vols. London [Leiden], 1778.brief aan een geleerd man. Groningen, 1770.

Album Studiosorum Academiae Lugduno Batavae MDLXXV- MDCCCLXXV Accedunt Nomina Curatorum et Professorum per eadem Secula. The Hague, 1875.

Allgemeine Literatur-Zeitung, 1791.

Anonymus Belga [De Wakker van Zon, P.] *De adel.* S.l., 1786.

Barbeyrac, J. "Préface du traducteur" in: S. Pufendorf *Le droit de la nature et des gens, ou système general des principes les plus importans de la morale, de la jurisprudence, et de la politique.* Fifth edition. 2 vols. Amsterdam, 1734. Vol.1, i-cxxi.

Beaufort, W.H. de, ed. *Brieven aan R.M. van Goens en onuitgegeven stukken hem betreffende.* 3 vols. Utrecht, 1884-1890.

[Bernard, F.] *Vrye gedachten van een burger over het verval van 't gemeenebest der Vereenigde Nederlanden.* [Holland], 1782.

Bibliothèque des Sciences et des Beaux Arts, 1757, 1765, 1766, 1771, 1772.

Brief van een heer te Utrecht aan zyn vriend te Rotterdam: behelzende een echt verhaal van het voorgevallene op maandag den eersten september, met den hoog eerwaarden heere Petrus Hofsteede, en 't schreeuwende geval, eenige dagen te voren, van Mr. Elias Lusac. S.l., 1783.

Canter de Munck, J. *De tegenswoordige regeeringsvorm der Zeven Vereenigde Provintien gehandhaafd en verdeedigd (...) tegen het ontwerp der volksregeering, vervat in zeker werk, betyteld: Grondwettige herstelling van Nederlands staatswezen, etc.* Middelburg, 1787.

[Capellen. J.D. van der] *Aan het volk van Nederland* (1781). H.L. Zwitzer, ed. Amsterdam, 1987.

Constant, B. *De la liberté chez les modernes. Écrits politiques.* M. Gauchet, ed. Paris, 1980.

[Court, J. and P. de la] *Consideratien van staat, ofte polityke weeg-schaal, waarin met veele redenen, omstandigheden, exempelen, en fabulen wert overwogen; welke forme der regeeringe, in speculatie gebout op de praktyk, onder de menschen de beste zy.* Beschreven door V.H. Fourth edition. Amsterdam, 1662.

[Court, P. de la] *Aanwysing der heilsame politike gronden en maximen van de republike van Holland en West-Vriesland.* Leiden and Rotterdam, 1669.

[Court, P. de la] *The true interest and political maxims of the republic of Holland.* London, 1746. Reprinted New York, 1972.

Decker, C.W. *Proeve eener verhandeling, over de natuur en uitnemendheid der herstelde regeeringswyze van den Nederlandsche Republiek.* Amsterdam, 1787.

Encyclopédie, ou dictionnaire universel raisonné des connoissances humaines. Vol.42. Yverdon, 1775.

Encyclopédie ou dictionnaire raisonné des sciences et des arts. Articles choisis. A. Pons, ed. 2 vols. Paris, 1986.

Ferrner, B. "Bengt Ferrner's dagboek van zijne reis door Nederland in 1759". G.W. Kernkamp, ed. *Bijdragen en Mededeelingen van het Historisch Genootschap (gevestigd te Utrecht)*, 31 (1910) 314-509.

Formey, J.H.S. *Mélanges philosophiques.* 2 vols. Leiden, 1754.

Formey, J.H.S. *La France littéraire ou dictionnaire des auteurs françois vivans.* Berlin, 1757.

[Goens, R.M. van] *De Ouderwetse Nederlandsche Patriot.* 65 numbers. [The Hague], 1781-1783.

Göttingische Anzeigen von gelehrten Sachen, 1772, 1793.

Grondwettige herstelling van Nederlands staatswezen zo voor het algemeen bondgenootschap, als voor het bestuur van elke byzondere provincie; geschikt om het voornaam doelwit aan te toonen, waar toe de poogingen van goede regenten en de requesten van vaderlandlievende burgers moeten strekken. 2 vols. Amsterdam, 1784-1786.

Grotius, H. *Inleidinge tot de Hollandsche Rechts-geleerdheid.* F. Dovring; H.F.D.W. Fischer and E.M. Meyers, ed. Leiden, 1965.

Haller, A. von. *Haller in Holland. Het dagboek van Albrecht von Haller van zijn verblijf in Holland (1725-1727).* G.A. Lindeboom, ed. Delft, 1958.

Hardenbroek, G.J. van. *Gedenkschriften (1747-1787).* F.J.L. Krämer and A.J. van der Meulen, ed. 6 vols. Amsterdam, 1901-1918.

Heedendaagsche Vaderlandsche Letter-Oefeningen, 1772.

Hogendorp, G.K. van. *Brieven en Gedenkschriften van Gijsbert Karel van Hogendorp.* F. and H. van Hogendorp, ed. 7 vols. The Hague, 1866-1903.

Hume, D. *Essays Moral, Political, and Literary.* E.F. Miller, ed. Indianapolis, 1985.

Journal des Sçavans, 1753.

Journal Encyclopédique, 1765.

Kluit, A. *Academische redevoering, over het misbruik van 't algemeen staatsrecht, of over de nadeelen en onheilen, die uit het misbruik in de beoefeninge voor alle burgermaatschappyen te wachten zyn, etc.* Leiden, 1787.

Kluit, A. *De souvereiniteit der Staten van Holland verdedigd tegen de hedendaagsche leer der volksregering, zoo als dezelve onder anderen wordt voorgedragen in een geschrift getiteld: Grondwettige herstelling van Nederlands staatswezen, etc.* Second enlarged edition. Leiden, 1788.

[Kluit, A.] *De rechten van den mensch in Vrankryk, geen gewaande rechten in Nederland. Of betoog dat die rechten by het volk van Nederland in volle kracht genoten worden en iets over onze vryheid en patriotismus.* Amsterdam, 1793.

Kossmann, E.H. and Mellink, A.F., ed. *Texts concerning the Revolt of the Netherlands.* Cambridge, 1974.

[Kumpel, J.W.] *De Philarche of vorsten-vriend.* 18 numbers. Rotterdam, 1785.

La Mettrie, J.O. de. *L'Homme machine.* Leiden, 1748.

Leeuwen, S. van. *Het Rooms-Hollands-Regt, waarin de Roomse wetten, met het huydendaagse Neerlands recht, in alles dat tot de dagelykse onderhouding kan dienen, met een bysondere kortheit, so wel in de vaste regts-stoffen, als in de manier van regts-vordering over een gebragt werden.* Eleventh printing. Amsterdam, 1744.

Leibniz, G.W. *The Political Writings of Leibniz.* P. Riley, ed. Cambridge, 1972.

Locke, J. *Two Treatises of Government.* P. Laslett, ed. Cambridge, 1970.

Lüder, A.F. *Geschichte des holländischen Handels. Nach Luzacs Hollands Rykdom bearbeitet.* Leipzig, 1788.

Marck, F.A. van der. *Nadere verklaring over de vryheid van den burgerstaat van Groningerland gegrondvest op deszelfs eige vaderlandsche wetten, tot opheldering van het 93ste en 94ste stuk der Nederlandsche Letter-Courant des jaars 1761.* Groningen, 1762.

Marck, F.A. van der. *Lectiones academicae, quibus selecta philosophiae practicae iurisque naturae capita et praecipue officia erga deum pertractantur.* Groningen, 1771.

Meerman, J. *De burgerlyke vryheid in haare heilzaame, de volks-vryheid in haare schadelyke gevolgen voorgesteld, inzonderheid met betrekking tot dit gemeenebest.* Leyden, 1793.

Missive van een oud regent, over de waare oorzaaken van den rampspoedigen en gevaarlyken staat van de Republiecq. S.l., [1786].

Molhuysen, P.C., ed. *Bronnen tot de geschiedenis der Leidsche Universiteit.* 7 vols. The Hague, 1913-1924.

Montesquieu, Ch. de Secondat, Baron de. *Oeuvres complètes.* R. Caillois, ed. 2 vols. Paris, 1949-1951.

Nederlands wonder-toneel, geopend in de jaren 1747 en 1748. Vertonende een korte en zakelyke aaneenschakeling van alle de wonderlyke gebeurtenissen welke de Vereenigde Provintien in de twee gemelde jaren zyn overgekomen, etc. 2 vols. Leiden, 1749.

Nieuwe Nederlandsche Jaerboeken, 1770, 1783.

Nouvelle Bibliothèque Germanique, 1748, 1749, 1750, 1753, 1757.

Onpartydige beschouwing, van de voorledene en tegenwoordige staatsgesteldheid van Holland, etc. Amsterdam, [1787].

Ontwerp om de Republiek door eene heilzaame vereeniging der belangen van regent en burger, van binnen gelukkig, en van buiten gedugt te maaken. Leyden, 1785.

Pufendorf, S. *Les devoirs de l'homme et du citoyen, tels qu'ils lui sont prescrits par la loi naturelle. Traduits du latin...par Jean Barbeyrac.* 2 vols. Trevoux, 1741.

Roques, P. "Examen de l'avertissement de l'imprimeur qui a publié le livre intitulé, l'Homme machine". *Nouvelle Bibliothèque Germanique,* vol.5, second part, 1748-1749, 328-357.

Rousseau, J.J. *Oeuvres complètes.* B. Gagnebin and M. Raymond, ed. 4 vols. Paris, 1959-1969.

Samenspraak tusschen de geest van een oudtydschen vaderlander en een hedendaagsch vryburger, etc. S.l., [1784].

Schneewind, J.B., ed. *Moral Philosophy from Montaigne to Kant. An Anthology.* 2 vols. Cambridge, etc., 1990.

Smith, A. *Lectures on Jurisprudence.* R.L. Meek; D.D. Raphael and P.G. Stein, ed. Indianapolis, 1982.

Smith, A. *An Inquiry into the Nature and Causes of the Wealth of Nations.* 2 vols. R.H. Campbell and A.S. Skinner, ed. Indianapolis, 1981.

De spiegel der vryheid, waarin ten klaarsten word getoond hoe gemakkelyk de verlooren vryheid zonder oprigten van vry-corpsen of het waapenen der burgeryen weerom gevonden kan worden. Door een vrye Dordsche burger. [Dordrecht], 1783.

Verhandeling over den alouden en teegenswoordigen staat van vryheid en regeering van Nederland. S.l., [1783].

Vogel, K. de. *Katechismus van het Stadhouderschap, etc.* 2 vols. Rotterdam, [1786-1787].

Vreede, G.W., ed. *Mr. Laurens Pieter van de Spiegel en zijne Tijdgenoten (1737-1800).* 4 vols. Middelburg, 1874-1877.

Wolff, C. *Vernünftige Gedanken von den Kräften des menschlichen Verstandes und ihrem richtigen Gebrauche in Erkenntnis der Wahrheit* (1713). H.W. Arndt, ed. Hildesheim, 1965.

Wolff, C. *Ausführliche Nachricht von seinen eigenen Schriften, die er in der deutschen Sprache von den verschiedenen Theilen der Weltweisheit herausgegeben auf Verlangen ans Licht gestellet* (1733). H.W. Arndt, ed. Hildesheim and New York, 1973.

Wolff, C. *Gesammelte kleine philosophische Schriften* (1736-1740). 6 vols. Hildesheim and New York, 1981.

Wolff, C. *Grundsätze des Natur- und Völckerrechts, worinn alle Verbindlichkeiten und alle Rechte aus der Natur des Menschen in einem beständigen Zusammenhange hergeleitet werden* (1754). M. Thomann, ed. Hildesheim and New York, 1980.

Wolff, C. *Des weyland Reichs-Freyherren von Wolff übrige theils noch gefundene kleine Schriften und einzelne Betrachtungen zur Verbesserung der Wissenschaften* (1755). Hildesheim, etc., 1983.

Wolff, C. *Briefe aus den Jahren 1719-1753. Ein Beitrag zur Geschichte der kaiserlichen Academie der Wissenschaften zu St. Petersburg* (1860). J.E. Hofmann, ed. Hildesheim and New York, 1971.

C. Secondary Printed Sources

Accarias, J. "Un publiciste dauphinois du XVIIIe siècle. Jacques Accarias de Sérionne. Sa famille, sa vie, ses ouvrages". *Bulletin de l'Académie delphinale*, fourth series, III, 1889, 487-533.
Ahsmann, M. and Feenstra, R. *Bibliografie van hoogleraren in de rechten aan de Leidse universiteit tot 1811.* Amsterdam, etc., 1984.
Airiau, J. *L'Opposition aux Physiocrates à la fin de l'ancien régime.* Paris, 1965.
Algemene Geschiedenis der Nederlanden. 15 vols. Haarlem, 1977-1983.
Bachmann, H.M. *Die naturrechtliche Staatslehre Christian Wolffs.* Berlin, 1977.
Bailyn, B. *The Ideological Origins of the American Revolution.* Cambridge, Mass., 1967.
Baker, K.M. *Inventing the French Revolution. Essays on French Political Culture in the Eighteenth Century.* Cambridge, 1990.
Ball, T.; Farr, J. and Hanson, R.L., ed. *Political Innovation and Conceptual Change.* Cambridge, 1989.
Barber, W.H. *Leibniz in France from Arnauld to Voltaire. A study in French reactions to Leibnizianism, 1670-1760.* Oxford, 1955.
Bartstra, J.S. *Vlootherstel en legeraugmentatie 1770-1780.* Assen, 1952.
Beck, L.W. *Early German Philosophy. Kant and his Predecessors.* Cambridge, Mass., 1969.
Beer, E.S. de. "The Huguenots and the Enlightenment". *Proceedings of the Huguenot Society of London*, 21 (1965-1970) 179-195.
Berg, J. van den. "Orthodoxy, rationalism and the world in eighteenth-century Holland" in: D.Baker, ed. *Sanctity and Secularity: the Church and the World.* Oxford, 1973.
Bergh, G.C.J.J. van den. *The Life and Work of Gerard Noodt (1647-1725). Dutch Legal Scholarship Between Humanism and Enlightenment.* Oxford, 1988.
Berkel, K. van. *In het voetspoor van Stevin. Geschiedenis van de natuurwetenschap in Nederland 1580-1940.* Meppel and Amsterdam, 1985.
Bie, J.P. de. *Het leven en de werken van Petrus Hofstede.* Rotterdam, 1899.
Bierens de Haan, J. *Van Oeconomische Tak tot Nederlandsche Maatschappij voor Nijverheid en Handel 1777-1952.* Haarlem, 1952.
Biografisch lexicon voor de geschiedenis van het Nederlandse protestantisme. 3 vols. Kampen, 1983-1988.
Blakemore, S. *Burke and the Fall of Language. The French Revolution as*

Linguistic Event. Hanover and London, 1988.

Blom, H.W. and Wildenberg, I.W. *Pieter de la Court in zijn tijd. Aspecten van een veelzijdig publicist. Voordrachten gehouden op het De la Court symposium, Erasmus Universiteit Rotterdam, 26 april 1985.* Amsterdam and Maarssen, 1986.

Bödeker, H.E. "Aufklärung als Kommunikationsprozeß". *Aufklärung. Interdisziplinäre Halbjahresschrift zur Erforschung des 18. Jahrhunderts und seiner Wirkungsgeschichte,* 2 (1987) number 2, 89-111.

Bodel Nyenhuis, J.T. *De Wetgeving op Drukpers en Boekhandel in de Nederlanden tot in het begin der XIXde eeuw.* Amsterdam, 1892.

Boogman, J.C. "The Union of Utrecht, its Genesis and Consequences". *Bijdragen en Mededelingen betreffende de Geschiedenis der Nederlanden,* 94 (1979) 377-407.

Boogman, J.C. *Raadpensionaris L.P. van de Spiegel: een reformistisch-conservatieve pragmaticus en idealist.* Amsterdam, etc., 1988.

Bos, J. *Rijklof Michael van Goens (1748-1810). Literator, politicus, piëtist. Catalogus van de tentoonstelling in de Koninklijke Bibliotheek te 's-Gravenhage 4 maart - 15 april 1988.* The Hague, 1988.

Bosch, J.W. "Quelques remarques sur l'influence de *l'Esprit des loix* dans l'oeuvre des juristes belges et néerlandais au XVIIIe siècle" in: *Album J. Balon.* Namur, 1968.

Bots, H. and Mijnhardt, W.W., ed. *De Droom van de Revolutie. Nieuwe benaderingen van het Patriottisme.* Amsterdam, 1988.

Bots, H.; Postumus Meyjes, G.H.M. and Wieringa, F., ed. *Vlucht naar de Vrijheid. De Hugenoten en de Nederlanden.* Amsterdam and Dieren, 1985.

Bots, H. and Vet, J. de. "Les Provinces-Unies et les Lumières". *Dix-Huitième Siècle,* 10 (1978) 101-122.

Bots, J. *Tussen Descartes en Darwin. Geloof en Natuurwetenschap in de achttiende eeuw in Nederland.* Assen, 1972.

Boutelje, G.A. *Bijdrage tot de kennis van A. Kluit's opvattingen over onze oudere vaderlandsche geschiedenis.* Groningen and The Hague, 1920.

Brake, W.Ph. te. "Staking a new claim to an old revolution: A review article". *Tijdschrift voor Geschiedenis,* 104 (1991) 15-23.

Braun, L. *Geschichte der Philosophiegeschichte.* Bearbeitet und mit einem Nachwort versehen von U.J. Schneider. Darmstadt, 1990.

Brouwer, H. "Rondom het boek. Historisch onderzoek naar leescultuur, in het bijzonder in de achttiende eeuw. Een overzicht van bronnen en benaderingen, resultaten en problemen". *Documentatieblad Werkgroep Achttiende Eeuw,* 20 (1988) 51-120.

Brugmans, H. "De Koopman. Mercurius als Spectator" in: *Tiende Jaarboek der Vereniging Amstelodamum.* Amsterdam, 1912.

Bruneau, C. "Commerce honnête et commerce déshonnête" in: *Mélanges d'histoire littéraire offerts à Daniel Mornet.* Paris, 1951.

Buijnsters, P.J. "Les Lumières hollandaises". *Studies on Voltaire and the Eighteenth Century,* 87 (1972) 197-215.

Buijnsters, P.J. *Nederlandse literatuur van de achttiende eeuw. Veertien verkenningen.* Utrecht, 1981.

Buijnsters, P.J. *Spectatoriale geschriften.* Utrecht, 1991.

Calinger, R.S. "The Newtonian-Wolffian controversy (1740-1759)". *Journal of the History of Ideas,* 30 (1969) 319-330.

Cassirer, E. *The Philosophy of the Enlightenment.* Princeton, 1979.

Castendijk, R.J. *Jan Wagenaar en zijn 'Vaderlandsche Historie'.* Schiedam, 1927.

Christie, I.R. *Stress and Stability in Late Eighteenth-Century Britain. Reflections on the British Avoidance of Revolution.* Oxford, 1984.

Cioranescu, A. *Bibliographie de la littérature française du dix-huitième siècle.* 3 vols. Paris, 1969.

Colenbrander, H.T. *De Patriottentijd, hoofdzakelijk naar buitenlandsche bescheiden.* 3 vols. The Hague, 1897-1899.

Collot d'Escury, H. *Holland's Roem in Kunsten en Wetenschappen, met Aanteekeningen en Bijdragen.* 8 vols. The Hague and Amsterdam, 1825-1844.

Cranston, M. *Jean-Jacques. The Early Life and Work of Jean-Jacques Rousseau 1712-1754.* London, 1983.

Cranston, M. *Philosophers and Pamphleteers. Political Theorists of the Enlightenment.* Oxford and New York, 1986.

Darnton, R. *The Business of Enlightenment. A Publishing History of the Encyclopédie 1775-1800.* Cambridge, Mass. and London, 1979.

Darnton, R. *The Great Cat Massacre and Other Episodes in French Cultural History.* New York, 1984.

De Monté Ver Loren, J.Ph. and Spruit, J.E. *Hoofdlijnen uit de ontwikkeling der rechterlijke organisatie in de noordelijke Nederlanden tot de Bataafse omwenteling.* Deventer, 1972.

Derathé, R. "Les réfutations du 'Contrat Social' au XVIIIe siècle". *Annales de la Société Jean-Jacques Rousseau,* 32 (1950-1952) 7-54.

Derathé, R. *Jean-Jacques Rousseau et la Science Politique de son Temps.* Second edition. Paris, 1979.

Dickinson, H.T. *Liberty and Property. Political Ideology in Eighteenth-Century Britain.* London, 1977.

Dijk, E.A. van; Trijsburg, J.; Wertheim, W.F. and Wertheim-Gijse

Weenink, A.H., ed. *De wekker van de Nederlandse natie. Joan Derk van der Capellen 1741-1784.* Zwolle, 1984.

Dubosq, Y.Z. *Le livre français et son commerce en Hollande de 1750 à 1780. D'après des documents inédits.* Amsterdam, 1925.

Duke, A.C. and Tamse, C.A., ed. *Too Mighty to be Free. Censorship and the Press in Britain and the Netherlands.* Zutphen, 1987.

Duynstee, W.J.A.J. *Geschiedenis van het natuurrecht en de wijsbegeerte van het recht in Nederland.* Amsterdam, 1940.

Eeghen, I.J. van. *De Amsterdamse boekhandel 1680-1725.* 5 vols. Amsterdam, 1960-1978.

Evenhuis, R.B. *Ook dat was Amsterdam. IV. De kerk der hervorming in de achttiende eeuw: de grote crisis.* Baarn, 1974.

Fajn, M. "Marc-Michel Rey: Boekhandelaar op de Bloemmarkt (Amsterdam)". *Proceedings of the American Philosophical Society*, 118 (1974) 260-268.

Falvey, J.F. "La Mettrie, l'Homme plus que Machine and La Machine terrassée: a question of authorship". *Modern Language Notes*, 75 (1960) 670-681.

Feenstra, R. and Waal, C.J.D. *Seventeenth-Century Leyden Law Professors and their Influence on the Development of the Civil Law. A Study of Bronchorst, Vinnius and Voet.* Amsterdam and Oxford, 1975.

Fockema Andreae, S.J. "Montesquieu en Nederland". *De Gids*, 112 (1949) 176-183.

Forbes, D. "Sceptical Whiggism, Commerce, and Liberty" in: A.S. Skinner and T. Wilson, ed. *Essays on Adam Smith.* Oxford, 1975.

Frängsmyr, T. "Christian Wolff's mathematical method and its impact on the eighteenth century". *Journal of the History of Ideas*, 36 (1975) 653-668.

Frijhoff, W.Th.M. *La société Néerlandaise et ses Gradués, 1575-1814. Une Recherche Sérielle sur le Statut des Intellectuels à partir des Registres Universitaires.* Amsterdam, 1981.

Fritschy, J.M.F. *De patriotten en de financiën van de Bataafse Republiek. Hollands krediet en de smalle marges voor een nieuw beleid (1795-1801).* The Hague, 1988.

Gabriëls, A.J.C.M. *De heren als dienaren en de dienaar als heer: het stadhouderlijke stelsel in de tweede helft van de achttiende eeuw.* Leiden, 1990.

Galama, S. *Het Wijsgerig Onderwijs aan de Hogeschool te Franeker 1585-1811.* Franeker, 1954.

Gay, P. *The Enlightenment: An Interpretation.* 2 vols. New York, 1967-1969.

Gay, P. *The Party of Humanity. Essays in the French Enlightenment.* New York, 1971.

Geyl, P. *De Patriottenbeweging 1780-1787.* Amsterdam, 1947.

Geyl, P. *Pennestrijd over Staat en Historie. Opstellen over de Vaderlandsche Geschiedenis aangevuld met Geyl's Levensverhaal (tot 1945).* Groningen, 1971.

Gibbs, G.C. "The role of the Dutch Republic as the intellectual entrepôt of Europe in the 17th and 18th centuries". *Bijdragen en Mededelingen betreffende de Geschiedenis der Nederlanden,* 86 (1971) 323-349.

Gobbers, W. *Jean-Jacques Rousseau in Holland. Een onderzoek naar de invloed van de mens en het werk (ca.1760-ca.1810).* Ghent, 1963.

Goslinga, W.J. *De Rechten van den Mensch en Burger. Een Overzicht der Nederlandsche Geschriften en Verklaringen.* The Hague, 1936.

Granpré Molière, J.J. *La Théorie de la Constitution anglaise chez Montesquieu.* Leiden, 1972.

Grijzenhout, F. *Feesten voor het Vaderland. Patriotse en Bataafse feesten 1780-1806.* Zwolle, 1989.

Grijzenhout, F.; Mijnhardt, W.W. and Sas, N.C.F. van, ed. *Voor Vaderland en Vrijheid. De revolutie van de patriotten.* Amsterdam, 1987.

Groenveld, S. and Leeuwenberg, H.L.Ph., ed. *De Unie van Utrecht. Wording en werking van een verbond en een verbondsacte.* The Hague, 1979.

Gunn, J.A.W. *Beyond Liberty and Property. The Process of Self-Recognition in Eighteenth-Century Political Thought.* Kingston and Montreal, 1983.

Haakonssen, K. "Hugo Grotius and the History of Political Thought". *Political Theory,* 13 (1985) 239-265.

Haase, E. *Einführung in die Literatur des Refuge. Der Beitrag der französischen Protestanten zur Entwicklung analytischer Denkformen am Ende des 17. Jahrhunderts.* Berlin, 1959.

Haitsma Mulier, E.O.G. *The Myth of Venice and Dutch Republican Thought in the Seventeenth Century.* Assen, 1980.

Haitsma Mulier, E.O.G. "'Hoofsche papegaaien' of 'redelyke schepsels': Geschiedschrijvers en politiek in de Republiek in de eerste helft van de achttiende eeuw". *Bijdragen en Mededelingen betreffende de Geschiedenis der Nederlanden,* 102 (1987) 450-475.

Haitsma Mulier, E.O.G. "A controversial republican: Dutch views of Machiavelli in the seventeenth and eighteenth centuries" in: G. Bock; Q. Skinner and M. Viroli, ed. *Machiavelli and Republicanism.* Cambridge, etc., 1990.

Hampsher-Monk, I. "Review Article: Political Languages in Time - The

Work of J.G.A. Pocock". *British Journal of Political Science*, 14 (1984) 89-116.

Hanou, A.J.A.M. *Sluiers van Isis. Johannes Kinker als voorvechter van de Verlichting, in de vrijmetselarij en andere Nederlandse genootschappen, 1790-1845. Een wetenschappelijke proeve op het gebied van de letteren.* Deventer, 1988.

Hanou, A.J.A.M. "Enkele kanttekeningen bij de studie van de Verlichting". *Literatuur*, 7 (1990) 155-161.

Harnack, A. *Geschichte der Königlichen Preussischen Akademie der Wissenschaften zu Berlin.* 3 vols. Berlin, 1900.

Hasquin, H. "Jacques Accarias de Sérionne. Economiste et publiciste français au service des Pays-Bas Autrichiens". *Etudes sur le XVIIIe Siècle*, 1 (1974) 159-170.

Hastings, H. "Did La Mettrie write *Homme plus que Machine?*". *Publications of the Modern Language Association of America*, 51 (1936) 440-448.

Hazard, P. *European Thought in the Eighteenth Century. From Montesquieu to Lessing.* Gloucester, Mass., 1973.

Hellmuth, E., *Naturrechtsphilosophie und bürokratischer Werthorizont. Studien zur preußischen Geistes- und Sozialgeschichte des 18. Jahrhunderts.* Göttingen, 1985.

Hellmuth, E., ed. *The Transformation of Political Culture. England and Germany in the Late Eighteenth Century.* Oxford, etc., 1990.

Himsbergen, E.J. van. "Grondwettige Herstelling" in: *Figuren en Figuraties. Acht opstellen aangeboden aan J.C. Boogman.* Groningen, 1979.

Hirschman, A.O. *The Passions and the Interests. Political Arguments for Capitalism before Its Triumph.* Princeton, 1978.

Hoeven, H. van der. *Gijsbert Karel van Hogendorp. Conservatief of liberaal?* Groningen, 1976.

Hont, I. and Ignatieff, M., ed. *Wealth and Virtue. The Shaping of Political Economy in the Scottish Enlightenment.* Cambridge, etc., 1983.

Hovy, J. *Het voorstel van 1751 tot instelling van een beperkt vrijhavenstelsel in de Republiek (propositie tot een gelimiteerd porto-franco).* Groningen, 1966.

Hugenholtz, F.W.N. "Adriaan Kluit en het onderwijs in de mediaevistiek" in: P.A.M. Geurts and A.E.M. Janssen, ed. *Geschiedschrijving in Nederland. Studies over de historiografie van de Nieuwe Tijd.* 2 vols. The Hague, 1981.

Huisman, C. *Neerlands Israel. Het natiebesef der traditioneel-gereformeerden in de achttiende eeuw.* Dordrecht, 1983.

Hunt, L. *Politics, Culture, and Class in the French Revolution*. London, 1986.

Hutchison, T. *Before Adam Smith. The Emergence of Political Economy 1662-1776*. Oxford, 1988.

Huussen jr., A.H. "1787. De Nederlandse revolutie?" *Bijdragen en Mededelingen betreffende de Geschiedenis der Nederlanden*, 104 (1989) 684-690.

Israel, J.I. *Dutch Primacy in World Trade, 1585-1740*. Oxford, 1990.

Jacob, M.C. *The Radical Enlightenment. Pantheists, Freemasons and Republicans*. London, etc., 1981.

Jacob, M.C. "In the Aftermath of Revolution: Rousset de Missy, Freemasonry, and Locke's Two Treatises of Government" in: *L'Età dei Lumi. Studi storici sul settecento Europeo in onore di Franco Venturi*. 2 vols. Naples, 1985.

Jacob, M.C. "Christianity and the Newtonian Worldview" in: D.C. Lindberg and R.L. Numbers, ed. *God and Nature. Historical Essays on the Encounter between Christianity and Science*. Berkeley, etc., 1986.

Jacob, M.C. and Mijnhardt, W.W., ed. *The Dutch Republic in the Eighteenth Century. Decline, Enlightenment, and Revolution*. Ithaca and London, 1992.

Jansen, C.J.H. *Natuurrecht of Romeins recht. Een studie over leven en werk van F.A. van der Marck (1719-1800) in het licht van de opvattingen van zijn tijd*. Leiden, 1987.

Jansen, C.J.H. "Over de 18e eeuwse docenten natuurrecht aan Nederlandse universiteiten en de door hen gebruikte leerboeken". *Tijdschrift voor Rechtsgeschiedenis*, 55 (1987) 103-115.

Janssens-Knorsch, U. *Matthieu Maty (1718-1776) and the Journal Britannique 1750-1755. A French view of English literature in the middle of the 18th century*. Amsterdam, 1975.

Janssens-Knorsch, U. *The Life and 'Mémoires Secrets' of Jean Des Champs (1707-1767). Journalist, Minister, and Man of Feeling*. Amsterdam and Maarssen, 1990.

Jong Hzn., M. de. *Joan Derk van der Capellen. Staatkundig levensbeeld uit de wordingstijd van de moderne democratie in Nederland*. Groningen and The Hague, 1921.

Kampinga, H. *De opvattingen over onze oudere vaderlandsche geschiedenis bij de Hollandsche historici der XVIe en XVIIe eeuw*. The Hague, 1917.

Keohane, N.O. *Philosophy and the State in France. The Renaissance to the Enlightenment*. Princeton, 1980.

Klippel, D. "Naturrecht als politische Theorie. Zur politischen Bedeutung des deutschen Naturrechts im 18. und 19. Jahrhundert" in: H.E. Bödeker and U. Herrmann, ed. *Aufklärung als Politisierung - Politisierung der Aufklärung*. Hamburg, 1987.

Kors, A.C. and Korshin, P.J., ed. *Anticipations of the Enlightenment in England, France, and Germany*. Philadelphia, 1987.

Kossmann, E.H. *Politieke Theorie in het Zeventiende-eeuwse Nederland*. Amsterdam, 1960.

Kossmann, E.H. *Verlicht Conservatisme: over Elie Luzac*. Groningen, 1966.

Kossmann, E.H. *The Low Countries 1780-1940*. Oxford, 1978.

Kossmann, E.H. *Politieke theorie en geschiedenis. Verspreide opstellen en voordrachten*. Amsterdam, 1987.

Kox, A.J., ed. *Van Stevin tot Lorentz. Portretten van achttien Nederlandse natuurwetenschappers*. Amsterdam, 1990.

Kramnick, I. "Republican Revisionism Revisited". *American Historical Review*, 87 (1982) 629-664.

Krauss, W. "Ein Akademiesekretär vor 200 Jahren: Samuel Formey" in: W. Krauss, *Studien zur deutschen und französischen Aufklärung*. Berlin, 1963.

Krauss, W. "La Correspondance de Formey". *Revue d'Histoire Littéraire de la France*, 63 (1963) 207-216.

Kruseman, A.C. *Aanteekeningen betreffende den Boekhandel van Noord-Nederland in de 17de en 18de eeuw*. Amsterdam, 1893.

Kundert, W. "Andreas Weiss (1713-1792). Professor des Naturrechts und des öffentlichen Rechts in Basel und Leiden". *Tijdschrift voor Rechtsgeschiedenis*, 49 (1981) 101-126.

Laspeyres, E. *Geschichte der volkswirtschaftlichen Anschauungen der Niederländer und ihrer Litteratur zur Zeit der Republik*. Leipzig, 1863.

Leeb, I.L. *The Ideological Origins of the Batavian Revolution. History and Politics in the Dutch Republic 1747-1800*. The Hague, 1973.

Lerner, R. *The Thinking Revolutionary. Principle and Practice in the New Republic*. Ithaca and London, 1987.

Lindeboom, G.A. *Herman Boerhaave. The man and his work*. London, 1968.

Lindeboom, J. *Frederik Adolf van der Marck. Een achttiende-eeuwsch leeraar van het natuurrecht*. The Hague, 1947.

Lokin, J.H.A. and Zwalve, W.J. *Inleiding in de rechtsgeschiedenis*. Groningen, 1985.

Lough, J. "The earliest refutation of Rousseau's *Contrat social*". *French Studies*, 23 (1969) 23-34.

Mannheim, K. "Conservative Thought" in: P. Kecskemeti, ed. *Karl*

Mannheim. *Essays on Sociology and Social Psychology*. London, 1953.

Marcu, E. "Un Encyclopédiste oublié: Formey". *Revue d'Histoire Littéraire de la France*, 53 (1953) 296-305.

Marx, J. "Une revue oubliée du XVIIIe siècle: *La Bibliothèque Impartiale*". *Romanische Forschungen. Vierteljahresschrift für romanische Sprachen und Literaturen*, 80 (1968) 281-291.

Marx, J. "Un grand imprimeur au XVIIIe siècle: Elie Luzac fils (1723-1796)". *Revue Belge de philologie et d'histoire*, 46 (1968) 779-786.

Marx, J. "Une liaison dangereuse au XVIIIe siècle: Voltaire et J.H. Samuel Formey". *Neophilologus*, 53 (1969) 138-146.

Marx, J. "Elie Luzac et la pensée éclairée". *Documentatieblad Werkgroep Achttiende Eeuw*, 11/12 (1971) 74-105.

Marx, J. "La Bibliothèque Impartiale: étude de contenu (janvier 1750-juin 1754)" in: M. Couperus, *L'étude des périodiques anciens. Colloque d'Utrecht*. Paris, 1972.

Marx, J. "Charles Bonnet contre les lumières 1738-1850". *Studies on Voltaire and the Eighteenth Century*, 156-157 (1976).

Masterson, M.P. "Montesquieu's Stadholder". *Studies on Voltaire and the Eighteenth Century*, 116 (1973) 81-107.

Mauzi, R. *L'idée du bonheur dans la littérature et la pensée française au XVIIIe siècle*. Geneva and Paris, 1979.

May, H.F. *The Enlightenment in America*. Oxford, etc., 1978.

Meek, R.L. *Social Science and the Ignoble Savage*. Cambridge, etc., 1976.

Meulen, J. ter. "Liste bibliographique de 76 éditions et traductions du *De iure belli ac pacis* de Hugo Grotius" in: *Biblotheca Visseriana V*. Leiden, 1925.

Meylan, P. *Jean Barbeyrac (1674-1744) et les débuts de l'enseignement du droit dans l'ancienne Académie de Lausanne*. Lausanne, 1937.

Mijnhardt, W.W. *Tot Heil van 't Menschdom. Culturele genootschappen in Nederland, 1750-1815*. Amsterdam, 1987.

Molhuysen, P.C. "De voorrechten der Leidsche Universiteit". *Mededeelingen der Koninklijke Akademie van Wetenschappen*, Afd. Letterkunde, Deel 58, serie B, 1-32. Amsterdam, 1924.

Möller, H. *Vernunft und Kritik. Aufklärung im 17. und 18. Jahrhundert*. Frankfurt am Main, 1986.

Nefkens, Th.M. "De denkbeelden van De Borger omtrent de economische achteruitgang der Republiek in de achttiende eeuw". *Maandschrift Economie*, 36 (1971-1972) 485-506.

Nieuw Nederlandsch Biografisch Woordenboek. 10 vols. Leiden, 1911-1937.

Nijenhuis, I.J.A. *Een joodse philosophe. Isaac de Pinto (1717-1787) en de ontwikkeling van de politieke economie in de Europese Verlichting.* Amsterdam, 1992.

Othmer, S.C. *Berlin und die Verbreitung des Naturrechts in Europa. Kultur- und sozialgeschichtliche Studien zu Jean Barbeyracs Pufendorf-Übersetzungen und eine Analyse seiner Leserschaft.* Berlin, 1970.

Overmeer, P.C.H. *De economische denkbeelden van Gijsbert Karel van Hogendorp (1762-1834).* Tilburg, 1982.

Pagden, A., ed. *The Languages of Political Theory in Early Modern Europe.* Cambridge, etc., 1987.

Pangle, Th.L. *Montesquieu's Philosophy of Liberalism. A Commentary on The Spirit of the Laws.* Chicago and London, 1973.

Pater, C. de. *Petrus van Musschenbroek (1692-1761), een Newtoniaans natuuronderzoeker.* Leiden, 1979.

Pater, C. de, ed. *Willem Jacob 's-Gravesande. Welzijn, wijsbegeerte en wetenschap.* Baarn, 1988.

Pellisson, M. "La question du bonheur au XVIIIe siècle". *La Grande Revue*, 10 (1906) 473-498.

Peterse, J.M. "Publicist voor Oranje. R.M. van Goens en *De Ouderwetse Nederlandsche Patriot* (1781-1783)". *Bijdragen en Mededelingen betreffende de Geschiedenis der Nederlanden*, 103 (1988) 182-208.

Pocock, J.G.A. *Politics, Language and Time. Essays on Political Thought and History.* New York, 1973.

Pocock, J.G.A. *The Machiavellian Moment. Florentine Political Thought and the Atlantic Republican Tradition.* Princeton, 1975.

Pocock, J.G.A. "The problem of political thought in the eighteenth century: patriotism and politeness (with comments by E.O.G. Haitsma Mulier and E.H. Kossmann)". *Theoretische Geschiedenis*, 9 (1982) 3-36.

Pocock, J.G.A. *Virtue, Commerce, and History. Essays on Political Thought and History, Chiefly in the Eighteenth Century.* Cambridge, etc., 1985.

Pocock, J.G.A. "Clergy and Commerce. The Conservative Enlightenment in England" in: *L'Età dei Lumi. Studi storici sul settecento Europeo in onore di Franco Venturi.* 2 vols. Naples, 1985.

Pocock, J.G.A. "Conservative Enlightenment and Democratic Revolutions: The American and French Cases in British Perspective". *Government and Opposition*, 24 (1989-1990) 81-105.

Popkin, J.D. *News and Politics in the Age of Revolution. Jean Luzac's Gazette de Leyde.* Ithaca and London, 1989.

Porter, R. and Teich, M., ed. *The Enlightenment in National Context.* Cambridge, etc., 1981.

Rees, O. van. "Het collegie van Adriaan Kluit over de statistiek van Nederland". *Tijdschrift voor Staathuishoudkunde en Statistiek door B.W.A.E. Sloet tot Oldhuis*, 12 (1855) 245-262.

Reibstein, E. "Deutsche Grotius-Kommentatoren bis zu Christian Wolff". *Zeitschrift für ausländisches öffentliches Recht und Völkerrecht*, 15 (1953-1954) 76-102.

Reichardt, R. and Schmitt, E., ed. *Handbuch politisch-sozialer Grundbegriffe in Frankreich 1680-1820*. Munich, 1985-. Thirteen volumes have appeared so far.

Reitsma, H. "'Altoos gedenkwaardig'. De herdenkingsliteratuur naar aanleiding van tweehonderd jaar Nederlandse Revolutie". *Theoretische Geschiedenis*, 16 (1989) 255-275.

Richter, M. *The Political Theory of Montesquieu*. Cambridge, etc., 1977.

Rijn, G. van. *Atlas van Stolk. Katalogus der historie-, spot- en zinneprenten betrekkelijk de geschiedenis van Nederland, verzameld door A. van Stolk Czn.* 12 vols. Amsterdam, 1895-1933.

Ritter, E. "Die Aufklärung und die Berliner Hugenotten". *Beiträge zur romanischen Philologie*, 9 (1970) 52-61.

Röd, R. *Geometrischer Geist und Naturrecht. Methodengeschichtliche Untersuchungen zur Staatsphilosophie im 17. und 18. Jahrhundert.* Munich, 1970.

Rorty, R.; Schneewind, J.B. and Skinner, Q., ed. *Philosophy in history. Essays on the historiography of philosophy.* Cambridge, etc., 1984.

Roscher, W.G.F. *Geschichte der National-Oekonomik in Deutschland.* Munich, 1874.

Roth, G. "Samuel Formey et son projet d'*Encyclopédie réduite*". *Revue d'Histoire Littéraire de la France*, 54 (1954) 371-374.

Rowen, H.H. *John de Witt, Grand Pensionary of Holland, 1625-1672.* Princeton, 1978.

Rowen, H.H. *The Princes of Orange. The Stadholders in the Dutch Republic.* Cambridge, etc., 1988.

Sassen, F. *Geschiedenis van de wijsbegeerte in Nederland tot het einde van de negentiende eeuw.* Amsterdam and Brussels, 1959.

Sassen, F. *Johan Lulofs (1711-1768) en de reformatorische verlichting in de Nederlanden.* Amsterdam, 1965.

Schama, S. *Patriots and Liberators. Revolution in the Netherlands 1780-1813.* New York, 1977.

Schieder, T. *Friedrich der Große. Ein Königtum der Widersprüche.* Frankfurt am Main, etc., 1983.

Schneiders, W., ed. *Christian Wolff 1679-1754. Interpretationen zu seiner Philosophie und deren Wirkung. Mit einer Bibliographie der Wolff-Literatur.* Hamburg, 1983.

Schneppen, H. *Niederländische Universitäten und deutsches Geistesleben von der Gründung der Universität Leiden bis ins späte 18. Jahrhundert.* Münster, 1960.

Schöffer, I. "The Batavian Myth during the Sixteenth and Seventeenth Centuries" in: J.S. Bromley and E.H. Kossmann, ed. *Britain and the Netherlands. Volume V. Some Political Mythologies.* The Hague, 1975.

Schöffer, I. "Adriaan Kluit, een voorganger". *Tijdschrift voor Geschiedenis*, 101 (1988) 3-16.

Schofield, T.P. "Conservative Political Thought in Britain in Response to the French Revolution". *Historical Journal*, 29 (1986) 601-622.

Schulte Nordholt, J.W. *The Dutch Republic and American Independence.* Chapel Hill and London, 1982.

Schutte, G.J. *De Nederlandse Patriotten en de koloniën. Een onderzoek naar hun denkbeelden en optreden, 1770-1800.* Groningen, 1974.

Schutte, G.J. "Willem IV en Willem V" in: C.A. Tamse, ed. *Nassau en Oranje in de Nederlandse geschiedenis.* Alphen aan den Rijn, 1979.

Schutte, G.J. "'A Subject of Admiration and Encomium'. The History of the Dutch Republic as Interpreted by Non-Dutch Authors in the Second Half of the Eighteenth Century" in: A.C. Duke and C.A. Tamse, ed. *Clio's Mirror. Historiography in Britain and the Netherlands.* Zutphen, 1985.

Scott, H.M., ed. *Enlightened Absolutism. Reform and Reformers in Later Eighteenth-Century Europe.* Houndmills and London, 1990.

Sekora, J. *Luxury. The Concept in Western Thought, Eden to Smollett.* Baltimore and London, 1977.

Shackleton, R. *Montesquieu. A Critical Biography.* Oxford, 1961.

Sher, R.B. *Church and University in the Scottish Enlightenment. The Moderate Literati of Edinburgh.* Princeton, 1985.

Shklar, J.N. *Men and Citizens. A Study of Rousseau's Social Theory.* Cambridge, etc., 1985.

Shklar, J.N. *Montesquieu.* Oxford and New York, 1987.

Skinner, Q. *The Foundations of Modern Political Thought.* 2 vols. Cambridge, 1978.

Smit, J.W. "The Netherlands in Europe in the Seventeenth and Eighteenth Centuries" in: J.S. Bromley and E.H. Kossmann, ed. *Britain and the Netherlands in Europe and Asia.* London and New York, 1968.

Sorell, A. *Descartes.* Oxford, etc., 1987.

Star Numan, O.W. *Cornelis van Bynkershoek. Zijn leven en zijne geschriften.* Leiden, 1869.

Stolleis, M., ed. *Staatsdenker im 17. und 18. Jahrhundert. Reichspublizistik, Politik, Naturrecht.* Frankfurt am Main, 1977.

Stouten, J. "On tolerance in the *Nederlandsche Letter-Courant* (1759-1763)". *Problèmes d'Histoire du Christianisme*, 13 (1984) 57-65.

Swarzbach, B.E. "Voltaire et les Huguenots de Berlin: Formey et Isaac de Beausobre" in: P. Brockmeier; J. Desné and J. Voss, ed. *Voltaire und Deutschland. Quellen und Untersuchungen zur Rezeption der französischen Aufklärung.* Stuttgart, 1979.

Thadden, R. von and Magdelaine, M., ed. *Die Hugenotten 1685-1985.* Munich, 1985.

Theeuwen, P.J.H.M. "Pieter 't Hoen (1744-1828). Politiek journalist en Utrechts patriot" in: *O Vrijheid! Onwaardeerbaar pand! Aspecten van de patriottenbeweging in stad en gewest Utrecht. Themanummer Jaarboek Oud-Utrecht 1987.* Utrecht, 1987.

Thieme, H., ed. *Humanismus und Naturrecht in Berlin - Brandenburg - Preussen. Ein Tagungsbericht.* Berlin and New York, 1979.

Thomann, M. "Influence du *Ius Naturae* de Christian Wolff" in: M. Thomann, ed. *Christian Wolff, Ius Naturae.* 8 vols. Hildesheim and New York, 1968-1972.

Tijn, Th. van. "Pieter de la Court. Zijn leven en economische denkbeelden". *Tijdschrift voor Geschiedenis*, 69 (1956) 304-370.

Tribe, K. *Governing Economy. The Reformation of German Economic Discourse 1750-1840.* Cambridge, etc., 1988.

Trousson, R. "Deux lecteurs de Rousseau au XVIIIe siècle: Madame de Charrière et Elie Luzac". *Lias*, 5 (1978) 191-255.

Tuck, R. *Natural Rights Theories. Their Origin and Development.* Cambridge, etc., 1981.

Tuck, R. "History of Political Thought" in: P. Burke, ed. *New Perspectives on Historical Writing.* Oxford, 1991.

Tully, J., ed. *Meaning and Context. Quentin Skinner and his Critics.* Oxford, 1988.

Turner, F.M. *The Greek Heritage in Victorian Britain.* New Haven and London, 1981.

Valkhoff, P. "Elie Luzac". *Neophilologus*, 4 (1919) 10-21 and 106-113.

Vartanian, A. "Elie Luzac's refutation of La Mettrie". *Modern Language Notes*, 64 (1949) 159-161.

Vartanian, A. *La Mettrie's L'Homme Machine. A Study in the Origins of an Idea.* Princeton, 1960.

Veen, T.J. and Kop, P.C., ed. *Zestig juristen. Bijdragen tot een beeld van de geschiedenis der Nederlandse rechtswetenschap.* Zwolle, 1987.

Velema, W.R.E. "Homo Mercator in Holland. Elie Luzac en het achttiende-eeuwse debat over de koophandel". *Bijdragen en Mededelingen betreffende de Geschiedenis der Nederlanden,* 100 (1985) 427-444.

Velema, W.R.E. "God, de deugd en de oude constitutie. Politieke talen in de eerste helft van de achttiende eeuw". *Bijdragen en Mededelingen betreffende de Geschiedenis der Nederlanden,* 102 (1987) 476-497.

Velema, W.R.E. "In Praise of the Stadholder. Elie Luzac and the Modernization of Orangism" in: W.H. Fletcher, ed. *Papers from the Second Interdisciplinary Conference on Netherlandic Studies.* Lanham, etc., 1987.

Velema, W.R.E. "The Rise and Fall of Morality. Elie Luzac on the History of the *Science des Moeurs*". *Theoretische Geschiedenis,* 14 (1987) 143-156.

Velema, W.R.E. "Revolutie, contrarevolutie en het stadhouderschap, 1780-1795". *Tijdschrift voor Geschiedenis,* 102 (1989) 517-533.

Vercruysse, J. "Marc-Michel Rey imprimeur philosophe ou philosophique". *Documentatieblad Werkgroep Achttiende Eeuw,* 34-35 (1977) 93-121.

Vermij, R.H., ed. *Bernard Niewentijt. Een zekere, zakelijke wijsbegeerte.* Baarn, 1988.

Vermij, R.H. *Secularisering en natuurwetenschap in de achttiende eeuw: Bernard Nieuwentijt.* Amsterdam, 1991.

Vile, M.J.C. *Constitutionalism and the Separation of Powers.* Oxford, 1967.

Voisine, J. "J. Formey (1711-1797). Vulgarisateur de l'Oeuvre de Rousseau en Allemagne" in: *Mélanges d'Histoire Littéraire offerts à Daniel Mornet.* Paris, 1951.

Vries, J. de. *De economische achteruitgang der Republiek in de achttiende eeuw.* Leiden, 1980.

Wade, I.O. *The Structure and Form of the French Enlightenment.* 2 vols. Princeton, 1977.

Wessels, L.H.M. "Jan Wagenaar (1709-1773). Bijdrage tot een herwaardering" in: P.A.M. Geurts and A.E.M. Janssen, ed. *Geschiedschrijving in Nederland. Studies over de historiografie van de Nieuwe Tijd.* 2 vols. The Hague, 1981.

Wessels, L.H.M. "Jan Wagenaar's 'Remarques' (1754): a reaction to Elie Luzac as a pamphleteer. An eighteenth-century confrontation in the Northern Low Countries". *Lias,* 11 (1984) 19-82.

Wessels, L.H.M. "Tradition et lumières in politicis. Quelques remarques sur l'argumentation et la position idéologique des patriotes à l'aube de la révolution (1780-1787)". *Documentatieblad Werkgroep Achttiende Eeuw*, 19 (1987) 171-192.

Whelan, F.G. "Vattel's Doctrine of the State". *History of Political Thought*, 9 (1988) 59-90.

Wieacker, F. *Privatrechtsgeschichte der Neuzeit, unter besonderer Berücksichtigung der deutschen Entwicklung*. Göttingen, 1967.

Wielema, M.R. "Christian Wolff in het Nederlands. De achttiende-eeuwse vertalingen van zijn Duitstalige oeuvre (1738-1768)". *Geschiedenis van de Wijsbegeerte in Nederland*, 1 (1990) 55-72.

Wielema, M.R. "'s-Gravesande en de metafysica". *Wijsgerig Perspectief*, 29 (1988-1989) no.1, 16-20.

Wildenberg, I.W. *Johan en Pieter de la Court (1622-1660 en 1618-1685). Bibliografie en receptiegeschiedenis. Gids tot de studie van een oeuvre.* Amsterdam and Maarssen, 1986.

Wilson, A.M. *Diderot*. New York, 1972.

Winch, D. *Adam Smith's politics. An essay in historiographic revision.* Cambridge, etc., 1978.

Wit, C.H.E. de. *De strijd tussen aristocratie en democratie in Nederland 1780-1848. Kritisch onderzoek van een historisch beeld en herwaardering van een periode.* Heerlen, 1965.

Wit, C.H.E. de. *De Nederlandse revolutie van de achttiende eeuw. Oligarchie en proletariaat.* Oirsbeek, 1974.

Wit, C.H.E. de. *Het ontstaan van het moderne Nederland 1780-1848 en zijn geschiedschrijving.* Oirsbeek, 1978.

Wood, G.S. *The Creation of the American Republic 1776-1787.* Chapel Hill, 1969.

Wood, G.S. "Conspiracy and the paranoid style: causality and deceit in the eighteenth century" *William and Mary Quarterly*, 39 (1982) 401-441.

Worst, I.J.H. "Staat, constitutie en politieke wil. Over F.W. Pestel en de variëteit van het achttiende-eeuwse orangisme". *Bijdragen en Mededelingen betreffende de Geschiedenis der Nederlanden*, 102 (1987) 498-515.

Zee, Th.S.M. van der; Rosendaal, J.G.M.M. and Thissen, P.G.B., ed. *1787. De Nederlandse revolutie?* Amsterdam, 1988.

Zwager, H.H. *Nederland en de Verlichting.* Bussum, 1980.

Zwalve, W.J. "Frederik Adolf van der Marck en Marcus Tullius Cicero. Enige opmerkingen over de crisis van het natuurrecht tegen het einde van de achttiende eeuw" in: *Acht Groningse juristen en hun Genootschap. 225 jaren Pro Excolendo Iure Patrio.* Groningen, 1986.

Zwalve, W.J. "Het Recht en de Verlichting. De juridische hoogleraar Frederik Adolf van der Marck (1719-1800)" in: G.A. van Gemert; J.

Schuller tot Peursum-Meyer and A.J. Vanderjagt, ed. *"Om niet aan onwetendheid en barbarij te bezwijken". Groningse geleerden 1614-1989.* Hilversum, 1989.

III. UNPUBLISHED SECONDARY SOURCES

Manen, H. van. "De Nederlandsche Letter-Courant. De betekenis van 18e-eeuwse tijdschriften voor de studie van de Nederlandse Verlichting". Unpublished M.A.-thesis, University of Amsterdam, 1989.

Marcu, E. "Formey and the Enlightenment". Unpublished Ph.D.-thesis, Columbia University, 1952.

Nijenhuis, I.J.A. "The University of Leiden: natural law and the study of the science of state household management in Holland". Unpublished paper presented to the Seventh International Congress on Enlightenment, Budapest, July 26 - August 2, 1987.

Tuck, R. "Moral Science and the Seventeenth-Century Origins of the Enlightenment". Unpublished paper presented to the conference 'Images of the Enlightenment', New York, April 6-8, 1990.

Versprille, A.J. "Remarks on Leiden archival materials concerning Elie Luzac". Unpublished note. Gemeentearchief Leiden, 1966.

INDEX